"*Carl F. H. Henry on the Holy Spirit* is a welcomed study that shines new and needed light on one of the twentieth century's most important evangelical theologians. What's welcomed is that Jesse Payne does not attempt to recast Henry as a primary pneumatological theologian, but rather lets the reader see how his pneumatology served to deepen and brighten Henry's focal doctrine of revelation. This approach is something all 'people of the book' should cherish."

Jason G. Duesing, provost and professor of historical theology, Midwestern Baptist Theological Seminary

"Jesse Payne's work on the role of the Holy Spirit in the theology of Carl F. H. Henry provides a fresh and convincing correction to the perception that Henry's theology was one-sided, lacking a developed pneumatology. Instead, Payne's careful and thoughtful research enables us to see that the Holy Spirit played an essential role in Henry's theological construction. Guiding readers through Henry's treatment of the doctrine of revelation, the church, and Christian ethics, we find that Henry's thought was thoroughly dependent on and inconceivable apart from the Holy Spirit. Helping all of us to see our need for the word of God and the Wind of God, Payne's volume fills an important role in our interpretation and understanding of this evangelical giant. I count it a privilege to recommend this fine book."

David S. Dockery, Distinguished Professor of Theology, Southwestern Baptist Theological Seminary; president, International Alliance for Christian Education

"Many think of the theology and life of Carl Henry as all head and no heart, but Payne corrects this misunderstanding of the man and his theology. Henry's theology wasn't limited to propositional revelation but he also recognized, as Payne ably shows, that we desperately need the Holy Spirit for illumination, for the life of the church, and for personal ethics. Payne can be thanked for addressing an area of Henry's theology that has been neglected."

Thomas R. Schreiner, James Buchanan Harrison Professor of New Testament Interpretation and professor of biblical theology, The Southern Baptist Theological Seminary

"Here is a fresh, insightful study of Carl F. H. Henry's pneumatology. Based on a close reading of Henry's voluminous writings as well as his interaction with competing voices, Payne shows the importance of the Holy Spirit both in Henry's thought and in the evangelical movement he loved and nurtured. Highly recommended!"

Timothy George, Distinguished Professor of Divinity, Beeson Divinity School, Samford University; general editor, Reformation Commentary on Scripture

"Jesse Payne has performed a profound service for evangelicalism by disclosing the spirituality of America's greatest propositional theologian. Digging deep into both well-known and less-consulted writings, Payne demonstrates irrefutably that Carl F. H. Henry is likewise a 'theologian of the Spirit.' This rings true, not only with regard to Henry's teachings on the locus of revelation, but also the loci of the church and Christian ethics. Well done!"

Malcolm B. Yarnell III, Research Professor of Theology, Southwestern Baptist Theological Seminary; author of *God the Trinity* and *Who Is the Holy Spirit?*

"Carl Henry had an uncanny but winsome knack for seeing where the American church failed to live out the whole counsel of Scripture. As Jesse Payne's incisive and readable *Carl F. H. Henry on the Holy Spirit* makes clear, one of Henry's constant exhortations was for churches and individual Christians to depend utterly on the Spirit for effective ministry and transformative virtue. Admirers of Henry and students of evangelicalism will want to read this book."

Thomas S. Kidd, Vardaman Distinguished Professor of History, Baylor University

"Evangelicalism will not experience renewal apart from a renewed dependence on the work of the Holy Spirit. And yet, evangelicals have often struggled to understand the Spirit, veering at times either to excess or to neglect. Who better to help navigate these pitfalls than evangelicalism's architect, Carl F. H. Henry? In this book, Jesse Payne provides an accessible and well-researched study of Henry's pneumatology, examining the work of the Spirit in revelation, the church, and the Christian life. For pastors and theologians alike, this is a work not only of historical scholarship but of discipleship, as we learn from Henry about the crucial role of the Spirit in our lives today."

Geoffrey Chang, assistant professor of historical theology and curator of the Spurgeon Library, Midwestern Baptist Theological Seminary

CARL F. H. HENRY *on* THE HOLY SPIRIT

CARL F. H. HENRY *on* THE HOLY SPIRIT

JESSE M. PAYNE

STUDIES IN HISTORICAL AND SYSTEMATIC THEOLOGY

Carl F. H. Henry on the Holy Spirit
Studies in Historical and Systematic Theology

Lexham Academic, an imprint of Lexham Press
1313 Commercial St., Bellingham, WA 98225
LexhamPress.com

Print ISBN 9781683594871
Digital ISBN 9781683594888
Library of Congress Control Number 2021933222

Lexham Editorial: Todd Hains, Kara Roberts, Abigail Salinger, Mandi Newell
Cover Design: Bryan Hintz
Typesetting: Justin Marr

To Marissa, the lovely
Macy, the kind
and Violet, the merry

CONTENTS

—

ACKNOWLEDGMENTS

—

Thank you to Dr. Jason Duesing and Dr. Owen Strachan for overseeing the dissertation that led to this book. I first heard the name Carl F. H. Henry in Dr. Duesing's master's level Baptist history course. I immediately knew two things: I wanted to study Henry further, and I wanted to do so under Dr. Duesing's supervision. Little did I know that, about a decade later, this book would come to fruition. It has been a privilege to learn from Dr. Duesing's academic and institutional service. I was grateful to have Dr. Strachan speak into these pages, as he has contributed much to studies of Henry. Numerous other professors deserve recognition, including Dr. John Mark Yeats, Dr. Thor Madsen, Dr. Rodney Harrison, and Dr. Radu Gheorghiță. And thank you to the unsung heroes: the Midwestern Baptist Theological Seminary Doctoral Office and the librarians and research assistants at Midwestern Seminary, Trinity Evangelical Divinity School's Rolfing Library, and the Billy Graham Center Archives at Wheaton College.

One of the greatest blessings of Midwestern's PhD program has been the development of friendships with fellow students that traverse state and national borders. Thank you for your insight and encouragement over our years of study together.

To Lakeland Baptist Church, thank you for your steadfast support while this book was underway. I am forever grateful for you. And to First Baptist Church of Burkburnett, thank you for the privilege of being your pastor. I pray that the Spirit reflected upon in these pages would be very active in our life as a church.

My parents, Mike and Jodi Payne, have supplied love, support, and encouragement throughout my writing. My heart bursts with appreciation for you both. To my siblings Ryan and Carly, their spouses Kelsey and Jason, and our extended family, thank you for being a refreshing support system throughout this journey. Kyle, Mitzi, Tanner, Travis, and Kayla Lyons have been tremendous blessings in countless respects.

To Todd Hains and the stellar team at Lexham Press, thank you for believing in this project and for your cheerful assistance along the way. Despite juggling countless editorial demands, Todd was quick to reply to my stream of questions with kindness and humor—ingredients that made this process a true joy. It's been a delight partnering with gifted men and women who love the Lord, love their work, and love the church.

And to those for whom words are hardly enough: thank you to Marissa, Macy, and Violet. Marissa has been my closest companion through every level of theological education, and her investment of time and patience rendered this book possible. She is a godly force of grace, beauty, and wisdom, and her willingness to listen to me process these pages out loud deserves a heavenly reward. Macy and Violet, you have made this season of writing all the sweeter. Thank you for being understanding when I needed to work and for being persistent when I needed to play.

Finally, thank you to the God of all grace (1 Pet 5:10). The words of Gregory of Nazianzus in *Oration 31* have been before me throughout this process, and I pray these pages echo his call: "We receive the Son's light from the Father's light in the light of the Spirit: that is what we ourselves have seen and what we now proclaim. ... We shall extol the Spirit; we shall not be afraid."[1]

---

1. St. Gregory of Nazianzus, *On God and Christ: The Five Theological Orations and Two Letters to Cledonius*, trans. Frederick Williams and Lionel Wickham, Popular Patristics Series 23, eds. John Behr and Augustine Casiday (New York: St. Vladimir's Seminary Press, 2002), 118–119.

ABBREVIATIONS

—

CFHHP   Carl F. H. Henry Papers
The Carl F. H. Henry Papers, including correspondence, notes, and sermons, are housed in Rolfing Library at Trinity Evangelical Divinity School in Deerfield, Illinois. Citations for these documents provide box and file references, which are accurate as of December 2018. According to library staff, the papers were in an active state of organization and classification at the time of writing. Researchers should be aware that further organizational efforts may relocate some documents.

GRA   *God, Revelation and Authority*

Come, Holy Ghost, our hearts inspire,
Let us Thine influence prove;
Source of the old prophetic fire,
Fountain of Light and Love.

Come, Holy Ghost, for moved by Thee
The prophets wrote and spoke,
Unlock the Truth, Thyself the Key,
Unseal the sacred Book.

Expand Thy wings, celestial Dove,
Brood o'er our nature's night;
On our disordered spirits move,
And let there now be light.

God, through Himself, we then shall know,
If Thou within us shine;
And sound, with all Thy saints below,
The depths of love divine.

—Charles Wesley, 1740

1
—

CARL F. H. HENRY ON ...
THE HOLY SPIRIT?

In the January 30, 1961, issue of *Christianity Today*, editor Carl F. H. Henry devoted a section to what he feared was a growing neglect of the Holy Spirit in modern theology. He wrote, "In twentieth century Christianity the Holy Spirit is still a *displaced person*. ... Whenever the Church makes the Spirit of God a refugee, the Church—not the Spirit—becomes the vagabond."[1] He was convinced that inattention to the Spirit would result in believers wandering helplessly throughout a lost world. Six years later, in the pages of the same magazine, Henry reiterated that the church is ever-dependent upon the Lord and Life-Giver, the Holy Spirit:

> If the Church is stricken today, it is not the soul that is dying. The Spirit is alive. There may yet be healing. There may yet be resurrection. It will depend on whether the churches really want this outpouring of the Holy Spirit in our day. Do we? Or do we merely want to get along as we have always done?[2]

---

1. Carl F. H. Henry, "I Believe ... ," *Christianity Today* (January 30, 1961): 23 (italics original).

2. "The Spirit of Pentecost: Will a Powerless Church Recover Its God-Given Soul?" unsigned editorial in *Christianity Today* (April 14, 1967): 29. Henry's writing at *Christianity Today* presents an interesting historiographical challenge. While many articles bear his name, he wrote a vast number of editorials that do not. Henry discussed writing these often, and many display his voice, vocabulary, and distinctive style. While none of my arguments are dependent upon these editorials, I draw from them in this book because of their value in examining Henry's thought. To neglect them would risk discounting a large body of relevant thought contained therein. When citing a *Christianity Today* editorial from Henry's tenure, the common convention in the academic literature has been to cite Henry as the author. Miles S Mullin II, in his article "Evangelicalism as Trojan Horse: The Failure of Neo-Evangelical Social Theology and the Decline of Denominationalism" adopted this approach, while also noting that the reference is an editorial in the citation. I will follow Mullin's technique by referencing Henry as the author while also indicating when the article is an editorial. Because the editorials were technically anonymous, there is no way to entirely prove that Henry

Henry posed questions like these consistently to thousands of readers throughout his tenure at *Christianity Today* (1956–1968). He devoted the entire January 4, 1963, issue to the Spirit, along with numerous other articles and editorials throughout his twelve years at the helm. Further, he addressed the topic of the Holy Spirit in academic works such as *Christian Personal Ethics* and the six-volume *God, Revelation and Authority*, as well as in journal articles, monographs, and unpublished documents and correspondence. Henry was tapping into an evangelical impulse toward the Spirit that had characterized the movement since its earliest days,[3] but since had seemed to dissipate in the haze of modernism.

But the Holy Spirit was never a subject of mere academic inquiry for Henry. He had a deep desire for the ongoing presence of the Spirit of God. In his 1986 autobiography, Henry recalled his own dependence upon the Spirit throughout his decades of ministry:

> I have always been open to some so-called mystical aspects of the Christian life ... when God becomes my God, when divine revelation penetrates not only the mind but rather the whole self, when the Spirit personally illumines the believer, dynamic fellowship with God opens possibilities of spiritual guidance in which the Holy Spirit personalizes and applies the biblical revelation individually to and in a redeemed and renewed life.[4]

Henry recognized that the Spirit was not only vital for personal growth, but for kingdom growth, too. Though remembered as an ambitious institutional builder, Henry maintained that, apart from the Spirit, evangelicalism's efforts would amass to nothing:

> It is a truism—though one we continually need to learn—that there can be no effective Christian work apart from the empowering of

---

was the sole author. However, because he himself wrote extensive editorials and as Editor had final say on what every editorial did and did not contain, it seems this is an appropriate way to utilize the available evidence while also being responsible and transparent about the sources. Editorials have been screened for Henry's tendencies; out of caution, those that do not correspond to his other work (voice, vocabulary, style, and content) have not been used.

3. Thomas S. Kidd, *Who Is an Evangelical? The History of a Movement in Crisis* (New Haven: Yale University Press, 2019), 4–5; 20–23; 56–58. See also Kidd, "The Bebbington Quadrilateral and the Work of the Holy Spirit," *Fides et Historia* 47.1 (2015): 54–57.

4. Carl F. H. Henry, *Confessions of a Theologian* (Waco, TX: Word Books, 1986), 52–53.

the Holy Spirit. We can build congregations. We can supply impressive buildings. We can accomplish organization. We can promote and finance activity on a scale unprecedented, and we can harness new and effective instruments. Ministers and workers can even have the most detailed kind of training. But the fact remains that the work of regeneration is still the work of the sovereign Spirit, and a genuine reviving of Christian life, vigor, and evangelism may be expected only as the Holy Ghost gives life and power to all that we bring for his service.[5]

Throughout his career, Henry returned to the present reality of the Spirit and the need for Christians to remain utterly dependent upon him in the interim between Pentecost and Parousia. Nothing of eternal consequence was possible without the Spirit's power and blessing.

QUESTIONS OF HENRY AND PNEUMATOLOGY

This book offers a critical examination of the pneumatological thought of Carl F. H. Henry, the "theological architect" of the twentieth-century neo-evangelical movement,[6] and undoubtedly one who left a lasting imprint on American evangelicalism.[7] The broad research questions

---

5. "The Spirit and the Church," unsigned editorial in *Christianity Today* (March 30, 1959): 20.

6. Peter Goodwin Heltzel, *Jesus and Justice: Evangelicals, Race, and American Politics* (New Haven: Yale University Press, 2009), 71. Miles S. Mullin II provides a helpful definition of neo-evangelicalism: "During the 1940s and 1950s, a new ethos materialized among northern, conversion-oriented Protestants and they were drawn together in a mood of cooperation and an impulse toward greater cultural engagement. Leaders were determined to reject the quietism of yesteryear and engage culture at a variety of levels, including redressing problematic issues in American society. They were convinced that evangelicalism had something to contribute to the national discourse in every area: intellectual, theological, social, political, and so on. They referred to their movement as the 'new evangelicalism.' Historians would label it neo-evangelicalism." See Miles S. Mullin II, "Evangelicalism as Trojan Horse: The Failure of Neo-Evangelical Social Theology and the Decline of Denominationalism," *Criswell Theological Review* 12.1 (2014): 51.

7. For helpful overviews of American evangelicalism (and the debate surrounding its terminology), see Kidd, *Who Is an Evangelical?*; George Marsden, *Understanding Fundamentalism and Evangelicalism* (Grand Rapids: Eerdmans, 1991), 1-6; Mark A. Noll, "Evangelicalism at Its Best," in *Where Shall My Wond'ring Soul Begin? The Landscape of Evangelical Piety and Thought*, ed. Mark A. Noll and Ronald F. Thiemann (Grand Rapids: Eerdmans, 2000); Douglas Sweeney, *The American Evangelical Story: A History of the Movement* (Grand Rapids: Baker Academic, 2005), 17-25. Other valuable resources include David Bebbington, *Evangelicalism in Modern Britain: A History from the 1730s to the 1980s* (London: Unwin Hyman Ltd., 1989); Judith L. Blumhofer and Joel A. Carpenter, eds., *Twentieth-Century Evangelicalism: A Guide to the Sources*

this book will seek to answer are: How does Carl F. H. Henry approach pneumatology throughout his writings? Is his thought developed? If so, in what way(s)? Further, are those who conclude that he had a weak pneumatology justified in doing so? Specifically, this book will argue that despite criticism that he possessed an underdeveloped pneumatology, Carl F. H. Henry understood the Holy Spirit to play a vital role in three key areas: revelation, ecclesiology, and ethics. In this, he believed that a Spirit-inspired Bible (revelation) would order a Spirit-enlivened body (ecclesiology) composed of Spirit-filled believers (ethics). Though revelation, ecclesiology, and ethics are at times treated in separate theological categories, sometimes with little relationship between them, Henry saw pneumatology as a thread uniting them together.

This chapter will give a preliminary overview of the research questions at hand. First, two rationales for the usefulness of this study will be provided. A defense will be given as to why Carl F. H. Henry, despite the sea of published literature devoted to his work, is worthy of further examination. Then, a case will be made as to why Henry's pneumatology in particular, despite the many topics he addressed, deserves greater attention and exploration. Following these rationales, a brief survey of the literature surrounding Henry's pneumatological views will be presented. Finally, the chapter will conclude with an overview of the book's argumentation and methodology.

WHY CARL F. H. HENRY?

The researcher of Carl F. H. Henry should be warned: there is (seemingly) no end to the writing of books, articles, and dissertations on Henry. As a key figure in twentieth-century American Protestantism, Henry has been evaluated by a wide range of scholars. If Henry is evangelicalism's theological Michelangelo, he certainly has a fair number of both admirers and detractors.[8]

(New York: Garland, 1990); Michael A. G. Haykin and Kenneth Stewart, eds., *The Advent of Evangelicalism: Exploring Historical Continuities* (Nashville: B&H Academic, 2008); Douglas Sweeney, "The Essential Evangelicalism Dialectic: The Historiography of the Early Neo-Evangelical Movement and the Observer-Participant Dilemma," *Church History* 60.1 (March 1991): 70–84.

8. Gabriel Fackre, "Carl F. H. Henry," in *A Handbook of Christian Theologians*, ed. Dean G. Peerman and Martin E. Marty, enl. ed. (Nashville: Abingdon, 1984), 583.

Despite the broad recognition of Henry's thought and importance (even among those who disagree with his conclusions), there is much to be done in understanding and applying his theological program and entrusting it to a new generation. Timothy George's 2004 prediction that "a new generation of evangelicals ... will still find [Henry] worthy of serious attention in the future" is coming to fruition.[9] Multiple volumes over the last fifteen years have emerged commending Henry as a figure deserving further attention, four of which are recognized below.

Gregory Thornbury, in his *Recovering Classic Evangelicalism: Applying the Wisdom and Vision of Carl F. H. Henry*, believes Henry to be "a key to evangelicalism's past" and may "be a cipher to its future."[10] He argues that issues important to Henry remain important today, and that re-engaging Henry will assist evangelicals in retrieving the best that evangelicalism has to offer in order to recover from its theological deterioration.

Essential Evangelicalism: The Enduring Influence of Carl F. H. Henry, edited by Matthew J. Hall and Owen Strachan, gives five reasons Henry is worth engaging today: he provided a model of orthodox engagement with an unorthodox world; he can give young evangelicals a framework for navigating secularism; he articulated a vision for gospel-centered social justice; he modeled evangelical ecumenism framed by confessional identity; and he understood theology and evangelism to be inseparable.[11] The editors "freshly commend Henry's work" because his vision and depth offer a strong foundation for contemporary evangelicals.[12] They acknowledge the current situation and hope that a new generation might change it:

Carl Henry is a distant reality for many modern Christians. Perhaps we should amend that: to a good many folks, he is unknown. He is recognized primarily among scholars, seminarians, and some pastors. Those who are aware of Henry know him to be a formidable theologian, a sometimes impenetrable writer, and an evangelical-at-large of the postwar twentieth century. ... Henry was

---

9. Timothy George, "Inventing Evangelicalism," *Christianity Today* (March 2004): 50.

10. Gregory Alan Thornbury, *Recovering Classic Evangelicalism: Applying the Wisdom and Vision of Carl F. H. Henry* (Wheaton, IL: Crossway, 2013), 31.

11. Matthew J. Hall and Owen Strachan, eds., *Essential Evangelicalism: The Enduring Influence of Carl F. H. Henry* (Wheaton, IL: Crossway, 2015), 17–23.

12. Hall and Strachan, *Essential Evangelicalism*, 19.

all these things. But he was more: a tireless evangelist, an incurable optimist, a gifted administrator, a loving father, a devoted husband, a fierce opponent, an eternal journalist, an unstoppable hatcher-of-grand-schemes, a Sunday school teacher.[13]

In pushing readers to delve into Henry's work at a new clip, the editors think "that one could profitably set down with Henry and spend a very long time following his trail of thought."[14] I have taken them up on the suggestion.

G. Wright Doyle, in his *Carl Henry: Theologian for All Seasons*, sees tremendous value in reengaging Henry's voice, especially because he has been neglected and misinterpreted over the previous few decades.[15] Doyle notes that recent monographs by Alister McGrath, John Frame, Scott Oliphant, and Douglas Kelly, all addressing issues Henry did before them, relegate him to footnotes or ignore him altogether.[16] Further, he laments that the 2007 *Dictionary of Major Biblical Interpreters* failed to include Henry anywhere in its index.[17] He desires to see a new generation of evangelicals recapture Henry's vision and apply it to the contemporary world.

Finally, Richard Mouw's foreword to the 2003 republication of Henry's 1947 *The Uneasy Conscience of Modern Fundamentalism* is instructive regarding Henry's aptness to speak to contemporary challenges (and, by extension, the value of reengaging his thought today). Mouw argues that Henry's clarion call in *The Uneasy Conscience of Modern Fundamentalism* needs to be heard anew:

> It must also be said that [Henry's] actual suggestions as to what is required in a well-formed biblical orthodoxy continue to ring true for many of us. While there is much to celebrate in the success of

---

13. Hall and Strachan, *Essential Evangelicalism*, 15–16.

14. Hall and Strachan, *Essential Evangelicalism*, 16.

15. G. Wright Doyle, *Carl Henry: Theologian for All Seasons—An Introduction and Guide to Carl Henry's God, Revelation, and Authority* (Eugene, OR: Pickwick, 2010), xi.

16. Doyle, *Carl Henry*, 16. However, Doyle also recognizes that other theologians have leaned upon Henry's work. See Millard Erickson, *Christian Theology* (Grand Rapids: Baker Academic, 1995); Gordon Lewis and Bruce Demarest, *Integrative Theology* (Grand Rapids: Zondervan, 1996); Wayne Grudem, *Systematic Theology: An Introduction to Biblical Doctrine* (Grand Rapids: Zondervan, 1994).

17. Doyle, *Carl Henry*, 16.

evangelicalism in recent years—both in grassroots ministries and in scholarly contributions—there are also reasons to worry a bit about tendencies in all sectors of contemporary evangelical life to dilute the proclamation of the Gospel, as well as to negotiate too-easy settlements between evangelical thought and various manifestations of "postmodern" culture. Carl Henry's antidote to the deviations from biblical truth in the 1940s speaks also to our own day.[18]

Mouw believes that "the agenda Henry laid out in [*The Uneasy Conscience of Modern Fundamentalism*] still deserves sustained attention."[19]

Beyond the works devoted to Henry's theological thought, others focus on him as a vital figure in the story of modern evangelicalism. Henry's importance to the broader narrative of American evangelicalism is well captured by Owen Strachan's *Awakening the Evangelical Mind: An Intellectual History of the Neo-Evangelical Movement*, Joel Carpenter's *Revive Us Again: The Reawakening of American Fundamentalism*, and Barry Hankins's *Uneasy in Babylon: Southern Baptist Conservatives and American Culture*.[20] These demonstrate that to understand modern evangelicalism, one must have a familiarity with Carl Henry—another rationale for investigating his theological views. Further, Albert Mohler's 2001 chapter on Henry in *Theologians of the Baptist Tradition* and Bob Patterson's 1983 *Carl F. H. Henry* both give attention to Henry's place in American evangelicalism.[21] Mohler sees Henry as virtually an institution unto himself, and believes Henry "represented the intellectual and cognitive defense of evangelical truth so central to the evangelical movement."[22] D. A. Carson understands Henry as a "towering figure" who is perennially relevant for evangelical thought.[23] Charles

---

18. Richard J. Mouw, foreword to *The Uneasy Conscience of Modern Fundamentalism*, by Carl F. H. Henry (Grand Rapids: Eerdmans, 1947; 2003), xiii.

19. Mouw, *Uneasy Conscience*, xiii.

20. See Joel A. Carpenter, *Revive Us Again: The Reawakening of American Fundamentalism* (New York: Oxford University Press, 1997); Barry Hankins, *Uneasy in Babylon: Southern Baptist Conservatives and American Culture* (Tuscaloosa: University of Alabama Press, 2002); Owen Strachan, *Awakening the Evangelical Mind: An Intellectual History of the Neo-Evangelical Movement* (Grand Rapids: Zondervan, 2015).

21. See R. Albert Mohler, "Carl F. H. Henry," in *Theologians of the Baptist Tradition*, ed. Timothy George and David S. Dockery (Nashville: B&H, 2001); Bob E. Patterson, *Carl F. H. Henry*, Makers of the Modern Theological Mind (Peabody, MA: Hendrickson Publishers, 1983).

22. Mohler, "Carl F. H. Henry," 282.

23. D. A. Carson, "The Compleat Christian: The Massive Vision of Carl F. H. Henry," *Trinity Journal* 35 (2014): 10.

Colson argued Henry's work needed further attention, as he believed that "when the history of the evangelical movement is finally written, Carl Henry will emerge as its dominant figure."[24] John Woodbridge captures well the role Henry played in the formation of evangelicalism and why he remains a figure of ongoing relevance:

> Indeed, what contours would the evangelical movement have assumed if Henry had not lent the considerable force of his mind and personality to its shaping and advocacy? ... To recount the story of the creation of *Christianity Today* (1956) without rehearsing the pivotal role Carl F. H. Henry played as the founding editor is difficult to imagine. To suppose that a number of world congresses on evangelism would have been held without the impetus he gave to them is likewise difficult to contemplate. To believe that the hundreds of evangelical leaders who attended the Evangelical Affirmations conference in 1989 would have done so if chairpersons other than Dr. Henry and Dr. Kenneth Kantzer had extended the invitation seems fanciful. Indeed, to review the history of the evangelical movement during the last half-century almost ineluctably draws one to assess Dr. Henry's place in history.[25]

Overall, these volumes, while disagreeing at points, all resound with a common refrain: Carl F. H. Henry still speaks to modern issues and challenges in evangelicalism. In many ways, Henry not only speaks to them, but anticipated them decades in advance. Carl R. Trueman is representative of the lot in recognizing that though Henry's work carries certain contextual tendencies and idiosyncrasies, the issues he tackled are timeless, which leads Trueman to commend Henry, "warts and all, for careful consideration."[26] This book will then carefully consider an aspect of Henry's thought that has not been sufficiently addressed.

---

24. Charles Colson, foreword to *Carl Henry at His Best: A Lifetime of Quotable Thoughts*, ed. Steve Halliday and Al Janssen (Portland: Multnomah, 1989), 13.

25. John D. Woodbridge, "Carl F. H. Henry: Spokesperson for American Evangelicalism," in *God and Culture: Essays in Honor of Carl F. H. Henry*, ed. D. A. Carson and John D. Woodbridge (Grand Rapids: Eerdmans, 1993), 379.

26. Carl R. Trueman, "Admiring the Sistine Chapel: Reflections on Carl F. H. Henry's *God, Revelation and Authority*," *Themelios* 25.2 (2000): 58.

WHY PNEUMATOLOGY?

Alongside addressing the value of analyzing Henry in particular, it is worth noting that pneumatology in general is a promising area of further study. Why is the present moment an appropriate and necessary time to reflect upon Henry's view of the Spirit? While Michael Horton recognizes that "it is always the right time to give sustained reflection on the Holy Spirit's person and work," he believes it to be "especially appropriate in our contemporary climate."[27] Despite Henry's concerns that the Spirit was at risk of becoming a *persona non grata* in conservative evangelical thought, Veli-Matti Kärkkäinen, recognizing the global growth of pneumatological interest, argues that "in recent years, one of the most exciting developments in theology has been an unprecedented interest in the Holy Spirit. A renaissance concerning the doctrine and spirituality of the Holy Spirit has stirred much interest and even enthusiasm from all theological corners."[28] Rustin Umstattd recognizes that in the last century, "the Holy Spirit received a much-needed revival in interest from theologians who delineated his role in such diverse areas as salvation, sanctification, ecology, ecclesiology, eschatology, and ethics."[29] Of course, it was difficult for Henry to realize and appreciate this momentous change from his chronological vantage point, but scholars now concur that the twentieth century marks not a downturn in pneumatological zeal but a spike.[30]

---

27. Michael Horton, *Rediscovering the Holy Spirit: God's Perfecting Presence in Creation, Redemption, and Everyday Life* (Grand Rapids: Zondervan, 2017), 14. In context, Horton's primary concern is that modern theologies tend to depersonalize, universalize, and immanentize the Holy Spirit. He is unsurprised that in this pluralistic age, it is the person of the Holy Spirit who is "even more susceptible to ideological and subjective manipulation and abstraction ... the Spirit becomes the obvious choice for a culture that eschews the particularity of the Father and the Son and the historical associations attending this particularity." Horton sees clearly the danger of this trajectory: "Assimilated to the world or to one's own inner spirit, such 'Spirit'-centered movements drift easily into neo-paganism. In short, exuberant talk about the Spirit may become just one more way of talking about ourselves." See Horton, *Rediscovering the Holy Spirit*, 22–23.

28. Veli-Matti Kärkkäinen, *Pneumatology: The Holy Spirit in Ecumenical, International, and Contextual Perspective*, 2nd ed. (Grand Rapids: Baker Academic, 2018), 1.

29. Rustin Umstattd, *The Spirit and the Lake of Fire: Pneumatology and Judgement* (Eugene, OR: Wipf & Stock, 2017), ix.

30. Of course, emphasizing the growth of both scholarly and grassroots attention to the Holy Spirit in the twentieth century risks insinuating that little reflection had been given to the third person of the Triune Godhead for some time. On this point, Sinclair Ferguson provides a helpful reminder when he writes, "[T]he assumption which became virtually an article of orthodoxy among evangelicals as well as others, that the Holy Spirit had been discovered almost *de novo* in the twentieth century, is in danger of the heresy of modernity,

Stanley Grenz sees this surge of pneumatological interest beginning in the 1950s. Since then,

> The church has witnessed an unparalleled explosion of interest in the Holy Spirit. Interest in the Spirit was once the domain of fringe groups such as the Montanists of Tertullian's day, the "enthusiasts" of the Radical Reformation, or the Pentecostals of the early 1900s. Today, however, Christians of many denominations want to know and appropriate the Holy Spirit.[31]

Gene L. Green believes that two historical developments advanced pneumatological reflection in the twentieth century.[32] He reaches back further than Grenz and recognizes that the rise of Pentecostalism among early-century American Protestants fostered renewed pneumatological interest and engagement. Moving into the latter half of the twentieth century, he understands Vatican II (1962–1965) as an important development that spurred fresh dialogue regarding the intersection of pneumatology, ecclesiology, and spirituality throughout Roman Catholicism. Pertaining to these movements within both Protestant and Roman Catholic circles, Horton argues that "there can be little doubt that [they] have influenced and even altered the faith and practice of global Christianity in a variety of ways."[33]

More germane to this book is the historical interaction between American charismatic movements and evangelicalism.[34] Henry's vision for

---

and is at least guilty of historical short-sightedness ... [Calvin, Owen, and Kuyper] richly demonstrate the attention which much earlier centuries gave to honoring [the Spirit] along with the Father and Son." See Sinclair B. Ferguson, *The Holy Spirit*, Contours of Christian Theology, ed. Gerald Bray (Downers Grove, IL: InterVarsity Press, 1996), 12. Horton agrees when he writes, "Whatever forgetfulness of the Holy Spirit may be evident in Protestantism generally and in Reformed circles particularly must be part of a forgetfulness of the rich treasures of our own past." See Horton, *Rediscovering the Holy Spirit*, 19.

31. Stanley J. Grenz, *Theology for the Community of God* (Grand Rapids: Eerdmans, 2000), 359.

32. Gene L. Green, "Introduction: The Spirit over the Earth: Pneumatology in the Majority World," in *The Spirit over the Earth: Pneumatology in the Majority World*, ed. Gene L. Green, Stephen T. Pardue, and K. K. Yeo (Grand Rapids: Eerdmans, 2016), 4.

33. Horton, *Rediscovering the Holy Spirit*, 20.

34. This book will use common classifications for "Pentecostal" and "charismatic," which have been well outlined by Wayne Grudem: "Pentecostal" refers to those denominations who trace their history back to the Pentecostal revival(s) in roughly the first decade of the twentieth century, while "charismatic" refers to those connected to the renewal movements in the mid-twentieth century in both Protestant and Catholic traditions. See Wayne Grudem,

evangelicalism (specifically his focus on the life of the mind) was incongru-
ous with what he understood to be certain charismatic tendencies, despite
the momentum these groups were gaining. As George Marsden explains:

> The burgeoning charismatic movement also changed the charac-
> ter of much of evangelicalism in important ways. The emphasis
> shifted both toward the experiential aspects of Christianity, a sense
> of closeness to Jesus through the Spirit dwelling within, and toward
> its therapeutic aspects. ... Such developments had to be viewed with
> mixed feelings by the former reformers of fundamentalism who had
> attempted to build an evangelical coalition around Billy Graham in
> the 1960s.[35]

Douglas Sweeney concurs with Marsden when he notes that:

> The swelling number of Pentecostals and charismatics within the
> evangelical ranks also added to the conflict over evangelicalism's
> nature and destiny. Beginning especially in the '60s, evangeli-
> cal leaders were faced with widespread conflict over things like

---

preface to *Are Miraculous Gifts for Today? Four Views* (Grand Rapids: Zondervan, 1996), 11.
Russell Spittler agrees when he argues that, "The decade of the 1990s [found] Pentecostals
concluding their first century, charismatics their first generation." See Russell P. Spittler,
"Are Pentecostals and Charismatics Fundamentalists? A Review of American Uses of These
Categories," in *Charismatic Christianity as a Global Culture*, ed. Karla Poewe (Columbia: The
University of South Carolina Press, 1994), 105. Other scholars collapse the terms together
and use "Pentecostal" in an umbrella fashion to encompass both, which Henry occasionally did as well. For example, Allan Anderson, in his *An Introduction to Pentecostalism: Global
Charismatic Christianity* from Cambridge University Press, uses the term "Pentecostalism"
in an "all-embracing way" to include the charismatic movement. One sees the collapse of
these two terms even in the title and subtitle of the book. He does, however, see value in
recognizing that classic Pentecostalism almost always carries some relationship to a specific
denomination, while the same is not necessarily true of charismatics. So even in utilizing the
terms synonymously, he recognizes the need for some level of demarcation between the two.
See Anderson, *An Introduction to Pentecostalism: Global Charismatic Christianity* (Cambridge:
Cambridge University Press, 2004), 1. Both groups embrace and endorse the full suite of
New Testament supernatural gifts and seek to utilize them today. While most Pentecostals
see baptism in the Spirit as a necessary subsequent experience to conversion manifested by
speaking in tongues, there is not total agreement among charismatics on this point (though
many would endorse the Pentecostal perspective).
35. Marsden, *Understanding Fundamentalism and Evangelicalism*, 78–79.

speaking in tongues, faith healing, and power evangelism—not to mention charismatic, or "contemporary," worship.[36]

Molly Worthen also sees the 1960s as an important decade for the realignment of evangelicals and charismatics. Due to multiple forces, some in the fundamentalist-evangelical stream were "reconsidering" their traditionally closed stance to charismatic interests, including present-day miracles and tongues.[37] While Henry's assessment of this movement will be treated in chapter 2, it is important to demonstrate at the outset that pneumatological discussions were not ancillary to his theological context, but, in some ways, defined the era.[38] In an observation closer to home for Henry, Richard Lovelace thinks with the advent of neo-evangelicalism, "there · appeared to be a small outpouring of the Spirit at the midcentury mark," a

---

36. Douglas Sweeney, "One in the Spirit? Evangelicals Are Still Searching for the Elusive Ideal of Unity," *Christian History and Biography* 92 (2006): 43.

37. Molly Worthen, *Apostles of Reason: The Crisis of Authority in American Evangelicalism* (Oxford: Oxford University Press, 2014), 141-42. The terminology of "fundamentalist-evangelical" stream is used to indicate the fluid nature of the movement and how they identified themselves, though by the '60s the fault lines were fairly clear. In defining classic fundamentalism, George Marsden writes, "Fundamentalism was a loose, diverse, and changing federation of co-belligerents united by their fierce opposition to modernist attempts to bring Christianity into line with modern thought." While fundamentalists often shared a number of theological traits, including millenarianism and a commitment to the Old Princeton School regarding biblical inerrancy, it was their militaristic opposition to modern thought and theology that defined the movement. See George Marsden, *Fundamentalism and American Culture: The Shaping of Twentieth Century Evangelicalism: 1870–1925* (New York: Oxford University Press, 1980), 4-5.

38. While not directly related to Henry himself, pneumatological interest also intensified at Henry's Fuller Theological Seminary in the late-twentieth century (well after Henry's departure), kindled by C. Peter Wagner, Fuller professor of church growth. Though Henry was nearing the end of his public ministry during this episode, he was likely aware of the developments at an institution that he invested many years into and helped shape theologically in its early days. For more on the Holy Spirit and the Third Wave movement, see C. Peter Wagner, *The Third Wave of the Holy Spirit: Encountering the Power of Signs and Wonders* (Ann Arbor, MI: Vine Books, 1988). For the relationship between Fuller seminary and the Third Wave movement, see Lewis B. Smedes, ed., *Ministry and the Miraculous: A Case Study at Fuller Theological Seminary* (Pasadena, CA: Fuller Seminary Press, 1987); Worthen, *Apostles of Reason*, 145-47. For an account of the pneumatological trajectory at another theological seminary during the twentieth century (in contrast to that of Fuller), see Jason G. Duesing, "'Power in the Seminary': 20th Century Pneumatological Distinctives at Southwestern Baptist Theological Seminary," White Paper 11 (Fort Worth: The Center for Theological Research at Southwestern Baptist Theological Seminary, 2006): 1-16.

revival of sorts that emulated previous awakenings in the nation's history.[39] Whether inside or outside his immediate circles, the airwaves were filled with talk of the Spirit, and Henry was there in the middle.

Despite this global rise in pneumatological attention from both Protestant and Catholic corners, further work remains, especially among evangelicals. As Stephen Wellum observes:

> Regarding the subject of the third person of the Godhead, we must, sadly, admit that even today he is still the neglected person in Trinitarian discussion. Even though great strides have taken place in recent years to think through Scriptural teaching and to theologize about the Spirit's person and work, for many in the evangelical church a robust understanding and living out of the Spirit's work in our lives is still lacking.[40]

The value of this book is found at the intersection of these two rationales: understanding how Carl F. H. Henry, one of American evangelicalism's greatest minds and central figures, approached the doctrine of the Spirit will help evangelicals in particular appreciate their past and contribute to the future in this era of pneumatological resurgence.

Further, because Carl F. H. Henry is an accomplished figure in the history of evangelicalism, a deep exploration of his views of a particular theological locus—in this case, pneumatology—is valuable. Significant attention has been given to numerous areas of Henry's thought. For example, Henry's understanding of the kingdom of God,[41] political

---

39. Richard F. Lovelace, *Dynamics of Spiritual Life: An Evangelical Theology of Renewal* (Downers Grove, IL: InterVarsity Press, 1979), 53. For more on this mid-century "evangelical boom," see Collin Hansen and John Woodbridge, *A God-Sized Vision: Revival Stories that Stretch and Stir* (Grand Rapids: Zondervan, 2010), 157-77; Owen Strachan, "Light from the Third Great Awakening: Harold Ockenga and the Call to Future Pastor-Theologians," *Journal of Biblical and Theological Studies* 3.1 (2018): 93-95. George Marsden also recognizes that at mid-century, "the United States was experiencing one of the most widespread religious revivals in its history." Marsden sees this revival extending beyond evangelicalism to encompass other traditions and a wide range of Americans. See George Marsden, *The Twilight of the American Enlightenment: The 1950s and the Crisis of Liberal Belief* (New York: Basic Books, 2014), 97.

40. Stephen J. Wellum, "The Glorious Work of God the Holy Spirit," *Southern Baptist Journal of Theology* 16.4 (2012): 2.

41. See Russell D. Moore, "Kingdom Theology and the American Evangelical Consensus: Emerging Implications for Sociopolitical Engagement" (PhD diss., The Southern Baptist

thought,[42] epistemology,[43] social concern,[44] doctrine of Scripture,[45] role in evangelicalism,[46] and engagement with modern theology (especially Karl Barth)[47] have all received dissertation-level treatments. It is not difficult to find resources examining Carl F. H. Henry's thought on a variety of topics. Henry on the doctrine of revelation? Take your pick. Henry on cultural engagement? Countless options. Henry on public policy, science, philosophy, or history? You get the point. But, Henry on … the Holy Spirit? Not as much, and for understandable reasons.

Despite the varied studies of Henry on a litany of subjects, there has been no sustained, academic analysis of his pneumatology. One possible reason for this is because many researchers of Henry have been connected to conservative Baptist traditions, and pneumatological questions were not at the forefront of their inquiry. Instead, they were asking questions of Henry that were relevant to their particular theological agendas and traditions, primarily regarding the nature of Scripture and the relationship of the covenant community to the world.

Another key reason for a lack of attention to Henry's pneumatology is that pneumatology is not explicitly at the forefront of his work. It is impossible to turn to one volume or chapter to gain a comprehensive

---

Theological Seminary, 2002).

42. See David L. Weeks, "The Political Thought of Carl F. H. Henry" (PhD diss., Loyola University of Chicago, 1991).

43. See Robert Carswell, "A Comparative Study of the Religious Epistemology of Carl F. H. Henry and Alvin Plantinga" (PhD diss., The Southern Baptist Theological Seminary, 2007); Jonathan Waita, "Carl F. H. Henry and the Metaphysical Foundations of Epistemology" (PhD diss., Dallas Theological Seminary, 2012).

44. See Murray Dempster, "The Role of Scripture in the Social-Ethical Writings of Carl F. H. Henry" (PhD diss., The University of Southern California, 1969); Jerry M. Ireland, "Evangelism and Social Concern in the Theology of Carl F. H. Henry" (PhD diss., Liberty University, 2015).

45. See Michael D. White, "Word and Spirit in the Theological Method of Carl Henry" (PhD diss., Wheaton College, 2012); Jonathan Wood, "Revelation, History, and the Biblical Text in the Writings of Carl F. H. Henry" (PhD diss., Southwestern Baptist Theological Seminary, 2015).

46. See Phyllis Alsdurf, "*Christianity Today* Magazine and Late Twentieth-Century Evangelicalism" (PhD diss., The University of Minnesota, 2004); Benjamin Thomas Peays, "Carl F. H. Henry's Understanding of the Formation of Evangelical Self-Identity from 1945 to 1948" (PhD diss., Trinity Evangelical Divinity School, 2015).

47. See John B. Mann, "Revelation of the Triune God through Word and Spirit: A Theological Critique of Karl Barth and Carl Henry" (PhD diss., Southwestern Baptist Theological Seminary, 2018); R. Albert Mohler, "Evangelical Theology and Karl Barth: Representative Models of Response" (PhD diss., The Southern Baptist Theological Seminary, 1989).

understanding of Henry's pneumatology. Instead, one must do a bit of triangulation between his doctrine of God, his writings about the Spirit, and other writings on issues like evangelism and ecclesiology, which are not pneumatological per se but still address the Spirit. Henry's pneumatology is there, but it does not present itself easily. It requires construction. Nonetheless, he does address the doctrine of the Spirit, and pneumatology plays a relevant role in his overall theological method and vision. In this, Henry's pneumatology is similar to Calvin's:

> The Holy Spirit hovers, as it were, over every facet of Calvin's theology—the inspiration of Scripture, the creation of the world, the justification and sanctification of the Christian, and the superintendence of the church—yet he is rarely the direct object of Calvin's theological eye. From cover to cover of the *Institutes* the Holy Spirit's presence is luminous yet hidden, and everywhere implicit.[48]

Overall, though pneumatology is not primary for Henry, it is not insignificant. As Owen Strachan notes:

> It is right to pay attention to Henry's major contributions, as an increasing number of scholars are. In doing so, however, we would be unwise to neglect other areas of his scholarly work. ... A historical-theological curiosity may justly animate such investigation, as may an earnest and appropriate desire to fill out contemporary understanding of leading scholars of the past. If we ought not confine our study of figures like Henry to their subsidiary views, neither should we ignore them.[49]

---

48. Robert W. Caldwell, *Communion in the Spirit: The Holy Spirit as the Bond of Union in the Theology of Jonathan Edwards*, Paternoster Studies in Evangelical History and Thought (Eugene, OR: Wipf & Stock, 2006), 41. Henry himself was fond of Calvin's pneumatology. In Volume 4 of *God, Revelation and Authority*, Henry devoted an entire "Supplementary Note" to Calvin's understanding of how the Spirit works in illumination. Henry did not provide much analysis, but rather allowed Calvin to speak freely by collating selective quotes from Calvin's *Institutes*, especially regarding the Spirit's illuminating work in both general and special revelation. See Carl F. H. Henry, *God, Revelation and Authority*, 6 vols. (Waco, TX: Word Books, 1976–1983; Wheaton, IL: Crossway, 1999), 4:290–95. Hereafter *GRA*.

49. Owen Strachan, "Carl F. H. Henry's Doctrine of the Atonement: A Synthesis and Brief Analysis," *Themelios* 38.2 (2013): 216.

This book is an effort to retrieve a subsidiary, yet significant, area of Henry's corpus—that of pneumatology. Henry's understanding of the Spirit informs how one understands his views of Scripture, the church, ethics, and the Christian mission in a secular society—all areas he addressed at length. An exploration into Henry's pneumatology is a worthy contribution because it will give readers a better understanding of a relatively untapped area of his theology, while also shedding light on his own spirituality, thus giving readers a better grasp of Henry himself. Further, by understanding how Henry approached the doctrine of pneumatology, readers will gain insight into the various conversations between mid-century evangelicals regarding the person and work of the Spirit. Just as it took centuries for the Princeton theologian B. B. Warfield to recognize Calvin as "the theologian of the Holy Spirit," it has taken too long for scholars to recognize Henry as, though not *the* theologian of the Spirit, certainly *a* theologian of the Spirit.[50]

THE SCHOLARLY STORY SO FAR

With the above rationales outlined, we can overview the relevant literature surrounding Carl F. H. Henry's pneumatology. As mentioned above, not only have scholars not adequately addressed Henry's view of the Spirit, but some have critiqued him for overlooking the doctrine throughout his career. The scholarly story so far of Henry and the Spirt is either silence, criticism, or pneumatological appreciation limited to a single focus like revelation or ethics.

Some scholars have been silent regarding Henry's attention to the Spirit and his interaction with charismatic and Pentecostal traditions. For example, C. Douglas Weaver, in his sweeping *Baptists and the Holy Spirit: The Contested History with Holiness-Pentecostal-Charismatic Movements*, does not converse with Henry's evaluation of these movements, though (as will be shown in chapter 2) he had much to say about them (both positive and negative). Henry makes no appearance in Weaver's index.[51] Weaver's book

---

50. B. B. Warfield, "John Calvin the Theologian," in *Calvin and Augustine*, ed. Samuel G. Craig (Philadelphia: Presbyterian and Reformed, 1956), 487.

51. C. Douglas Weaver, *Baptists and the Holy Spirit: The Contested History with Holiness-Pentecostal-Charismatic Movements* (Waco, TX: Baylor University Press, 2019), 565.

is a magisterial account of the interactions between Baptists and various holiness groups with an impressive trail of meticulous research. It is arguably the strongest resource to date on how American Baptists have interacted with these traditions. Therefore, it is curious that Henry, a formidable Baptist theologian of the twentieth century—who did not tuck away his views of the Jesus People or the charismatic movement but published them in various places—is absent from the story. Of course, this is not because Weaver would discount Henry's important role in American evangelicalism, but instead is likely because Henry is so rarely consulted on issues beyond inerrancy and social engagement.

Other scholars offer critique. Albert Mohler and James Leo Garrett both see Henry's pneumatology as deficient. While Mohler sees ecclesiology as Henry's most "glaring omission," he also believes Henry "gave little attention to the Holy Spirit, and, except in his work in personal ethics, to the Christian life and devotion."[52] Garrett argues similarly that Henry has "given little attention to other doctrines, notably the Holy Spirit, the Christian life, and the church."[53] I offer an alternative interpretation of Henry by demonstrating that while Mohler and Garrett are undoubtedly correct that these elements were not dominant in his published work, he nonetheless expounded on them in greater degree than has been appreciated, and that pneumatology played a vital role in his articulations of revelation, ecclesiology, and ethics.

Further, while not pertaining to Henry's pneumatology specifically (though certainly connected to his understanding of the Spirit's work vis-à-vis inspiration and illumination), his views of propositional revelation have been challenged by scholars. Kevin Vanhoozer believes Henry "depersonalized" the written word of God and sees his propositional framework as "reductionistic."[54] Anthony Thiselton would likely group Henry into the "many" who "treat the whole Bible as consisting of 'closed' texts always in propositional form."[55] M. James Sawyer thinks Henry's mentor, Gordon

---

52. Mohler, "Carl F. H. Henry," 292.

53. James Leo Garrett, *Baptist Theology: A Four-Century Study* (Macon, GA: Mercer University Press, 2009), 519.

54. Kevin J. Vanhoozer, *The Drama of Doctrine: A Canonical-Linguistic Approach to Christian Theology* (Louisville: Westminster John Knox Press, 2005), 45, 268.

55. Anthony C. Thiselton, *Hermeneutics: An Introduction* (Grand Rapids: Eerdmans, 2009), 312.

Clark, "inculcated" twentieth-century evangelicals with a veiled rationalism attuned only to biblical propositions while downplaying the "existential dynamic of the Holy Spirit" in the life of the believer.[56] Henry, who "endorsed with approval his mentor's position," then became a key conduit of this supposedly Spirit-stunted view of special revelation to the evangelical masses.[57] However, this book will seek to absolve Henry of the strongest critiques from those who challenge his understanding of the relationship between word and Spirit.[58] To be sure, Henry's work was not unassailable. His thought is worthy of pushback, and its imperfections should not be ignored by his admirers. There is constructive aid in the criticisms of the committed evangelical scholars mentioned above and beyond. Still, I remain unconvinced of certain aspects of these critiques; by showcasing Henry's engagement with the Spirit, perhaps some of these disagreements will develop further and adopt a new appreciation for the supernatural side of Henry's articulation of propositional revelation.

Despite these critiques, Henry also has pneumatological defenders. Michael D. White calls the "oft-made claim that Henry ignores the work of the Holy Spirit" a "caricature."[59] Thornbury also challenges Henry's critics at this point:

> As we saw in a previous chapter, one of the oft-cited criticisms of Henry by postfoundationalist thinkers is that he does not emphasize the role of the Holy Spirit in advancing his theory of propositional revelation. After many years of reading and studying Henry, I can say that I honestly have no idea how someone who has actually read *God, Revelation and Authority* can say that.[60]

---

56. M. James Sawyer, "The Father, the Son, and the Holy Scriptures?" in *Who's Afraid of the Holy Spirit? An Investigation into the Ministry of the Spirit of God Today*, ed. Daniel B. Wallace and M. James Sawyer (Dallas: Biblical Studies Press, 2005), 254–68.

57. Sawyer, "The Father," 269. Sawyer also mentions Clark's influence on other evangelical theologians who contributed to the popularity of this view, including Ed Carnell, Paul Jewett, Edmund Clowney, and Billy Graham.

58. For more on Henry's approach to hermeneutics, see William C. Roach, *Hermeneutics as Epistemology: A Critical Assessment of Carl F. H. Henry's Epistemological Approach to Hermeneutics* (Eugene, OR: Wipf & Stock, 2015).

59. White, "Word and Spirit," 169. Vanhoozer defends Henry's view of propositional revelation at this point as well. See Vanhoozer, *The Drama of Doctrine*, 268.

60. Thornbury, *Recovering Classic Evangelicalism*, 132–33. For more on the nature of these specific critiques, see Chad Owen Brand, "Is Carl Henry a Modernist? Rationalism and

Thornbury also recognizes that "persistently in his explanation of inerrancy, Henry draws attention to the Spirit as an active and personal stim-
ulant toward understanding, discernment, and regeneration."[61] After
quoting a lengthy passage on the Spirit from Volume 4 of *God, Revelation
and Authority*, Thornbury states that "powerful observations such as these
characterize the prose of *GRA* and, once read, render ridiculous the notion
that Carl F. H. Henry embraced some sort of cold, rationalistic view of God,
the Spirit, and revelation."[62] And while "most theologians in Church history do not specifically refer to the 'authority of the Holy Spirit' in their
writings," John A. Studebaker recognizes that Henry had a developed concept of the Spirit's authority, and Studebaker places Henry next to Calvin
and Tertullian as theologians who exposit this element of pneumatology.[63]

Further, Malcolm Yarnell recognizes and appreciates Henry's "pneumatological epistemology."[64] He reviews Henry's understanding of propositional revelation and sees that "Henry is adamant that these doctrines
[inspiration, inerrancy, and infallibility] are pneumatological, and that
pneumatology is incredibly important."[65] Regarding Henry's pneumatology, Yarnell concludes:

> To summarize Henry's Spirit-based epistemology, the Holy Spirit,
> by inspiring the authors of an inerrant and infallible Bible and
> by illuminating or interpreting the Bible to us, makes Christ

---

Foundationalism in Post-War Evangelical Theology," *Trinity Journal* 20 (1999): 3–21. Carson
offers a similar defense of Henry vis-à-vis his postfoundationalist critics. He agrees with
Thornbury that many who critique Henry have misunderstood what Henry was arguing in
the first place, thereby mischaracterizing his views, leading to an unbalanced and unsym-
pathetic evaluation based on faulty original conclusions: "In short, not a few critics have
focused rather negatively on one element of Henry's thought—and even there not getting
Henry quite right—without attempting a broader (and necessarily more positive) evaluation
of the man." See Carson, "The Compleat Christian," 12.

61. Thornbury, *Recovering Classic Evangelicalism*, 143.

62. Thornbury, *Recovering Classic Evangelicalism*, 143–44.

63. John A. Studebaker, *The Lord Is the Spirit: The Authority of the Holy Spirit in Contemporary
Theology and Church Practice*, The Evangelical Theological Society Monograph Series (Eugene,
OR: Pickwick, 2008), 19.

64. Malcolm B. Yarnell III, "Whose Jesus? Which Revelation?" *Midwestern Journal of
Theology* 1.1–2 (2003): 45. Yarnell also draws upon Henry's work on the Spirit in other places.
For example, see Malcolm B. Yarnell III, "The Person and Work of the Holy Spirit," in *A
Theology for the Church*, ed. Daniel L. Akin, rev. ed. (Nashville: B&H Academic, 2014), 528–29.

65. Yarnell, "Whose Jesus? Which Revelation?," 44.

epistemologically available to us. The Holy Spirit, moreover, through Christian proclamation of the word, makes Christ soteriological available to us in regeneration. This relatively tight doctrine of revelation means one may not oppose personal experience or the Spirit or Jesus Christ to the Bible. One may not oppose the Jesus of experience to the Jesus of the Bible.[66]

Nonetheless, while acknowledging that Henry devoted thought to the Spirit, these writers limit their interaction with Henry's pneumatology to the doctrine of revelation. While important, this does not exhaust Henry's understanding of the Spirit. The data and evaluation of Henry's pneumatology, given his immense output and unpublished papers, is incomplete. Further, both Henry's pneumatological challengers and defenders do not answer relevant questions that can be posed by the data, including (but not limited to) how Henry's view of the Spirit impacted his understanding of the charismatic movement and how the fruit of the Spirit should manifest in one's life. This book will build on the defenders of Henry's pneumatology by examining the Spirit's role in inspiration and illumination in greater depth, and by extending it to ecclesiology and ethics as well by utilizing primary sources that they did not.

OVERVIEW, OUTLINE, AND METHODOLOGY

In summarizing the above, Carl F. H. Henry's pneumatology is a relevant field of further research because it has been argued that he possessed an insufficient doctrine of the Spirit. Because Henry is so vital to the history of American evangelicalism, investigating a subsidiary, yet significant, area of his corpus is a justifiable endeavor. Scholars contest whether Henry addressed pneumatology in a sufficient manner, and if so, whether the presentation is satisfactory given his overall theological goals. This book will seek to contribute to this conversation by demonstrating that not only did Henry believe pneumatology was an important field of inquiry, but also that pneumatology is an essential element to three areas of his theological program: revelation, ecclesiology, and ethics. In this, he believed that a Spirit-inspired Bible (revelation) would order a Spirit-enlivened body

---

66. Yarnell, "Whose Jesus? Which Revelation?," 46.

(ecclesiology) composed of Spirit-filled believers (ethics). In addressing these three areas, the book will attempt to show how pneumatology played a foundational role in how Henry understood and articulated each. Though not always explicitly stated, the Holy Spirit is embedded into—or, better yet, indwells—each of these areas to such an extent that it is not too much to say that his views regarding each are preceded by and dependent upon his understanding of the Spirit. Finally, the book will encourage contemporary evangelicals to give Henry a fresh hearing on the doctrine of the Spirit today.

In overviewing the book's arc, this final aim—giving Henry a fresh hearing—is important to emphasize at the beginning so as to prepare readers for the man they will meet and the value he offers. Henry was a cessationist, and his convictions as to why will be outlined in chapter 2. But, as will be expanded upon in the Conclusion, Henry shatters the stereotype of a ridged and curmudgeonly cessationist absorbed in a purely rational, black-and-white logic with no space for mystery or expectation of the Spirit. While some may suspect cessationists of subconsciously replacing the Spirit they cannot tame with a book they think they can, Henry—who has been characterized along these lines—demonstrates the faulty assumptions behind this impression. This is a secondary motive for surveying Henry's view of the Spirit: to depict with a flesh-and-blood figure that cessationism, while believing that certain supernatural sign-gifts ceased with the apostolic age, nonetheless can (and must!) exhibit a radical dependence on the Spirit and maintain a rich and active relationship with him that shapes their daily experience. No defense of cessationism is offered here as the particulars of that conversation lay outside of my scope. There are strong resources available for such an exploration.[67] I do, however, hope to exhibit the possibility of a dynamic and vivid Spirit-filled life for the cessationist both personally and corporately, with Henry serving

---

67. For a recent and accessible volume in favor of cessationism, see Thomas R. Schreiner, *Spiritual Gifts: What They Are & Why They Matter* (Nashville: B&H, 2018). For a standard text in the field, see Richard B. Gaffin, Jr., *Perspectives on Pentecost: New Testament Teaching on the Gifts of the Holy Spirit* (Grand Rapids: Baker, 1979). For two recent and respected volumes favoring the contrasting position, continuationism, see Gregg R. Allison and Andreas J. Köstenberger, *The Holy Spirit*, Theology for the People of God, ed. David S. Dockery, Nathan A. Finn, and Christopher Morgan (Nashville: B&H Academic, 2020); Andrew Wilson, *Spirit and Sacrament: An Invitation to Eucharismatic Worship* (Grand Rapids: Zondervan, 2018).

as a model. If you disagree with Henry and believe that the supernatural sign-gifts of the New Testament continue to operate in a normative fashion, I do hope you will continue reading and appreciate how one cessationist emphasized the Spirit in his theological vision and how he himself relied on the Spirit in his inner life. Henry might serve to shave off some of the rougher edges of certain unhelpful caricatures floating around in evangelical circles (both of Henry individually and of cessationism in general). If you think Henry is correct that certain miraculous gifts of the Spirit have ceased, he will press you to examine the extent to which you are actually anticipating the Spirit's activity *today*. Henry will ask of you more than you might expect: *more* recognition of the Spirit's role in Scripture, *more* desire for the Spirit's unity in the church, *more* dependency on the Spirit's power for evangelism and holiness, and *more* of the fruit of the Spirit in your posture and personal interactions. If reading Henry's work strengthens these pursuits, he will have succeeded.

This chapter has outlined the need for this particular study and has provided an overview of the existing literature pertaining to this topic. Chapter 2 will provide an overview of Henry's understanding of the Spirit's person and work, as well as the historical and theological context in which he was writing. Chapters 3 through 5 will address, in order, Henry's understanding of the Spirit's role in revelation, ecclesiology, and ethics. The Conclusion will unite these threads together and bolster the claim that Henry was indeed a theologian of the Spirit, and that his body of work can help a new generation of evangelicals to disagree well and work together toward a greater understanding of a desire for the Holy Spirit of God.

Throughout the book, we will examine primary sources from Henry that will help buttress the claim that he should be recognized as a theologian of the Spirit. Secondary sources will be consulted in order to further the conversation about the role of the Spirit in Henry's thought, especially as it pertains to the Bible, the church, and the Christian life. Special attention will be given to Henry's historical situation, especially his evaluations of the charismatic and Jesus People movements, as well as his interactions with Karl Barth and with advocates of ecumenism. This is necessary in order to demonstrate the considerable pneumatological climate in which Henry lived and to which he contributed. The following chapters will contain primary data relevant to the topic at hand from four main categories: academic volumes such as *God, Revelation and Authority* and *Christian Personal Ethics*; articles from *Christianity Today* and other journals; miscellaneous monographs; and unpublished material such as correspondence, notes, and sermons from the Carl F. H. Henry Papers housed in the Rolfing Library at Trinity Evangelical Divinity School in Deerfield, Illinois. As noted, while some have utilized one or a few of these sources, no project has yet incorporated them all into an evaluation of Henry's pneumatology.

2
—
CARL F. H. HENRY'S PNEUMATOLOGY (CONTOURS AND CONTEXT)

INTRODUCTION

Carl F. H. Henry's friend, Bernard Ramm, appreciated the mystery in analyzing the Holy Spirit:

> To profess to know a great deal about the Spirit of God is contrary to the nature of the Spirit of God. There is a hiddenness to the Spirit that cannot be uncovered. There is an immediacy of the Spirit that cannot be shoved into vision. There is an invisibility of the Spirit that cannot be forced into visibility. There is a reticence of the Spirit that cannot be converted into openness. For these reasons one feels helpless, inadequate, and unworthy to write a line about the Spirit.[1]

Or, as Graham Cole succinctly notes: "No one is master of the Spirit."[2]

Henry would claim to be no master of the Spirit, but he did attempt to bear witness to the biblical presentation of the third person of the Triune Godhead. He did so in his published works, and he also did so in the classroom. In what appear to be handwritten lecture notes, Henry bemoaned the fact that "seminaries have a semester or term on Christology, but [only]

---

1. Bernard Ramm, *Rapping about the Spirit* (Waco, TX: Word Books, 1974), 7. Quoted in Graham A. Cole, *He Who Gives Life: The Doctrine of the Holy Spirit*, Foundations of Evangelical Theology, ed. John S. Feinberg (Wheaton, IL: Crossway, 2007), 42.

2. Cole, *He Who Gives Life*, 41.

an hour lecture on the Spirit."[3] He then encouraged his students to read the works of Abraham Kuyper and George Smeaton on pneumatology.[4] Henry was concerned with "whether all that currently passes as pneumatology in religious circles is authentic," and was convinced that "if the resurgence of interest in the Holy Spirit is appropriate and necessary, no less so is a parallel interest in criteria for separating what is spiritually legitimate from what is counterfeit."[5] As with any theologian or commentator, Henry's portrait of the Spirit had both strengths and weaknesses. Nonetheless, he did take pneumatology seriously and sought to be a clear and credible voice for evangelicals during an era of pneumatological explosion.

Before defending the central thesis of this book—that Henry believed a Spirit-inspired Bible (revelation) would order a Spirit-enlivened body (ecclesiology) composed of Spirit-filled believers (ethics)—it is necessary to outline the broad contours of Henry's general pneumatological approach. Specifics in the areas of revelation, ecclesiology, and ethics will be reserved for subsequent chapters. First, this chapter will sketch a general outline of Henry's understanding of the Spirit's person and work. This is not an exhaustive account, nor does it consider every reference Henry made to the Spirit. Neither does it attempt to address every possible aspect of pneumatology that may be expected in a volume dedicated to that field. Instead, it aims to capture the *primary themes* that arise in *Henry's* work on the Spirit. Henry's pneumatology was active in his overall theological program, but its scale was limited as he did not devote ample attention to various facets contained in more expansive treatments. Therefore, the sections examining how Henry formulated the doctrine of the Spirit will be more descriptive

---

3. Carl F. H. Henry, untitled lecture notes, CFHHP (undated, unprocessed box). In his archives, Henry left another handwritten document on the Spirit which he titled "Pneumatology = The Holy Spirit." Both documents appear to be lecture notes, as they contain a typical speaking outline with various comments and the occasional illustration interspersed.

4. Specifically, Henry referenced Abraham Kuyper, *The Work of the Holy Spirit*, trans. Henri De Vries (New York: Funk & Wagnalls, 1900) and George Smeaton, *The Doctrine of the Holy Spirit* (Edinburgh: T&T Clark, 1882).

5. Henry, *GRA*, 6:371. Writing contemporaneously with Henry, Richard F. Lovelace shared a similar concern: "In what has already been said about the Jesus movement and the Charismatic renewal, it is clear that not everything which accompanies a renewed surge of vitality in the church is necessarily healthy, productive and purely of the Holy Spirit." See Lovelace, *Dynamics of Spiritual Life*, 239.

than constructive. Second, with the broad contours of Henry's pneumatology in place, the chapter will then situate Henry within his historical
and pneumatological context and lay out how he interpreted his own times
with regard to the charismatic and Jesus People movements.

THE UN-SYSTEMATIC THEOLOGIAN

Before evaluating the basic contours of Henry's pneumatology, it is important to reflect upon his theological methodology. Henry's pneumatology
unfolds across his corpus in a certain way due to his tendencies. Specifically,
the fact that Henry was not a traditional systematic theologian, nor an
expert biblical exegete, influenced his pneumatological writings.

Considering he did not write a traditional systematic theology, nor did
he structure his writings in the vein of most systematicians, few would
characterize Carl F. H. Henry as a systematic theologian in the traditional
sense.[6] Instead, Henry brought a journalistic slant to his work. He was
always in conversation with the preeminent voices of the day on a given
theological topic, and his writings often set various thinkers in conversation with one other, with Henry operating as umpire throughout.[7] Perhaps

---

6. According to John Webster, "Systematic theology aims at a comprehensive,
well-proportioned, and unified conceptual representation of Christian teaching. In conceptu-
alizing Christian doctrine in its full scope, systematic theology treats a relatively stable range
of topics, even though individual essays may adjust the proportions or placement of certain
elements of the whole, and may judge some topics outside their concern." See John Webster,
"Introduction: Systematic Theology," in *The Oxford Handbook of Systematic Theology*, ed. John
Webster, Kathryn Tanner, and Iain Torrance (Oxford: Oxford University Press, 2007), 12. Given
Webster's definition, Henry likely would not be considered a systematic theologian because
one would be hard-pressed to demonstrate that he attempted a "comprehensive" account of
Christian doctrine throughout his career, nor one "well-proportioned," as Henry's efforts
were spent heavily on revelation. Loci like eschatology were not given the same amount
of attention. Certainly, the range of Henry's writings, when collated together, address the
various divisions of traditional systematic theologies. However, even in this, it seems too
much to say that Henry ever attempted a "unified conceptual representation" of Christian
dogma. However, G. Wright Doyle argues that Henry was indeed a systematic theologian.
See Doyle, *Carl Henry: Theologian for All Seasons*, 93–94. It is fair to say that *God, Revelation
and Authority* is in the vein of systematic theology, if not a complete or comprehensive one.
Doyle is certainly correct in defending Henry against those who paint him as essentially a
"theological journalist." See Doyle, *Carl Henry: Theologian for All Seasons*, 93.

7. D. A. Carson, "The Compleat Christian," 14–15. Carson sees this as both a strength and
a weakness. He believes it to be one reason why Henry was simultaneously influential in
his day (because of his awareness of contemporary theological trends), while also sounding,
to some readers, dated today (as many of Henry's conversation partners have faded from
twenty-first-century discussions).

Henry's unique approach and organization is what leads Mohler to conclude that "the lack of systematic expression has left several theological
issues untouched and underdeveloped in Henry's system" (including, pre-
sumably, pneumatology).[8]

Not only was Henry not a traditional systematician, neither was he
known as an accomplished exegete. His strengths were in philosophy of
religion, epistemology, revelation, and modern theology. He was not particularly strong in biblical studies or biblical languages. Gregory Thornbury
thinks that "though Carl cited a lot of Bible verses in his work, context for
those references was not always provided, which, coupled with his relatively weak command of Hebrew, may have limited his exegesis."[9] Early
in his academic journey, Henry found the study of Hebrew to be "unre-
warding," and he ultimately forgot what little Hebrew he knew almost
as quickly as he acquired it.[10] Decades later, nearing the end of his career,
Henry still did not possess great confidence in his exegetical abilities, especially as he understood exegesis relating to systematic theology. In a 1990
letter to D. A. Carson, Henry remarked: "Only today did I catch up with
the essay you thoughtfully shared with me, on 'The Role of Exegesis in
Systematic Theology,' and I found it rewarding indeed. At point after point
I saluted your convictions, even if I am unable to do them justice in my
own work."[11] Beyond exegesis, Henry was also not a trained church his-
torian, and nowhere did he trace in depth the history of pneumatological
development.[12] Where Henry excelled, however, was in his overview of the

---

8. Mohler, "Carl F. H. Henry," 292.

9. Thornbury, *Recovering Classic Evangelicalism*, 23.

10. Henry, *Confessions of a Theologian*, 92–93. This, of course, does not mean that Henry
was unqualified to do exegesis at a scholarly level. Indeed, his master's thesis at Wheaton
College was devoted to an exegesis of the parables in Matthew 13. Further, Henry was appar-
ently equipped enough to guest teach on the Gospels from the Greek text while at Northern
Seminary. See Henry, *Confessions of a Theologian*, 92.

11. Carl F. H. Henry, letter to Don Carson, February 22, 1990, CFHHP (box 1990 [box 1],
file "Correspondence—Misc.").

12. That is, in relative comparison to what could be said about the historical development
of pneumatology. He did, however, reflect upon the early ecumenical creeds, which also
allowed him to address the development of the Spirit's place in these early statements. See
Henry, *GRA*, 5:201–206. Though not focused on pneumatology, Henry also devoted a chapter
to the Chalcedonian definition in *The Identity of Jesus of Nazareth*. However, the chapter was
focused on modern receptions of the definition in light of twentieth-century Christological
trends rather than on the definition's historical setting or development. See Carl F. H. Henry,
The Identity of Jesus of Nazareth (Nashville: Broadman & Holman, 1992), 89–113.

Spirit in light of modernist theology and the need for a dependence on the Spirit for the Christian life.

The above is in no way meant to question Henry's exegetical competence or theological method. He was an evangelical theologian par excellence. Rather, it is meant to help interpreters appreciate Henry's strengths and weaknesses, and to argue that these provide contextual clues as to the organization of his theological writings and how he approached the theological task, including pneumatology.

As demonstrated, Henry has been critiqued for neglecting pneumatology, perhaps because he offered no single volume on the topic, nor did he treat the doctrine in a concentrated way. Instead, Henry's comments on the Spirit are interspersed throughout various theological disciplines. However, this is not unlike how other theologians have approached the topic. As Kärkkäinen observes:

> Traditionally, pneumatology has not received a separate locus in Christian systematic theologies. Unlike the doctrine of the Trinity or the church, the discussion of the Spirit has not stood on its own feet, so to speak. Most often pneumatological topics have been incorporated into the doctrine of salvation (soteriology) and inspiration of Scripture. Pneumatology has also been connected routinely with the doctrine of the church.[13]

According to this remark, Henry is squarely within how other theologians have treated the Spirit—by incorporating pneumatology into multiple theological areas. In Henry's case, these are revelation, ecclesiology, and ethics. This is not a drawback to his approach but rather reaffirms him as one who took seriously the Spirit across the spectrum of his theological reflection. Based on Kärkkäinen's observation, Henry's pneumatological schema is unsurprising given how others have approached the subject throughout church history. Just as Henry's pneumatology was compared to Calvin's in chapter 1, it also resembled that of the Anglican theologian Richard Hooker, whose "discussion of the Holy Spirit is unsystematic although his dependence on the Holy Spirit for his theology is extensive."[14]

---

13. Kärkkäinen, Pneumatology, 9.
14. John K. Stafford, "Richard Hooker's Doctrine of the Holy Spirit" (PhD diss., The University of Manitoba, 2005), ii.

Before proceeding to the contours of Henry's pneumatology, one final preparatory remark is necessary to set the stage for how Henry engages the subject. Indeed, what follows applies to any account of the person and work of the Spirit, not only to that of Carl Henry. In *Christianity Today*, Henry remarked that "the office of the Spirit is that of testifying to Jesus Christ as our incarnate, crucified, and risen Savior. The Spirit does not put himself into the forefront so to speak."[15] In *The Holy Spirit: Shy Member of the Trinity*, F. Dale Bruner colorfully captures this activity of the Spirit:

> It has often been said that the Holy Spirit is the Cinderella of the Trinity, the great neglected person of the Godhead, and that if the church could rediscover the person and work of the Holy Spirit, it would, at the same time, rediscover the power of Pentecost and of the earliest Christians. I am not convinced. ... I do believe, however, that the Spirit's sign, desire, and work is that we be overcome again, thrilled again, excited, impressed and gripped again by the wonder, the majesty, the earthiness, the relevance of Jesus and his Word to our world. The Holy Spirit does not mind being Cinderella outside the ballroom if the Prince is honored inside his Kingdom.[16]

The above comments serve as important reminders to any exploration of the Spirit. Verses pertinent to pneumatology do not fall into neatly defined categories. The Spirit will not be examined for his own glory, for he seeks the glory of the Son. Therefore, any investigation of the Spirit must be undertaken with a willingness to encounter some level of mystery.

"THE FULL, FURIOUS WIND OF GOD": THE CONTOURS OF HENRY'S PNEUMATOLOGY

With these preliminary comments about Henry's methodology and the nature of pneumatological exploration in place, it is appropriate to proceed to the general contours of Henry's pneumatology. This section will provide

---

15. Unsigned editorial, "The Spirit and the Church," 20.

16. Frederick Dale Bruner and William Hordern, *The Holy Spirit: Shy Member of the Trinity* (Eugene, OR: Wipf & Stock, 2001), 16. Horton rejects the language of shyness as it pertains to the Spirit, though he may be operating off a different definition than Bruner. See Horton, *Rediscovering the Holy Spirit*, 16. Bruner stresses that he does not mean weakness or timidity. He means rather the Spirit's deference to Christ. Still, Horton wants to maintain that the Spirit is no "freelance operator" but is "integral to the divine drama from beginning to end." Both are true: the Spirit is integral to every work of God, and one key work is his pointing men to the glories of Christ.

an overview of Henry's understanding of the person and work of the Holy Spirit. In Volume 6 of *God, Revelation and Authority*, Henry referred to the Spirit as the "full, furious wind of God."[17] This section will utilize Henry's terminology in reference to both the Spirit's person and work.

THE FULL WIND OF GOD: THE PERSON OF THE SPIRIT

As referenced in the introduction to chapter 1, Carl F. H. Henry was abundantly clear that the Holy Spirit is a person, even if Henry believed him to be a displaced person in the life of the church.[18] In the same piece, Henry approvingly quoted an unnamed theologian: "When Christianity lost the Holy Spirit as the divine person who leads into all truth, the Spirit was soon misunderstood (by idealistic philosophy) only as Mind, indeed as human mind. The ability of distinguishing spirits was lost."[19]

Henry remarked in his 1957 *Christian Personal Ethics*:

> The Spirit is the dynamic principle of Christian ethics, the personal agency whereby God powerfully enters human life and delivers man from enslavement to Satan, sin, death, and law. The Spirit of God is not listed under "others" in the *dramatis personae* of redemption. He is a main character whose role is crucial for the life of holiness in all its phases.[20]

In the same chapter, Henry appealed to 1 Corinthians 2:10 to affirm that the Spirit is "the principle of knowledge" and that "nothing, not even the secrets of God, is beyond the Spirit's reach or scrutiny."[21] He recognized that the Spirit is not a secondary force grasping for divinity; rather he shares in God's very essence. On this point, Henry noted that "the Holy Spirit is no mere synonym for the example of Christ, not even a mystical metaphor for the Indwelling Christ."[22] Instead, the Spirit is a person, consubstantial with the Father and the Son, existing eternally as God the Spirit.

---

17. Henry, *GRA*, 6:336.
18. Henry, "I Believe ... ," 23.
19. Henry, "I Believe ... ," 23.
20. Carl F. H. Henry, *Christian Personal Ethics* (Grand Rapids: Eerdmans, 1957), 437.
21. Henry, *Christian Personal Ethics*, 450.
22. Henry, *Christian Personal Ethics*, 443.

Another defense of the Spirit's deity that Henry provided in *Christian Personal Ethics* concerns the Spirit's work of regeneration. He emphasized that the Spirit, as God, has united the Christian to Christ, not in a subjective way awaiting final consummation but in an objective sense—believers have been made alive by the Spirit here and now (Eph 2:5).[23] Because only God has the authority to make one at peace with himself, and Henry saw this role attributed to the Spirit in Scripture, Henry thus recognized the divinity of the Spirit. In *Christian Personal Ethics*, Henry routinely appealed to the Spirit as the "source of new life" by citing Scriptures such as Romans 8:2, 6 and 2 Corinthians 3:6.[24] Henry understood that if the Spirit was not the divine Spirit, but only a hazy energy of sub-divine substance, then salvation itself would be a futile concept.[25]

Henry also gave attention to the person of the Spirit in *God, Revelation and Authority*. In Volume 6, he reached back to show that the Old Testament paints a foundational portrait of the Holy Spirit, one distinct from the concept of impersonal force so prevalent in secular philosophy (both ancient and modern):

> We should emphasize, first of all, that mention of the Spirit is not unique to the New Testament. References to the divine Spirit are found in Greek secular philosophy, although, except in Stoicism, the concept has but a secondary role; the *pneuma* is generally regarded as a vital and impersonal force immanent in the universe and not clearly nonmaterial at that. The Old Testament, however, views

---

23. Henry, *Christian Personal Ethics*, 449.

24. Henry, *Christian Personal Ethics*, 454.

25. John Feinberg and Michael Reeves also stress this point. According to Feinberg, "As to the Holy Spirit, if he is not fully God, the implications for salvation are again serious. Scripture teaches that the Holy Spirit regenerates believers and indwells them and fills them, but if the Holy Spirit is a lesser God or no God at all, how can we be sure that he can do any of these things? Moreover, unless he is coequal in being and purpose with the Father and the Son, what guarantees that even if he tried to do such things, the Father and the Son would recognize his actions as appropriate and relate to us accordingly?" See John S. Feinberg, *No One Like Him: The Doctrine of God*, Foundations of Evangelical Theology, ed. John S. Feinberg (Wheaton, IL: Crossway, 2001), 440. Michael Reeves writes, "If the Spirit were not God, he could not [bring mankind into communion with the Father and Son]. It is because God is three persons—Father, Son, and Spirit—that we can have such communion. If God was in heaven and his Spirit a mere force, he would be more distant than the moon." See Michael Reeves, *Delighting in the Trinity: An Introduction to the Christian Faith* (Downers Grove, IL: IVP Academic, 2012), 90.

the divine Spirit as a revelation of the transcendent personal God, a supernatural reality not reducible to an impersonal principle intrinsically immanent in the cosmos or man. God's Spirit is neither pantheistically related to man's spirit nor a supernatural power immanent in man and the world. The Spirit is, rather, a transcendent personal reality. This Old Testament view is foundational to the teaching elaborated more fully in the Christian era.[26]

Moving into the New Testament, Henry's favorite evidence for the personhood and divinity of the Spirit was the baptismal formula of Matthew 28:19 and the apostolic benediction of 2 Corinthians 13:13–14. According to Henry, "the juxtaposition of the names of the Father and the Son and the Spirit ... keeps the three personal names prominent before the people. The passages that mention the divine persons imply personal equality. ... By addressing three persons of the Godhead the apostolic benediction implies their distinct personality and common divinity."[27] Henry also appealed to 2 Thessalonians 2:13, Romans 1:1–4, and 1 Peter 1:2 to buttress this argument. Further, in the March 12, 1965, issue of *Christianity Today*, Henry published the text of a radio address previously given by J. Gresham Machen, in which Machen made precisely the same point regarding the divine name of Father, Son, and Spirit. According to Machen:

> For one thing, the great Trinitarian passages in the Bible really imply the personality of the Spirit. When, for example, our Lord in the "Great Commission" at the end of the Gospel according to Matthew command the apostles to make disciples of all the nations, "baptizing them in the name of the Father, and of the Son, and of the Holy Ghost," can he possibly mean that although the Father and the Son are persons, the Holy Ghost is a mere impersonal aspect of the being of the Father or of the Son? The perfect coordination of the

---

26. Henry, *GRA*, 6:371.

27. Henry, *GRA*, 5:198. Henry referenced 2 Corinthians 13:13 as the apostolic benediction here in *GRA*, but many translations cite the benediction as verse 14, in which Paul writes, "The grace of the Lord Jesus Christ and the love of God and the fellowship of the Holy Spirit be with you all."

three—Father, Son, and Holy Spirit—would seem to make such an interpretation extremely unusual.[28]

Henry understood Trinitarianism to be central to biblical Christianity. In his chapter on the Trinity in *God, Revelation and Authority*, Henry stated:

At the heart of Christianity's revelation of God is a trinitarian form of monotheism. That the living God is triune—that three eternal persons coexist within the one divine essence—is the distinctive Christian affirmation about deity. Alongside the proper names of God and his perfectional names the Bible arrays the personal names Father, Son, and Holy Spirit. The doctrine of the Trinity is Christianity's unique declaration concerning the divine being and is definitive for Christian theism.[29]

Though modernist theology "had reduced the Spirit of God from a distinct person to a divine power or influence," Henry maintained that the Spirit is a divine person, the full wind of God, who moves and lives and acts as the third person of the Trinity.[30]

EVALUATION OF HENRY'S PRESENTATION
OF THE SPIRIT'S PERSON

Henry's thought on the Spirit's person was less developed than his thought on the Spirit's work. He affirmed the ecumenical creeds regarding the Spirit's divinity and highlighted the necessary implications that flow from a Trinitarian understanding of God. However, outside of the Scripture references above, Henry did not devote expansive thought to the Spirit's person. The main area of neglect in Henry's presentation was his attention specifically to the Spirit's divine attributes. Again, Henry was content to recognize that the Spirit shares the divine name in multiple triadic passages, a worthy defense of the Spirit as God. But more could be said. He did not thoroughly address attributes such as the Spirit's holiness,

---

28. J. Gresham Machen, "The Eternal Verities: The Holy Spirit," *Christianity Today* (March 12, 1956): 27.

29. Henry, *GRA*, 5:191.

30. Henry, *GRA*, 4:256.

omnipresence, omnipotence, and eternality.[31] As seen above, Henry's comment on 1 Corinthians 2:10 is a recognition of divine omniscience linked to the Spirit. However, beyond this, Henry did not address the Spirit's divine attributes at length.

The strongest aspect of Henry's presentation of the Spirit is its Trinitarian framework.[32] The Spirit's person should not be extracted from the Godhead and analyzed as if he exists in suspension from Father and Son. Thankfully, Henry avoided this approach. This allowed him to recognize the interconnectedness of Trinitarian theology with other doctrines such as justification and sanctification. If the Spirit were not God, these would be not only impossible but inconceivable. Christopher Holmes recognizes the necessity of a fully Trinitarian schema for a healthy pneumatology: "In sum, one's pneumatology is only as good as one's wider doctrine of the Trinity. The doctrine of the Trinity is the principle of intelligibility for pneumatology: without the Trinity, not only pneumatology but also all other doctrines lose their anchor."[33] Carl F. H. Henry got this right, and his Trinitarian impulse in discussing the person of the Spirit should be recognized, applauded, and emulated.

THE FURIOUS WIND OF GOD: THE WORK OF THE SPIRIT

Most of Carl F. H. Henry's attention to the Spirit is devoted to how the Spirit works both individually and corporately. In highlighting the "furious" wind of God, Henry was not using the word with a negative connotation, but rather highlighting the power and activity of the Spirit. While subsequent chapters will develop the Spirit's work at greater lengths (specifically in revelation, ecclesiology, and ethics), this section will mention the broad strokes of how Henry understood the Spirit to operate.

---

31. For a helpful treatment of the passages connecting these divine attributes directly to the Spirit, see Matthew Barrett, "'We Believe in the Holy Spirit': Revisiting the Deity of the Spirit," *Southern Baptist Journal of Theology* 16.4 (2012): 39–41.

32. On this topic of Trinitarian relations, Henry believed the Spirit proceeds from the Father and the Son. See Henry, *GRA*, 6:401. In this, he embraced the *filioque* clause traditional in Western conceptions of Trinitarian relations. For more, see Allison and Köstenberger, *The Holy Spirit*, 258–64. For an overview of the development and disagreements surrounding this doctrine, see A. Edward Siecienski, *The Filioque: History of a Doctrinal Controversy*, Oxford Studies in Historical Theology (Oxford: Oxford University Press, 2010).

33. Christopher J. Holmes, *The Holy Spirit*, New Studies in Dogmatics, ed. Michael Allen and Scott R. Swain (Grand Rapids: Zondervan, 2015), 213.

BAPTIZING, SEALING, AND FILLING

Perhaps the clearest framework for summarizing how Henry understood the Spirit to work in an individual's life is to utilize the terms he used in *Christian Personal Ethics*: baptizing, sealing, and filling.[34] According to Henry, the baptism of the Spirit is not a subsequent experience to salvation but happens at the moment of conversion. Indeed, baptism by the Spirit is precisely what 1 Corinthians 12:12–13 states: "For just as the body is one and has many members, and all the members of the body, though many, are one body, so it is with Christ. For in one Spirit we were all baptized into one body—Jews or Greeks, slaves or free—and all were made to drink of one Spirit."[35] Henry believed that upon conversion, believers are baptized into new spiritual realities, most importantly into the body of Christ. Contrary to Pentecostal or charismatic conceptions of a post-conversion baptism in the Spirit, Henry claimed, "[T]he biblical data nowhere teach that the Spirit's baptism of the believer occurs subsequent to the new birth."[36] As a result of his conviction that baptism by the Spirit happened at regeneration, he did not recognize speaking in tongues as validation for one's spiritual baptism. He also appealed to church history in his defense that glossolalia is no indication of the baptism of the Spirit by noting that "this view has no support from such Christian stalwarts of the past as Luther, Calvin, Knox, Wesley, Whitefield, Edwards, Carey, Judson and others."[37]

The Spirit also seals the believer. Henry drew his understanding of this aspect of the Spirit's work from passages such as Ephesians 1:13 and 4:30, 2 Corinthians 1:21, and Revelation 7:3. He thought this sealing encompassed three functions: confirmation, identification, and security.[38] The Spirit confirms believers are children of God, as seen in passages such as

---

34. Henry, *Christian Personal Ethics*, 451–56. Henry used similar language roughly thirty years later in *God, Revelation and Authority* (baptism, indwelling, and infilling). Though he modified the language, the concepts remained the same. See Henry, *GRA*, 6:385–87.

35. Henry, *Christian Personal Ethics*, 452.

36. Henry, *GRA*, 6:385. In this section, Henry anticipated the passages that some would use to defend a second "Spirit baptism." He briefly exegeted Acts 8:17; 9:17; 11:16; and 19:1–7, concluding that these "contrary inferences" are completely unjustifiable. See Henry, *GRA*, 6:385–386.

37. Henry, *GRA*, 4:287.

38. Henry, *Christian Personal Ethics*, 453. Ferguson agrees when he states, "Sealing may indicate a variety of things: it secures and may also authenticate an object with a view to some future occasion (for Paul, 'for the day of redemption')." See Ferguson, *The Holy Spirit*, 180–82.

Romans 8:16 and 1 John 5:10. He identifies and marks them as belonging not to the world but to God, as seen in John 14:17. Finally, he secures their final salvation, as seen in Ephesians 4:30 and Romans 8:23.[39]

Henry also understood the Spirit to fill the believer. This role occupied most of Henry's attention in both *Christian Personal Ethics* and *God, Revelation and Authority*. He saw the two above actions (baptizing and sealing) as "permanent and once-for-all," but the Spirit's filling requiring "daily renewal."[40] He highlighted the command in Ephesians 5:18 to be "filled with the Spirit" (and indicated the passive voice of the original text) to show that "the Spirit is eager to occupy us, and that if we are unfulfilled the fault is ours."[41] This filling was meant to be an ongoing experience, akin to drinking deeply from an ever-present stream of empowerment:

> In an otherwise arid land, the Jordan River was known as a lifeline but as a variably sufficient one; the "rivers of living water" mentioned by Jesus represent by contrast an inexhaustible supply of the Spirit that flows from him to the believer in constant renewal and refreshing. Normal Christian living is a life continually sustained by the Spirit.[42]

Again, in *Christian Personal Ethics*, he wrote that "this filling is not to be merely a spasmodic last resort in times of moral defeat and ethical exasperation. Rather, it is meant to be a daily and normal experience."[43] He stressed that the Spirit's filling does not mean that at salvation believers only receive a portion of the Spirit. Instead, Henry meant that it is possible that "the full claim of the Spirit may not yet be fully translated into life, and hence the call to the Spirit's fullness perpetually confronts the believer."[44] Therefore, he found it possible that "one may be a believer without this constant filling of the Spirit—a weak believer, not drawing on the spiritual resources at his disposal, but frustrating the Spirit's manifestations,

---

39. Henry, *Christian Personal Ethics*, 453.
40. Henry, *Christian Personal Ethics*, 453–54.
41. Henry, *Christian Personal Ethics*, 454.
42. Henry, *GRA*, 6:387.
43. Henry, *Christian Personal Ethics*, 454.
44. Henry, *Christian Personal Ethics*, 454.

and allowing the old nature to reassert itself in thought, feeling, word, and action."[45]

Associated with Henry's understanding of the Spirit's filling was his understanding of the spiritual gifts bestowed by God to the church: "The Spirit's fullness is connected with a considerable diversity of gifts, all bestowed for the edification of the whole body of believers."[46] He recognized that, in one sense, all Christians are "charismatic" in that they all receive at least one divine *charismata*.[47] He was careful, however, to focus on the Spirit's gracious endowment of the gifts rather than the individual's worthiness to receive them. Further, he stressed that these gifts were given for the common good, not individual glory (1 Cor 12:7). Regarding specific gifts themselves, Henry recognized that there are distinctions between them, but that "perhaps we should not impose too much systematic rigidity on the stipulated gifts, since in some respects they seem to overlap."[48] For a believer to discern his or her gift, simply "giving oneself under God to serve others may be the best way to discover what special gift or gifts one has."[49]

The Spirit's ministry of baptizing, sealing, and filling the believer does not exhaust Henry's understanding of the Spirit's work. Indeed, the remainder of this book is an exercise in detailing how Henry understood the Spirit to operate in the domains of revelation, ecclesiology, and ethics. Therefore, more will be said as the chapters unfold. However, one aspect of Henry's pneumatology deserves further comment here, as it helps interpret many of Henry's views outlined later.

As can be gathered from the above, regarding the nature of supernatural sign-gifts, Henry was a cessationist.[50] He believed that "miracles,

---

45. Henry, *Christian Personal Ethics*, 455.

46. Henry, *GRA*, 6:388.

47. Henry, *GRA*, 6:390.

48. Henry, *GRA*, 6:390. Henry briefly commented on various gifts in *GRA*, 6:392–94.

49. Henry, *GRA*, 6:391.

50. According to Richard Gaffin, cessationism is the conviction that the supernatural sign-gifts of the New Testament ceased with the close of the apostolic era, as their role of confirming the apostles' message was no longer necessary. See Richard B. Gaffin, "A Cessationist View," in *Are Miraculous Gifts for Today? Four Views*, ed. Stanley N. Gundry and Wayne A. Grudem (Grand Rapids: Zondervan, 1996), 41–42. In one of the twentieth century's key defenses of cessationism, B. B. Warfield argued that the miraculous sign-gifts "were part of the credentials of the Apostles as the authoritative agents of God in founding the church. Their function thus confined them to distinctively the Apostolic Church, and they necessarily passed away with

tongues, and prophecies appear as temporary phenomena."[51] The next section exploring Henry's historical situation contains more on his specific critiques of the charismatic movement, but it suffices to say here that Henry recognized a distinction between those gifts that ceased with the apostolic era and those that continue.[52] Henry shared his views on the topic not only in the academy but also from the pulpit. In one unpublished sermon on Philippians 3:1–12, Henry asked (regarding Philippians 3:10), "Does Paul, as some charismatics suggest, mean that we are to share in the power of Christ's resurrection by the gifts of healing and exotic tongues? I think not, though I shall not now argue the point."[53] He reserved detailed argumentation for his academic volumes, primarily *Christian Personal Ethics* and *God, Revelation and Authority*.

But before departing from these comments, it is important to provide expanded context for Henry's cessationist convictions, especially regarding miracles. From the above, Henry might be interpreted as claiming that God no longer performs miracles in the modern day. But to pigeonhole Henry as an anti-supernaturalist who disregarded God's ability to work however he pleases, including through the miraculous, would be to misread what he claimed. Henry understood God's omnipotence to be the grounds upon which he is "free to preserve the course and causality of nature, to work miracles, or even to do away with nature entirely if he wills."[54] Though Henry believed the supernatural sign-gifts were not normative for the church today and was unpersuaded that individuals possessed a divine bestowment of miraculous gifting, he believed that God operates in miraculous ways well beyond the apostolic age into the present. In his first published pamphlet written only a year after his conversion, Henry defined the "Spirit-directed life" as "living [in such a way] that we expect miracles

---

it." See B. B. Warfield, *Counterfeit Miracles* (New York: Charles Scribner's Sons, 1918), 6. While agreeing with Warfield's position, Gaffin provides helpful framing and intramural critique of Warfield's approach. See Gaffin, "A Cessationist View," 28–29.

51. Henry, *Christian Personal Ethics*, 440.

52. Henry, *GRA*, 6:397.

53. Carl F. H. Henry, "God's Call to the Higher Life," unpublished sermon, August 12, 1990, CFHHP (box 1990 [box 1], file "God's Call to the Higher Life").

54. Henry, *GRA*, 5:311.

to happen."[55] Roughly five decades later, Henry maintained that "God at his sovereign discretion can and does heal with or without faith."[56] He continued:

> According to some scholars, miracles ceased with the ending of the apostolic age once the New Testament revelation was inscripturated and apostolic testimony no longer required external accreditation by signs. The New Testament nowhere explicitly states whether miracles will cease or continue beyond its pages. No one will deny that medieval church history lent itself to legend on the premise that miracles continue, and many cults today exploit the miraculous. Just because genuine articles have been counterfeited, however, is no reason to discard the genuine article. It could be that the present crisis-time in the fortunes of Christian faith, an age that some consider the threshold of the final end-time, may see a recurrence of dramatic signs and wonders both genuine and counterfeit.[57]

From these and other corresponding comments, G. Wright Doyle is correct to conclude that "Carl Henry did not, like some theologians, deny the present activity of the Spirit in the church; he was open to the reality of miracles in this age."[58] Recognizing this about Henry is important as it nuances his pneumatological position and defends him against accusations of a crude cessationism unmoved by the miraculous.[59] He remained

---

55. Carl F. H. Henry, "The Mystery of Living Victoriously," CFHHP (box 1935, file "My First Printed Pamphlets 1934–1935").

56. Henry, *GRA*, 6:392.

57. Henry, *GRA*, 392–93.

58. G. Wright Doyle, "Carl Henry and the Chinese Church," *Evangelical Review of Theology* 38.1 (2014): 45.

59. With regard to healing and miracles, Henry personifies what Thomas Schreiner describes as "nuanced cessationism." Schreiner writes: "It isn't clear to me that particular people have a *gift* of healing or miracles. This certainly does not mean there aren't miracles today! God can still heal and do miracles according to his will, and he does! Cessationism doesn't mean there are no miracles in the present age, nor does it mean that we don't pray for healings or miracles. ... Yes, God works miracles, but they are relatively rare. Perhaps God is pleased in cutting-edge missionary situations to grant the same signs and wonders we see in the New Testament era. I think this is certainly possible and that is why I call my view a nuanced cessationism." See Schreiner, *Spiritual Gifts*, 164–65.

captivated by God's omnipotent activity in these latter days, and he actively sought to see and receive it.

EVALUATION OF HENRY'S PRESENTATION OF THE SPIRIT'S WORK

Similar to Henry's presentation of the Spirit's person, his presentation of the Spirit's work had both strengths and weaknesses. The strengths are found in his extended meditations on the Spirit's role of filling the believer. He had a grand vision of how the Spirit works, from the moment of conversion to the end of one's life. Though a cessationist, Henry believed in no paralyzed Spirit. Instead, Henry's cessationism was characterized by an explicit call for Christians to pursue more of the Spirit, not less. This will be examined at greater length in chapter 5.

Another strength in Henry's understanding of the Spirit's work was the connection he made between the Spirit and the church. He recognized the Spirit played an important role in the corporate body of Christ. In *Christian Personal Ethics*, Henry stated:

A powerless church, no less than a morally languid church, is a sign of a fellowship unfulfilled by the Spirit. ... When there is no effective manifestation of the Spirit in her ministry, her message of redemptive theology and morality is perilously near being merely a philosophical explanation of life. The church that has only theology and ethics, but is powerless, is the church with a stifled Spirit.[60]

Henry understood that the temple of the Spirit referred to the corporate body of Christ, not just the body of an individual (1 Cor 6:19); therefore, the Spirit's work was carried out in two realms: individual and collective. This will be examined at greater length in chapter 4.

Henry's presentation of the Spirit's work also had weaknesses. He did not give ample attention to the Spirit's work in creation, nor in how the Spirit operated more generally throughout the Old Testament.[61] Henry's

---

60. Henry, *Christian Personal Ethics*, 456.

61. For more, see Allison and Köstenberger, *The Holy Spirit*, 5–52, 295–301; James M. Hamilton, Jr., *God's Indwelling Presence: The Holy Spirit in the Old and New Testaments*, NAC Studies in Bible and Theology, ed. Ray Clendenen (Nashville: B&H, 2006); Michael Horton, "'Lord and Giver of Life': The Holy Spirit in Redemptive History," *Journal of the Evangelical Theological Society* 62.1 (2019): 47–63.

understanding of the Spirit's work was focused almost entirely on New Testament data. While the Spirit certainly comes into clearer light in the New Testament, to focus almost exclusively there is to enter the theater halfway through the film. According to Michael Horton, "Introducing the Holy Spirit too late in the story—at the application of redemption—we miss much of the action."[62] This critique accurately describes much of Henry's presentation of the Spirit's work.

CHARISMATICS AND JESUS PEOPLE: THE CONTEXT OF HENRY'S PNEUMATOLOGY

Chapter 1 demonstrated that there was an increased interest in the Spirit during the twentieth century, both in Protestant and Catholic traditions. Henry, whose career gained steam mid-century, was writing squarely in the middle of this wave. Eventually, the wave crashed onto Henry's specific theological shores. Axel R. Schäfer summarizes this transition and situates Henry in it, including the newfound tensions and challenges he faced:

> In particular, the growth of Pentecostal and charismatic groups within the evangelical family, to the detriment of Calvinist and reformist denominations, was a clear indication of this shift from a liturgical and legal-rational emphasis to the emotional and experiential aspects of Christianity. The focus on a sense of closeness to Jesus through an indwelling spirit, getting filled with the Holy Spirit, laying on of hands, and glossolalia was often more appealing to a generation reared in "situation ethics" and "make love, not war" rhetoric than the theological sophistication sought by Carl Henry and other postwar evangelicals.[63]

This section will examine this charismatic wave and how Henry addressed it. His approach to the charismatic and Jesus People movements shed light on his appreciation and criticisms of the new pneumatological context in which he was writing.

---

62. Horton, *Rediscovering the Holy Spirit*, 47.

63. Axel R. Schäfer, *Countercultural Conservatives: American Evangelicalism from the Postwar Revival to the New Christian Right* (Madison: The University of Wisconsin Press, 2011), 102.

PENTECOSTALS AND CHARISMATICS:

HISTORICAL CONTINUITIES

Dating back to the early twentieth century, Pentecostals and fundamentalists were not friendly.[64] However, by the mid-1940s, neo-evangelicalism had carved out space for Pentecostals, especially through the formation of the National Association of Evangelicals (NAE, 1942).[65] Whether this was because these were war years and a national desire for unity led to a truce between the groups, or because genuine theological solidarity demanded it, the fact remains that Henry and others were more open to Pentecostal groups than their fundamentalist forebears.[66] According to Matthew Sutton, when the NAE was established, "Many fundamentalists now accepted Pentecostals, whom they had once considered tongues-speaking, chandelier-swinging, faith-healing radicals, as part of mainstream American evangelicalism."[67] The NAE strategically did not take firm posi-

---

64. See Grant Wacker, "Travail of a Broken Family: Evangelical Responses to Pentecostalism in America, 1906–1916," *Journal of Ecclesiastical History* 47.3 (1996): 505–28. For an account focusing not on the differences but on the (strained) kinship between Pentecostals and fundamentalists, see Gerald W. King, *Disfellowshiped: Pentecostal Responses to Fundamentalism in the United States, 1906–1943*, Princeton Theological Monograph Series (Eugene, OR: Pickwick, 2011).

65. For example, J. Narver Gortner, president of the Pentecostal Glad Tidings Bible Institute, along with a group of his fellow Assemblies of God members, received a special invitation to an early meeting of the NAE as the organization was seeking to build its leadership base and network. However, tension was close at hand. Groups who differed on charismatic expression struggled to align in a meaningful way, even when both could agree on mutual theological statements. See Worthen, *Apostles of Reason*, 36–37. For more on the relationship between both Pentecostals and fundamentalists and Pentecostals and evangelicals, including how these groups related in the NAE, see Vinson Synan, *The Holiness-Pentecostal Tradition: Charismatic Movements in the Twentieth Century* (Grand Rapids: Eerdmans, 1997), 207–11.

66. Russell P. Spittler, "Are Pentecostals and Charismatics Fundamentalists?," 110. Though decades later, this openness can be seen in Henry's publication of Jack J. Chinn's article "May We Pentecostals Speak?" in the July 17, 1961, edition of *Christianity Today*. Chinn's article gives a thoughtful, irenic defense of Pentecostalism. Though Henry was not persuaded by the argument, he still found it valuable enough to include for *Christianity Today*'s readers. See Jack J. Chinn, "May We Pentecostals Speak?" *Christianity Today* (July 17, 1961): 8–9. While Kidd correctly recognizes that *Christianity Today* became "the magazine of record for non-Pentecostal evangelicals," this was not due to any editorial strategy to stifle Pentecostal voices or perspectives. See Kidd, *Who Is an Evangelical?* 87.

67. Matthew Avery Sutton, *American Apocalypse: A History of Modern Evangelicalism* (Cambridge: Harvard University Press, 2014), 286. Sutton also notes that Pentecostals serving in early NAE leadership further highlights the nature of this change. For more on the formation of the National Association of Evangelicals, see James DeForest Murch, *Cooperation without Compromise: A History of the National Association of Evangelicals* (Grand Rapids: Eerdmans, 1956).

tions on numerous theological issues, including Pentecostalism.[68] Still, Henry had reservations. Of course, this section evaluates Henry's critiques of the charismatic movement, not specifically Pentecostalism. However, a historical bridge exists between the two, and they share numerous characteristics. Tracing this story is important, as Henry's criticism of the charismatic movement is not unrelated to the spirit of Pentecostalism. Russell Spittler helps construct this bridge when he recognizes that three movements arose at the beginning of the twentieth century, each in reaction to the cultural and theological landscape at the close of the nineteenth century. These movements were, in historical succession: Pentecostalism, fundamentalism, and neo-orthodoxy.[69]

Faced with the dawn of a new era—technologically, politically, socially, and theologically—fundamentalism and neo-orthodoxy both reacted in an "intellectual style."[70] Early conservative Protestants published *The Fundamentals* (1910–1915), a logical, thorough defense of biblical truths under attack by modernism. Though the moniker "fundamentalist" would emerge later, *The Fundamentals* represented how fundamentalism would challenge modernism—through the use of ideas.[71]

---

68. Though the NAE statement did not take firm positions on issues like premillennialism or Pentecostalism, it still had a significant theological impact on the Pentecostal groups seeking affiliation. C. M. Robeck argues that this union led to the "evangelicalization" of Pentecostals. With these two streams coming together, "some Pentecostal groups have rewritten their statements of faith, and others have imported such 'evangelical' issues as 'inerrancy' into their theological arenas for the first time." See C. M. Robeck, "National Association of Evangelicals," in *Dictionary of Pentecostal and Charismatic Movements*, ed. Stanley M. Burgess, Gary B. McGee, and Patrick H. Alexander (Grand Rapids: Zondervan, 1990), 635–36. Originally quoted in Scott A. Ellington, "Pentecostalism and the Authority of Scripture," in *Pentecostal Hermeneutics: A Reader*, ed. Lee Roy Martin (Leiden: Brill, 2013), 151. Though there was certainly a Pentecostal-izing of evangelicalism in the latter twentieth century, the current flowed both ways. Pentecostals were challenged to address doctrinal issues, primarily the nature of Scripture, through exposure to the fundamentalist-evangelical tradition in the NAE.

69. Spittler, "Are Pentecostals and Charismatics Fundamentalists?," 107.

70. Spittler, "Are Pentecostals and Charismatics Fundamentalists?," 107. Joel Carpenter concurs with Spittler when he writes, "While these groups [Wesleyans and Pentecostals] emphasized moral and experiential answers to modern secularity's challenges, fundamentalism favored the cognitive and ideological battleground. Although the fundamentalists shared the other two movements' concerns for right living and the power of the Holy Spirit, they cared more about fighting for right doctrine." See Carpenter, *Revive Us Again*, 5.

71. Grant Wacker points out that "most historians have not treated fundamentalists very well." See Grant Wacker, *One Soul at a Time: The Story of Billy Graham*, Library of Religious Biography, ed. Mark A. Noll and Heath W. Carter (Grand Rapids: Eerdmans, 2019), 109. However, while fundamentalists have been maligned as dim-witted dunces, the caricature

Neo-orthodoxy also reacted in an intellectual style. Karl Barth's *Romans* commentary was representative of this strategy. Of course, Barth disagreed with fundamentalists on key theological issues, especially his "passion for paradox" (as compared with American fundamentalists' disdain for the same).[72] Still, fundamentalism and neo-orthodoxy both wanted to correct the waywardness of nineteenth-century biblical criticism through "an essentially cognitive rescue of the church from its lassitude."[73]

In contrast, Pentecostalism mounted not an intellectual rebuttal, but an experiential one. According to Spittler:

> Pentecostalism profoundly distrusted the intellectual enterprise. The Pentecostal critique focused not so much on diluted theology as upon withered piety. The fault lay not in wrong thinking so much as in collapsed feeling. Not the decline of orthodoxy but the decay of devotion lay at the root of the problem. It was not merely that the church was liberal, but that it was lifeless. What was needed was not a new argument for heads but a new experience for hearts. ... Fundamentalists and neo-orthodox Christians mount arguments, though the former does it in terms of creeds, the latter in terms of paradox. Pentecostals give testimonies. The one goes for theological precision, the other for experiential joy. There is a profound difference between the cognitive fundamentalist and the experiential Pentecostal.[74]

Fast-forwarding to Henry's day, one begins to discern the shape of his critique of the charismatic movement. Henry—never one to be mistaken as a neo-orthodox theologian—still shared their strategy. Carl Henry and Karl Barth were foes in the specifics, but friends in the general. Both believed the remedy to ailments in the world and the academy was theological. On the other hand, though not one-in-the-same, the charismatic movement

---

fails the historical test. Though there was a stream that downplayed formal academic training in the movement, Marsden argues that educational institutions were central to fundamentalism in the early- to mid-twentieth century. According to Marsden, "Fundamentalists are among those contemporary Americans who take ideas most seriously." See Marsden, *Understanding Fundamentalism and Evangelicalism*, 116.

72. Spittler, "Are Pentecostals and Charismatics Fundamentalists?," 107.

73. Spittler, "Are Pentecostals and Charismatics Fundamentalists?," 108.

74. Spittler, "Are Pentecostals and Charismatics Fundamentalists?," 108.

of the mid-twentieth century shared with Pentecostalism an exaltation of experience, sometimes at the expense of cognitive exercise. As D. Allen Tennison recognizes, "Experience is sometimes viewed as so important to their hermeneutic that Pentecostals have been strongly criticized for exegeting their experience rather than the Bible."[75] The charismatic movement inherited something of this experiential impulse, and it is here where Henry's criticisms of the movement were focused.

HENRY'S CRITICISMS OF THE CHARISMATIC MOVEMENT

Before exploring these criticisms, it should be noted that Henry was not altogether opposed to the charismatic movement.[76] He appreciated their desire for the Spirit's manifestation in one's life and their vibrancy in evangelism and worship. In an interview for *Evangelical Thrust*, Henry warned his fellow evangelicals:

Now I don't think we have a right to criticize—a right in full good conscience to criticize—the Charismatic Movement unless we are always as concerned as it is for the infilling of the Holy Spirit, and for demonstrating what an authentic experience of the Holy Spirit implies for Christian life. ... Paul pleads, "Be ye being filled ongoingly with the Holy Spirit of God." And we need to capture that.[77]

---

75. D. Allen Tennison, "Charismatic Biblical Interpretation," in *Dictionary for Theological Interpretation of the Bible*, ed. Kevin J. Vanhoozer, Craig G. Bartholomew, Daniel J. Trier, and N. T. Wright (Grand Rapids: Baker Academic, 2005), 107.

76. He also defended Pentecostalism (and the charismatic movement) from its most uncharitable critics. While some waved off Pentecostal and charismatic expressions as religious manifestations of the drug culture or other quasi-religious experiences, Henry rejected these caricatures. Though disagreeing with them, he defended their orthodoxy: "Although Pentecostalism lacks a systematic theology and its beliefs are not credally structured, it insists nonetheless on the objective existence of the triune God, the Lordship of Jesus Christ the God-man, the personal reality of the Holy Spirit, and the authority of the Bible." See Carl F. H. Henry, *Toward a Recovery of Christian Belief: The Rutherford Lectures* (Wheaton, IL: Crossway, 1990), 27.

77. Carl F. H. Henry, "Dr. Henry Tackles Pros and Cons of the Charismatic Movement," *Evangelical Thrust* (June 1978): 17. John S. Hammett shares this perspective when he writes, "Whatever their many faults may be, most Pentecostal churches rely upon and call upon the Spirit to empower them in an emphasis that Baptists would do well to ponder and learn from." See John S. Hammett, *Biblical Foundations for Baptist Churches: A Contemporary Ecclesiology* (Grand Rapids: Kregel, 2005), 75.

Further, Henry's criticisms of the charismatic movement do not mean that he himself disregarded dependency on the Spirit. He shied away from "Spirit-experience" language, but this was due to the extremes of a "Spirit-centered" theology, not because a genuine leading by the Spirit was not worthy of pursuit.[78] As shown, he emphasized dependency upon the Spirit in the Christian life. Instead, his criticism was focused on the theological foundation of the charismatic movement, a foundation he found to be porous and potentially dangerous.

THE BIBLICAL CRITIQUE

Henry's biblical critique was based on his inability to square the biblical text with the charismatic perspective. His reading kept him from embracing in the Spirit as a post-conversion experience validated by speaking in a mysterious language. Henry recognized that not all charismatics demanded glossolalia from adherents and that some were concerned with the general theological trajectory of the movement.[79] Still, he had genuine concerns borne out of a desire to see Christian theology honored and valued. This section will not rehearse the specific points above regarding Henry's cessationism other than to say that Henry believed the charismatic view of the Spirit was not too big but entirely too small: "The modern openness to charismatic emphasis is directly traceable to the neglect by mainstream Christian denominations of an adequate doctrine of the Holy Spirit."[80] In his estimation, their small vision of the Spirit led directly to the unhealthy enthusiasm sweeping the world. He thought the charismatic movement was unbalanced in that it myopically emphasized debatable points and missed the larger thrust of passages like 1 Corinthians 12. In Henry's estimation, charismatics were guilty of oversimplifying the issue of tongues, an issue he found to be "much more complex than many charismatic Christians imply or realize."[81] He believed that "[w]hatever the case may be, the charismatic movement can be safeguarded from excesses only by a biblical theology of the Holy Spirit, one that is sensitive to the

---

78. Carl F. H. Henry, untitled lecture notes, CFHHP (undated, unprocessed box).

79. Henry, *GRA*, 6:394.

80. Henry, *GRA*, 4:284.

81. Henry, *GRA*, 6:394.

entire New Testament teaching."[82] He thought relegating the Spirit's importance to glossolalia and miraculous healing was to discount so much of
the Spirit's daily ministry—the regular filling that empowered believers
in their normal rhythms of life. He believed that given the "scant attention given by the New Testament to glossolalia, the contemporary church's
extensive interest and even preoccupation with it are phenomenal."[83]

THE COGNITIVE-RATIONAL CRITIQUE

Beyond disagreements based on biblical data, Henry was also concerned
about the emphasis on personal experience that many charismatics cham-
pioned. This represents the theological aspect of Henry's critique. In *God,
Revelation and Authority*, Henry wrote:

> The welcome for the charismatic movement in some circles raises
> critically important issues whenever its emphasis on a sporadic
> divine creative force is preferred above a rational approach to
> Christianity. There can be no doubt that secular rationalism is the
> enemy of revealed religion, and, moreover, that a proper doctrine of
> the Holy Spirit who testifies to the centrality of the incarnate, cru-
> cified and risen Jesus is integral to biblical theism. But those who
> champion Spirit-Christianity often tend to dismiss the rationality
> of revelation as an intrusion into Christian theology of Greek phi-
> losophy, particularly of Platonism.[84]

In other words, Henry feared that those who embraced the charismatic
movement could potentially drift from a cognitive recognition of revealed
religion and eventually begin to question even the necessity of doctrinal
formulations of Christian truth.[85] If one's internal experiences are the

---

82. Henry, *GRA*, 6:397.

83. Henry, *GRA*, 4:286.

84. Henry, *GRA*, 4:288.

85. Despite this concern, Henry does not seem to have appreciated (nor anticipated)
the growing number of evangelical academics who either self-identify as Pentecostal or
charismatic, or who are sympathetic to these movements' characteristics. The post-war
economic expansion of the 1940s and 1950s granted increased educational and professional
mobility to many Pentecostal students, who also found increased acceptance in the wider
evangelical world (especially in the National Association of Evangelicals). This led to more
Pentecostal students completing terminal degrees at established institutions, which in turn
increased scholarly opportunities to those from a Pentecostal background. See Jonathan Olson,
"The Quest for Legitimacy: American Pentecostal Scholars and the Quandaries of Academic

ultimate barometer of reality, why any need for concrete dogma? Henry knew that when the importance of orthodox doctrine began to dissolve, disaster lay just around the corner.

The doctrine of justification provides an illuminating example of this point. Henry was concerned that justification by faith was going unappreciated in his day. One reason for this trend was the charismatic emphasis upon a post-conversion experience (whether baptism in the Spirit or a more general embrace of glossolalia):

> Some professedly evangelical denominations refuse to attach to the rubric of justification the decisive significance on which the Protestant Reformers and the evangelical mainstream insist. They focus instead on the centrality of sanctification, or on some post-conversion charismatic experience. ... In our time other issues are mixed with Christ as the ground of the sinner's divine acceptance: the rite of baptism, attendance at mass, charismatic speaking in tongues, or insistence on partial sanctification as at least a condition of justification.[86]

Henry bristled when crucial doctrines, such as justification by faith, were being devalued by charismatic groups that exalted personal experience. Not only did this discount the revelation provided by God in Scripture, but it was also the doorway down a dubious path. Henry thought that "to repudiate reason in the interest of spiritual reality can lead open-endedly into the realm of the supernatural and occult."[87] Of course, Henry was not accusing charismatics of dabbling in darkness, but he was giving a warning: it is concerning when one craves merely a supernatural feeling. The enemy is ready to fill the void. According to Henry, "The revival of witchcraft, Satan-worship, voodoo and astrology reflects an outreach toward the transcendent in an age of disenchantment with science and technology. In the absence of rational revealed religion such phenomena

---

Pursuit," *Intermountain West Journal of Religious Studies* 4.1 (2013): 96. Amos Yong argues that Pentecostalism might play a "central role" in the theological academy of the twenty-first century. See Amos Yong, "Pentecostalism and the Theological Academy," *Theology Today* 64 (2007): 244.

86. Carl F. H. Henry, "Justification: A Doctrine in Crisis," *Journal of the Evangelical Theological Society* 38.1 (1995): 57–58.

87. Henry, *GRA*, 4:288.

readily become counterreligious."[88] Henry traced this rise of interest in the occult among Christians directly to truncated teaching about the Spirit in evangelical churches:

> Many evangelical churches, while emphasizing the personality and deity of the Holy Spirit, have been on more familiar terms with the doctrine of the Spirit than with the Spirit's power. The removal of the Holy Spirit to the outermost margin of church influence has resulted in the rise of a great variety of cults, which compensate for this lack by an extreme and radical doctrine of the Spirit.[89]

This was one reason Henry gave his life to the task of theology. He wanted to protect Christ's sheep from deviant theologies that would promise enlightenment yet lead them astray.

Related to Henry's theological critique was his fear that unintelligible tongues would be given equal authority to Scripture. Henry stressed that "the divine Spirit speaks in Scripture, a fact not to be derogated by appealing instead to present-day charismatic utterances or experiences."[90] He continued: "The Spirit illumines the truth, not by unveiling some hidden inner mystical content behind the revelation ... but by focusing on the truth of revelation as it is."[91] Henry despised the language of the Spirit giving a "fresh word," which "suggested an immediate revelational authority different from that of the scripturally mediated word."[92] He saw this as a textbook slippery-slope scenario leading to a frightening state of affairs: when experience and Scripture are given equal authority, virtually anything can be justified as a "fresh word" from the Lord.[93]

---

88. Henry, *GRA*, 4:288.

89. Carl F. H. Henry, "The Acts of the Apostles: An Introduction to the Quarter's Lessons," in *The All Bible Graded Series of Sunday School Lessons: Studies in the Book of Acts*, ed. James DeForest Murch (Chicago: Scripture Press, 1951), 2. Copy in CFHHP (box 1951 [box 1], file "The Acts of the Apostles").

90. Henry, *GRA*, 4:283.

91. Henry, *GRA*, 4:283.

92. Henry, *GRA*, 4:284.

93. Henry was not making a novel argument with this line of thinking. According to Michael Horton, this was one of the main points at which Martin Luther critiqued the radical Anabaptist Thomas Müntzer almost five hundred years before. Horton writes, "The Reformers called this 'enthusiasm' (lit. 'God-within-ism'), because it made the external Word of Scripture subservient to the inner word supposedly spoken by the Spirit today within the individual or the church." The problem has not disappeared: "Tragically, 'enthusiasm'

HENRY'S CRITICISMS OF THE
JESUS PEOPLE MOVEMENT

While the charismatic movement was sweeping all sectors of Christianity throughout the world, a related movement was growing in sunny California that eventually spread to streets and campuses across the country. The Jesus People movement combined the features of the charismatic movement with the flavor of 1960s counterculture. Larry Eskridge defines the movement along similar lines:

> The typical Jesus People ethos was dominated by several core characteristics that mixed and matched influences from the evangelical and countercultural sides of the movement's parentage. ... [T]he new street Christians' literalistic interpretation of the Scriptures led them into a heavy emphasis on Pentecostal and charismatic phenomena such as glossolalia, prophecy, and "words of knowledge." ... At first sight, most or all of these characteristics could be seen as applying, to some extent, to a broad swath of American evangelicals and Pentecostals during the 1960s and 1970s. But what set the Jesus People apart from their straight evangelical and Pentecostal cousins was the intensity with which these characteristics marked them and were incorporated into a distinctly nonbourgeois unchurchy atmosphere that was far removed from respectable America's way of doing church.[94]

Richard Bustraan gives a concise definition that recognizes the family resemblance: the Jesus People movement "wed certain values of the 1960s American counterculture, namely hippiedom, together with values of Christianity, namely Pentecostalism."[95] Despite the discomfort

---

has become one of the dominant ways of undermining the sufficiency of Scripture, and it is evident across the spectrum ... Radical Protestants have emphasized a supposedly immediate, direct, and spontaneous work of the Spirit in our hearts apart from creaturely means. ... In other words, it is not that revelation, inspiration, and authority are denied but that the surprising, disorienting, and external voice of God is finally transformed into the 'relevant,' uplifting, and empowering inner voice of our own reason, morality, and experience." See Michael Horton, "Prologue: What Are We Celebrating?" in *Reformation Theology: A Systematic Summary*, ed. Matthew Barrett (Wheaton, IL: Crossway, 2017), 27–28. For more on Luther's critique of Anabaptism, see Nathan A. Finn, "Curb Your Enthusiasm: Martin Luther's Critique of Anabaptism," *Southwestern Journal of Theology*, 56.2 (2014): 163–81.

94. Larry Eskridge, *God's Forever Family: The Jesus People Movement in America* (Oxford: Oxford University Press, 2013), 54–55.

95. Richard Bustraan, *The Jesus People Movement: A Story of Spiritual Revolution Among the Hippies* (Eugene, OR: Pickwick, 2014), xvii. This is a revised version of Bustraan's doctoral

some traditional evangelicals felt at the emergence of such a movement, its momentum was unmistakable. According to Molly Worthen, "[T]he renewal movement's revolutionary approach to praying and glorifying God appealed to so many believers—especially young people—that even skeptics had to admit that worship would never be the same."[96] The message of the Jesus People was attractive to a growing youth culture that increasingly disdained the institutions (and authority) of previous generations. Their cameo appearance in the lyrics to Elton John's 1971 song "Tiny Dancer" indicates the extent to which mainstream culture had taken notice of the "Jesus freaks."

Similar to his posture toward certain aspects of the charismatic movement, Henry did not reject the Jesus People outright.[97] They "boldly emphasized that the Christian gospel carries in it a divine revelation and redemption absent from the counterculture no less from the technocratic society it assailed."[98] He was appreciative that the Jesus People movement was open to, and in some cases supported, older evangelical organizations such as InterVarsity Christian Fellowship, Campus Crusade for Christ, Young Life, and Youth for Christ.[99] Further, Henry appreciated the evangelistic vitality that radiated from the Jesus People:

---

dissertation at The University of Birmingham.

96. Worthen, *Apostles of Reason*, 143.

97. It is notable that Henry devoted as much attention to the Jesus People that he did, further buttressing the argument that pneumatological concerns were central to the context in which he was writing. He allotted an entire chapter in Volume 1 of *GRA* to "The Jesus Movement and Its Future," which lay squarely within a series of dense theological and philosophical chapters. Carl Trueman thinks this extended engagement with the Jesus People gives this section of *GRA* a "bizarre" and "dated feel." Why the interest, especially for modern readers, when, according to Trueman, the Jesus People "have proved about as significant for Christianity since the 1960s as Rolf Harris's Stylophone has been for the music of Kraftwerk"? But this is precisely the point: though the Jesus People Movement will enjoy only brief mention in most history books, Henry found the movement worthy of serious interaction. They were no fringe group in Henry's day; because of their growing influence among evangelicals, he needed to address them directly. See Carl Trueman, "Uneasy Consciences and Critical Minds: What the Followers of Carl Henry Can Learn from Edward Said," *Themelios* 30.2 (2005): 35. Elsewhere, Trueman levels a similar criticism against Henry's interaction with the Jesus People in *GRA*, but he is more appreciative of the content as historically illuminating and valuable. See Trueman, "Admiring the Sistine Chapel," 52.

98. Henry, *GRA*, 1:123.

99. Henry, *GRA*, 1:125. For more on the relationship between the Jesus People movement and the more traditional evangelical infrastructure, see John G. Turner, *Bill Bright and Campus Crusade for Christ: The Renewal of Evangelicalism in Postwar America* (Chapel Hill: University of North Carolina Press, 2008). Turner sees Explo '72 in Dallas as the tangible intersection of the two, coined by Billy Graham as the "Christian Woodstock." After Christian worship

There can be little doubt about the present evangelistic vitality of the Jesus movement. Critics have too often ignored the fact that if their own congregations reflected the spiritual earnestness characteristic of these young people—their interest in the Bible, their prayer meetings, their outreach to others—local pastors would soon experience revival in their churches.[100]

However, Henry's broad critique of the charismatic movement carried over specifically to the Jesus Movement. In January of 1972, he spoke at Loma Linda University on "Christianity and the Counter-Culture Revolution." The *Los Angeles Times* covered the address, in which Henry recognized that "it will not do just to disown and to scold disaffiliated youth, for we are called to exhibit a better way."[101] However, Henry also chastised the theological vacuity of the movement: "The weakest facet of the youth revolt is its mindlessness, its intellectual coherence. ... The Jesus freaks at least know that Jesus Christ is the way into the supernatural world, but even they have a limited future unless their evangelical faith is theologically informed."[102] In the pages of *GRA*, Henry challenged the "theological sterility" that pervaded the movement.[103] Contrary to claims by Jesus People, this actually harmed evangelism rather than helping it:

[The Jesus People movement's] doctrinal content as a whole is rather minimal. For this reason it easily falls pretty to certain emphases in evangelism that hurry over problems of the mind in calling people to spiritual decision; faith is somehow thought to dispense with valid syllogisms or to cover invalid ones. For all its thrust beyond the evangelical establishment churches, the Jesus movement tends to be

---

music (and, at one point, Johnny Cash), evangelical luminaries like Graham and Bright would preach a traditional gospel message. Turner believes the tone of the more conventional evangelical coalition ultimately won the day: "In many ways, however, Explo '72 symbolized a conservative evangelical appropriation of the Jesus Movement: carefully planned, toned down, and commercialized." See Turner, *Bill Bright and Campus Crusade for Christ*, 143. Molly Worthen agrees, as she believes that evangelicals were partly successful in "domesticating" charismatic practices, including those of the Jesus People. See Worthen, *Apostles of Reason*, 143.

100. Henry, *GRA*, 1:132.

101. Carl F. H. Henry, "Jesus Freaks Seen as Test of Christian Belief," *Los Angeles Times*, January 15, 1972, 29. Copy in CFHHP.

102. Henry, "Jesus Freaks."

103. Henry, *GRA*, 1:132.

intellectually shallow and doctrinally tolerant, accommodating sub-biblical and even heretical concepts for the sake of "Christian love."[104]

Again, similar to his critique of the charismatic movement, Henry found this to be dangerous not only for the receiver of the message but for the messengers themselves. The threat of theological hollowness with experiential enthusiasm was spiritually hazardous: "Whereas deference to the evangelical traditions ran the risk of straight-jacketing the Spirit, the experiential approach of the Jesus movement ran the risk of spiritual aberration and left many young believers vulnerable to cultic excesses."[105]

What can be made of Henry's critique of the Jesus People movement? First, he genuinely appreciated their evangelistic zeal and compassion for the destitute. But neither theology lacking compassion nor compassion lacking theology advances the ball in the right direction. If the fundamentalism Henry critiqued in *The Uneasy Conscience of Modern Fundamentalism* was guilty of the former, Henry found the Jesus Movement guilty of the latter. Indeed, Henry found one key similarity between fundamentalism and the Jesus Movement. With no stabilizing theology or intellectual capital to confront the ideas of the day, the Jesus People eventually became "isolationistic and escapist with regard to society," the same posture adopted by fundamentalists before them.[106]

Along these lines, as with the charismatic movement, Henry's critique was ultimately theological. Because the Jesus People "were not interested in systematic theology ... and had little regard for creeds or rules," Henry thought their enthusiasm for experience was shallow.[107] He found

---

104. Henry, *GRA*, 1:132.

105. Henry, *GRA*, 1:131.

106. Henry, *GRA*, 1:133. Axel Schäfer sees other ironic similarities between traditional fundamentalism and the religiously countercultural Jesus People, especially in the way that the latter adopted the traditional moral codes of the former. Whereas the secular counterculture was advocating increased permissiveness in virtually every realm of experience, the Jesus People "led sober, disciplined lives" not because of any "external enforcement" but by choice. See Schäfer, *Countercultural Conservatives*, 101.

107. Worthen, *Apostles of Reason*, 143. Henry critiqued other groups as well who demonstrated similar traits in their pursuit of the immediacy of the Spirit. For example, he challenged Frank Buchman's Moral Rearmament Movement by stating, "The movement's stress on religious immediacy tended to obscure the mediatorial work of Christ, however, and the objective authority of the Scripture. ... The theological outlook was simplistic and vulnerable, however, and the socio-political thrust highly individualistic." See Carl F. H. Henry, "Moral

his day's reinvigorated pneumatological conversations actually too little interested in the full biblical presentation of the Spirit. His message to the charismatic and Jesus People movements was that there was more to behold in pneumatology than they were willing to see. Just as the Spirit is unwilling to be the focal point in the Godhead, neither is he willing to be consigned to merely ecstatic religious experience. Further, these movements' emphasis on the Spirit (for the charismatics) or Jesus and the Spirit (for the Jesus People) led Henry to believe that their vision of the Triune God left something to be desired.[108]

A representative summation of Henry's evaluation of the Jesus People is found in a brief section of a relatively overlooked 1973 volume that interacted with various sentiments of the 1960s and '70s counter-culture movements. Despite concerns, his overall appraisal was positive. Granted, he thought "their existential orientation and shallow doctrinal logic left them vulnerable to extreme charismatic claims and to fanatical excesses."[109] But he did not harp on their deficiencies. Instead, he believed the movement had the merit of a genuine return to God for masses of young people who were "apostolically venturesome for the gospel."[110] He appreciated that "the Jesus-freak mood [was] yielding in many places to a Jesus-follower commitment."[111] He hoped the world would learn from their radiance, love, and confidence in the sin-destroying power of the gospel.[112] He was thankful that the Jesus People provided an alternative to "those who buck the whole gamut of teenage temptation without God and who while lacking new life in Christ mistakenly think they have plumbed all the exhilarating experiences young life has to offer."[113] By this time nearing the status of a senior evangelical statesman, Henry argued that the younger Jesus People generation had "much to say to the Christian community that they find

---

Rearmament," in *Baker's Dictionary of Christian Ethics*, ed. Carl F. H. Henry (Grand Rapids: Baker Book House Company, 1973), 433.

108. Henry, *GRA*, 1:132.

109. Carl F. H. Henry, "What Is Man on Earth For?" in *Quest for Reality: Christianity and the Counter Culture*, ed. Carl F. H. Henry (Downers Grove, IL: InterVarsity Press, 1973), 160.

110. Henry, "What Is Man on Earth For?," 160.

111. Henry, "What Is Man on Earth For?," 160.

112. Henry, "What Is Man on Earth For?," 160–61.

113. Henry, "What Is Man on Earth For?," 161.

so hard to understand."[114] While Henry's generally favorable estimation of the Jesus People might be surprising in light of his commitment to rigorous theological reasoning and his cessationist views, he maintained a tender heart for their movement, primarily because they caught something about the Spirit that marked them in a powerful way. While imperfect, he admired their passion and found it a potential corrective to strands of evangelicalism that had grown stagnant to the Spirit. This is why Henry was willing to excus" Christians who yielded to charismatic fanaticism more readily than he would excuse those who lived as if Pentecost never happened.[115]

CONCLUSION

This chapter has outlined the contours and context of Henry's pneumatology. It has provided an overview of the strengths and weaknesses of his pneumatological presentation. It has also demonstrated that pneumatology was not an ancillary concern to Henry's historical context; instead, in addressing issues pertaining to the Spirit, Henry was speaking to one of the pressing issues of his day. With the contours and context of Henry's pneumatology in place, the reader is better prepared to encounter the particulars of Henry's pneumatology, specifically in the areas of revelation, ecclesiology, and ethics. As mentioned, the book will follow a three-fold thesis thread—that Henry believed a Spirit-inspired Bible (revelation) would order a Spirit-enlivened body (ecclesiology) composed of Spirit-filled believers (ethics). It is to the first element of this thesis—pneumatology and revelation in Henry's thought—that the book will now turn.

---

114. Henry, "What Is Man on Earth For?," 161.
115. Henry, *GRA*, 3:22.

3

—

A SPIRIT-INSPIRED BIBLE (PNEUMATOLOGY AND REVELATION)

INTRODUCTION

Perhaps the quintessential passage of Henry is found in Volume 2 of *God, Revelation and Authority* (GRA). On the doctrine of revelation, Henry was shy in neither substance nor style:

> Divine revelation palpitates with human surprise. Like a fiery bolt of lightning that unexpectedly zooms toward us and scores a direct hit, like an earthquake that suddenly shakes and engulfs us, it somersaults our private thoughts to abrupt awareness of ultimate destiny. By the unannounced intrusion of its omnipotent actuality, divine revelation lifts the present into the eternal and unmasks our pretensions of human omnicompetence. As if an invisible Concorde had burst the sound barrier overhead, it drives us to ponder whether the Other World has finally pinned us to the ground for a life-and-death response. Confronting us with a sense of cosmic arrest, it makes us ask whether the end of our world is at hand and propels us unasked before the Judge and Lord of the universe. Like some piercing air-raid siren it sends us scurrying from life's preoccupations and warns us that no escape remains if we neglect the only sure sanctuary. Even once-for-all revelation that has occurred in another time and place fills us with awe and wonder through its ongoing significance, and bears the character almost of a fresh miracle.[1]

---

1. Henry, *GRA*, 2:17.

This served as a portal into *GRA*'s fifteen theses, which Henry unpacked in Volumes 2–6. *GRA* is less a systematic exposition of theology and more an extended prolegomenon on the nature of Scripture. Specifically, Henry emphasized Scripture's divine origin and the logical implications thereof. This chapter will demonstrate that pneumatology served as an aquifer that gave Henry's doctrine of revelation its vibrancy and vitality. In this, his concept of special revelation was inconceivable apart from pneumatology. The chapter will conclude with a case study that sets Henry in conversation with Karl Barth on inspiration and illumination so as to better distill the particularities of Henry's view in comparison with the growing alternative of his day.

THE PRIORITY OF (SPECIAL) DIVINE
REVELATION: A CENTRAL THEME

Before examining Henry's understanding of a Spirit-inspired Bible vis-à-vis pneumatology, it is important to highlight the centrality of divine revelation to his theological program. While he is rightly remembered for calling fundamentalists away from social neglect, much of his theological legacy remains in the realm of revelation and Scripture. He summarized his view in his "The Priority of Divine Revelation: A Review Article":

> The Christian doctrine [of revelation] is that the living personal God directly and objectively manifests himself by intelligible words, commands and acts. God's redemptive revelation is given once for all at definite times and places, but he also is continually disclosed in nature and history and in and to the mind and conscience of man universally. The inspired Biblical writings present us with logically consistent and supernaturally authoritative teaching, authenticated by miracle and by fulfilled prophecy. The prophetic and apostolic divine revelation, now complete, and the pre-eschatological revelation given in Jesus Christ, and the content of this revelation, gathered up for us in the Bible, as B. B. Warfield said, now serve as God's full and final revelation. The historic Christian view is that revelation is given in the form of verbal truths inerrantly conveyed in the inspired prophetic-apostolic writings.[2]

---

2. Carl F. H. Henry, "The Priority of Divine Revelation: A Review Article," *Journal of the Evangelical Theological Society* 27.1 (1984): 78.

Henry's understanding of revelation can be summarized in two axioms from his 1989 Rutherford Lectures at The University of Edinburgh: "The basic axioms of the Christian religion are two. The basic ontological axiom is *the living God*; the basic epistemological axiom is *divine revelation* ... [these] axioms illumine reality literally and factually."[3] He articulated the same axioms and their implications over a decade earlier in his address at the April 9, 1976 meeting of the American Theological Society:

> The primary ontological axiom of theology is the living God; the primary epistemological axiom is divine self-revelation. ... It is manifestly impossible to discover reliable data about deity unless God voluntarily discloses himself; if he did not want to be known, God could easily hide himself. ... God in his revelation is the foundational ground of truth, the primary source of all that may properly be said about him and his intentions, the supreme authority beyond which no appeal is possible. The distinctive orientation of the biblical doctrine of the Word of God issues from the transcendence of the God of Genesis and of the Gospels to the world and man, and redemptive self-disclosure in word and deed.[4]

Henry's career was spent explaining and defending this view, including the propositional nature of God's divine revelation in the Scriptures.

While special revelation enjoyed the majority of Henry's attention, he also affirmed the presence of God's general revelation.[5] He took a mediating position between Aquinas, who placed a premium on general revelation,

---

3. Henry, *Toward a Recovery of Christian Belief*, 68–69 (italics original).

4. Carl F. H. Henry, "What Is the Proper Task of Theology?," CFHHP (box 1975 [box 2], file "Writings—'What is the Proper Task of Theology?'—American Theological Society Meeting Papers, April 9, 1976").

5. According to Henry, "The classic Christian view, moreover, states that divine revelation is addressed by the Logos to mankind generally through nature, history, and conscience [general revelation], and is mediated more particularly through the sacred history and Scriptures, which find their redemptive climax in Jesus of Nazareth [special revelation]." See "Revelation in History," unsigned editorial in *Christianity Today* (October 9, 1964): 31. Contra Barth, Henry argued, "A general revelation of the Creator in his creation is integral to Christian doctrine founded upon Scripture and beyond that upon the factualities of the universe. Anyone who denies this doctrine places himself not only in unmistakable contradiction to the Bible and to the great theological traditions of Christendom that flow from its teaching, but also against the living God's disclosure in cosmic reality and in mankind to which Scripture testifies (Rom 1:19–21)." See Henry, *GRA*, 2:83–84.

and Barth, who sought to demolish the concept altogether. Though much can be said regarding Henry's views on the philosophical and epistemological relationships between nature, science, history, and the biblical text, this chapter will be limited to evaluating the Holy Spirit's role in special revelation, namely the Old and New Testaments of the Christian Bible.[6] Because of the breadth of Henry's work on the doctrine of revelation, this limitation is necessary to remain focused on the relationship between pneumatology and revelation, specifically the Spirit's role in inspiration and illumination.

THE CENTRAL TEXT AND THE CENTRAL TOOL

Because Henry's most developed work on inspiration and illumination is found in *GRA*, and because *GRA* is so vital to his articulation of these topics, a brief excursus on the nature of *GRA* will be provided. However, *GRA* came later in Henry's career, and Henry had been articulating his thoughts on inspiration and illumination well before its publication. While *GRA* is the central text for evaluating Henry's concept of revelation, *Christianity Today*, with its large readership and accessible prose—as opposed to *GRA*'s thick theological presentation—proved to be the central tool for the dissemination of Henry's views. Following these brief sketches of the roles *GRA* and *Christianity Today* played in Henry's program, this chapter will explore the particularities of Henry's understanding of inspiration and illumination.

THE CENTRAL TEXT: *GOD, REVELATION AND AUTHORITY*

According to Gabriel Fackre, "In twentieth-century theology, the status of Scripture has been the absorbing interest of the evangelical community."[7] He understands Henry to have been not only "the century's most influential evangelical thinker," but also one of the key stewards of this evangelical attention to Scripture.[8] The primary focus of this stewardship was Henry's *magnum opus—God, Revelation and Authority*, written between 1976–1983.

---

6. For more on this topic, see Jason S. Stanghelle, "God, History, and Authority? History and Revelation in the Thought of Carl F. H. Henry," *Trinity Journal* 35 (2014): 39–59; Wood, "Revelation, History, and the Biblical Text in the Writings of Carl F. H. Henry."

7. Gabriel Fackre, *The Doctrine of Revelation: A Narrative Interpretation*, Edinburgh Studies in Constructive Theology (Edinburgh: Edinburgh University Press, 1997), 153–54.

8. Fackre, *The Doctrine of Revelation*, 154.

This six-volume set offered evangelicals a grand and sweeping defense of biblical authority, inspiration, and inerrancy, even as modernity and neo-orthodoxy were redefining and chipping away at each.[9]

According to Hall and Strachan, "*GRA* is to the Christian academy what Tolstoy is to the literary guild."[10] It remains unmatched among its evangelical counterparts in its interaction with modern theology and its engagement with a dizzying array of topics. As Thornbury states, "When one picks up and reads [Henry's] massive six-volume *God, Revelation and Authority*, what one appreciates is the breadth of Henry's scholarship. Biblical studies, contemporary theology, sociology, psychology, history, and politics are all represented in his research."[11] Perhaps Henry's friend Millard Erickson was recalling *GRA* when he told Gregory Thornbury, "You know I love Carl Henry's work. It's extremely important. I hope someday that it is translated into English."[12]

Despite the text's density, *GRA* garnered ample praise. Roger Nicole was "very well impressed" with Volumes 3 and 4 and found them to "constitute an excellent presentation of the doctrine of inspiration."[13] J. I. Packer told Henry that *GRA* was "massive and magisterial, epoch-making as a venture in evangelical theology on the grand scale."[14] Packer ended his letter with a plea for more from Henry's pen: "I hope to attempt a 3-vol. text for students, but you write on Barth's scale (the only one of us who does, now that Berkouwer's star is going down)—and the more you can give us of such writing the better for the church and the world."[15] Henry told William Mueller that he had received numerous "gratifying tributes" even from those "who do not in all respects share [his] positions."[16] Even President

---

9. For a brief yet profitable overview of *GRA*, see Trueman, "Admiring the Sistine Chapel," 48–58.

10. Hall and Strachan, "Editors' Preface," in *Essential Evangelicalism*, 18.

11. Gregory Alan Thornbury, "Vain Philosophy? Carl F. H. Henry's Plea for a Philosophically Informed Ministry," in Hall and Strachan, *Essential Evangelicalism*, 144.

12. Thornbury, *Recovering Classic Evangelicalism*, 24.

13. Roger Nicole, letter to Carl F. H. Henry, September 28, 1979, CFHHP (box "*God, Revelation and Authority* 1976–1983" [box 1], file "Vol. III + Vol. IV Reviews").

14. J. I. Packer, letter to Carl F. H. Henry, February 2, 1980, CFHHP (box "*God, Revelation and Authority* 1976–1983" [box 1], file "Vol. III + IV Reviews").

15. J. I. Packer, letter to Carl F. H. Henry, February 2, 1980.

16. Carl F. H. Henry, letter to William A. Mueller, June 25, 1985, CFHHP (box "*God, Revelation and Authority* 1976–1983" [box 1], file "Comments").

Jimmy Carter expressed to Henry that, upon receiving a copy of *GRA*, he appreciated Henry's thoughtfulness and looked forward to reading the volume.[17]

Despite the thoroughness of *GRA*, Paul House believes that further work remains in understanding Henry's views. He thinks Henry "leaves us much space to develop his ideas on authority, inspiration, and inerrancy—the subject of *God, Revelation and Authority*, volume 4."[18] This chapter is an effort to that end—to better understand the pneumatological underpinnings in Henry's presentation of special revelation.

THE CENTRAL TOOL: CHRISTIANITY TODAY

Though *GRA* was Henry's final word on the topic at hand, it was not the only vehicle through which Henry advanced his views. Instead, the fortnightly *Christianity Today* provided a leaner and more digestible option, especially for those swimming in the depths of day-to-day ministry with little time to tackle a theological tome. In Henry's twelve years at the helm of the magazine (1956–1968), he leveraged articles, editorials, and guest contributors to advance his traditional views of inspiration and illumination while also defending them against erosion by theological modernism and neo-orthodoxy.[19]

---

17. Jimmy Carter, letter to Carl F. H. Henry, December 7, 1979, CFHHP (box "*God, Revelation and Authority* 1976–1983" [box 1], file "Comments").

18. Paul House, "Hope, Discipline, and the Incarnational Scholar," in Hall and Strachan, *Essential Evangelicalism*, 125.

19. For an overview of *Christianity Today*'s role in American Protestantism, see Phyllis E. Alsdurf, "The Founding of *Christianity Today* Magazine and the Construction of An American Evangelical Identity," *Journal of Religious and Theological Information* 9 (2010): 20–43; Wacker, *One Soul at a Time*, 76–81. Of course, the story concluded with no fairy-tale ending. Henry remained bothered by how his departure unfolded in 1968. His final "Editor's Note" was terse: "My time has come to say farewell to 160,000 fortnightly readers and to go into journalistic exile. This issue officially terminates my twelve-year editorship, in line with executive-committee action a year ago. ... The new editor, Dr. Harold Lindsell, assumes duties in September, and thereafter will determine all content. I shall go off the Board and have no voice in future policy formulation." See Carl F. H. Henry, "Editor's Note," *Christianity Today* (July 5, 1968): 2. From his perspective, he was (at various times) misled, unappreciated, under-resourced, and choked by oversight. Perhaps he had a case. Still, Henry's theological voice and vision for the magazine conflicted with other leaders and board members, which introduced tension early in the magazine's life. The falling-out remained one of the deepest disappointments of his career. See Henry, *Confessions of a Theologian*, 275–87. For more on the tension surrounding Henry's final days at *Christianity Today*, see Gary Dorrien, *Social Ethics in the Making: Interpreting an American Tradition* (Chichester: Wiley-Blackwell, 2009), 455–56.

When Henry accepted the editorship of the magazine, Billy Graham expressed confidence in his friend:

> Beloved Carl ... I am more convinced than ever that this magazine is desperately needed throughout the world. ... How thankful we are that the Lord has led you to take this great responsibility. I believe it is one of the most strategic posts in Christendom today. You are going to need the wisdom of Solomon, the patience of Job, the courage of Elijah and the faith of Abraham—you have all of these qualities.[20]

Three months prior, as the two were formulating the magazine's aim, Graham told Henry that "the full inspiration of Scripture ... should be maintained at all costs."[21] Henry would devote the next twelve years to ensuring the magazine remained faithful to this vision.

According to Henry, *Christianity Today*'s primary audience was "every gospel minister in the English-speaking world."[22] He hoped his articulation of special revelation would be embraced by the clergy and then, through their ministries, trickle into the pews. The magazine played an integral role in the intellectual infrastructure of neo-evangelicalism. Through it, Henry spoke to over one hundred sixty thousand ministers every two weeks in the magazine's first year, something even Billy Graham could not claim.[23]

While *Christianity Today* addressed social and political issues, Henry never relinquished the opportunity to address biblical authority,

---

20. Billy Graham, letter to Carl F. H. Henry, March 10, 1956, CFHHP (box 1956, file "Correspondence—Graham, Billy"). Henry quoted from this letter in *Confessions of a Theologian*, 155. Despite Graham's confidence, he was concerned that Henry's headiness would spill into the pages of the magazine, leading to confusion among readers who did not share Henry's intellectual capacity. According to Timothy George, "After the first issue of *Christianity Today*, Billy Graham wrote a six-page critique reporting an impression of Henry's editorial as an example of 'obscurity reaching for profundity.' As a matter of fact, Henry was reading more widely, and thinking more deeply, than practically anyone else in the evangelical orbit. ... In the process he was introducing a new generation of evangelicals to a world of thought—and to a way of thinking—not available on the ordinary circuit of Bible conferences, summer camp meetings and youth revivals." See Timothy George, "Evangelicals and Others," *First Things* (February 2006): 18–19.

21. Billy Graham, letter to Carl F. H. Henry, January 10, 1956, CFHHP (box 1956, file "Correspondence—Graham, Billy").

22. Henry, *Confessions of a Theologian*, 155.

23. Henry, *Confessions of a Theologian*, 174.

inspiration, illumination, and inerrancy. Though *GRA* provided a more substantive engagement with the theology behind his views of special revelation, *Christianity Today* allowed a more succinct articulation of them.

SPIRIT-INSPIRED WRITERS AND
SPIRIT-INSPIRED WORDS:
HENRY'S VIEW OF INSPIRATION

In 1974, James Leo Garrett did not include Carl F. H. Henry in an article entitled "Representative Modern Baptist Understandings of Biblical Inspiration."[24] Why this decision? Garrett thought that "biblical inspiration constitutes only a very small proportion of Henry's total writings."[25] Of course, in 1974, Garrett had a fair point. He cannot be critiqued for not having Volume 4 of *GRA* at his disposal, as he made this evaluation before its publication. And he was correct that biblical inspiration represents only one of many issues that Henry addressed. But with time, it becomes clear that inspiration *would* represent a key element in Henry's thought. Though the smallest of the five, Lake Ontario is still a Great Lake, and though a "small proportion" of his total writings, Henry's work on inspiration is still extensive (and became even more so after Garrett's estimation). As John Mann argues, "The inspiration of Scripture is arguably where Henry's work has been the most influential in current theological conversations."[26]

Henry thought that "few Christian tenets are now more misunderstood and more misrepresented than the doctrine of the inspiration of Holy Scripture."[27] He defined biblical inspiration as "a supernatural influence upon divinely chosen prophets and apostles whereby the Spirit of God assures the truth and trustworthiness of their oral and written proclamation. Historic evangelical Christianity considers the Bible as the essential textbook because, in view of this quality, it inscripturates divinely revealed truth in verbal form."[28] In *GRA*, Henry relied primarily upon 2 Timothy 3:16

---

24. James Leo Garrett, "Representative Modern Baptist Understandings of Biblical Inspiration," *Review & Expositor* 71 (1974): 195.

25. Garrett, "Representative Modern Baptist Understandings," 195.

26. John B. Mann, "Revelation of the Triune God Through Word and Spirit: A Theological Critique of Karl Barth and Carl Henry" (PhD diss., Southwestern Baptist Theological Seminary, 2018), 144.

27. Henry, *GRA*, 4:136.

28. Henry, *GRA*, 4:129.

and 2 Peter 1:19–21 to defend his view. And defend he would, for "to maintain silence about the divine inspiration of Scripture is, in effect, to attenuate the work of God and to minimize the ministry of the Spirit."[29]

Henry rejected a mechanical dictation view of inspiration. He believed "the writers of Scripture are not unhistorical phantoms whom the divine Spirit controls like mechanical robots."[30] Henry was frustrated by theologians like Hans Küng who correlated traditional views of inspiration with the mechanical dictation theory.[31] He found this to be not only an unfair caricature of his position, but also a view embarrassingly unfamiliar with established literature on the subject, including works by A. A. Hodge and B. B. Warfield, which "insisted on a necessary differentiation between scriptural inspiration and verbal dictation."[32]

Mohler is correct when he states that Henry's theory of biblical inspiration "steers a middle course between the so-called 'dynamic' and 'dictation' theories."[33] Henry was cautious about "dual" or "co-authorship" language, as that could insinuate that God worked with man rather than through man to produce Scripture.[34] He understood the writers to be legitimate supporting actors in the production of Scripture—here he agreed with Barth's terminology of the writers as *auctores secundarii*—whose "various differences of personality and style carry over into the sacred literature."[35] As mentioned, one of Henry's constant frustrations with his contemporaries was their seeming inability (or unwillingness) to recognize that his view of Scripture did not necessitate a disavowal of the human agent. Henry stressed the Spirit's ability to speak God's words clearly without hijacking the person through whom He spoke:

> The Spirit of God made full use of the human capacities of the chosen writers so that their writings reflect psychological, biographical, and even sociohistorical differences. In discussing biblical inspiration, nonevangelical theologians [here Henry specifically targeted

---

29. Henry, *GRA*, 4:161.
30. Henry, *GRA*, 4:138.
31. Henry, *GRA*, 4:141.
32. Henry, *GRA*, 4:141.
33. Mohler, "Carl F. H. Henry," 288–89.
34. Henry, *GRA*, 4:142.
35. Henry, *GRA*, 4:142.

Emil Brunner] repeatedly misrepresent the evangelical view as somehow requiring a violation of or disregard for the humanity of the writers of Scripture.[36]

While Henry maintained that the Spirit inspired authors, he also thought biblical inspiration extended to the very words the writers penned: "When the Scripture speaks of inspiration, it does not stop short with the inspiration of only the person; rather it affirms something specific also about the written texts."[37] God did not merely heighten the internal awareness of the writers, but he superintended his own words through theirs. As Henry remarked in one unpublished address: "Divine inspiration is, therefore, not simply a relationship of the Spirit to the persons (prophets/apostles) but extends to their writings: Scripture is inspired; God breathed out not apostles but Scripture."[38] One of Henry's strongest concerns was to maintain that the Bible is a "linguistic revelatory deposit."[39] For Henry, the written text is the ultimate locus of inspiration, not merely the human author's mind or thoughts. Further, this quality of the text is plenary—it extends to every word of the Old and New Testaments.

COROLLARIES OF BIBLICAL INSPIRATION: INERRANCY AND INFALLIBILITY

Two corollaries flow from Henry's doctrine of inspiration. First, Henry was an avowed advocate of biblical inerrancy. His work on inerrancy, specifically his chapter on the topic in Volume 4 of *GRA*, remains "one of the most thorough treatments in evangelical literature."[40] Because he understood inspiration to extend to the very words of Scripture, how could inerrancy

---

36. Henry, *GRA*, 4:148–49. Henry was clear to argue that, contra Barth, "the Holy Spirit's employment of human writers does not at all require or demand error in what they wrote." See Henry, *GRA*, 4:151.

37. Henry, *GRA*, 4:143.

38. Carl F. H. Henry, "The Authority of the Scriptures," CFHHP (box 1977 [box 2], file "Writings—The Bible and the Crisis of Authority").

39. Henry, *GRA*, 4:144.

40. Mohler, "Carl F. H. Henry," 289. Henry believed inerrancy to be the logical conclusion of biblical inspiration. He understood inerrancy to be a quality reserved for the original autographs of Scripture: "Verbal inerrancy implies that the original writings or prophetic-apostolic autographs alone are error-free." See Henry, *GRA*, 4:207.

be avoided? Would the God who does not lie (Heb 6:18) fail to communicate truth via texts?

Henry grounded inerrancy in inspiration. As Michael White recognizes, "While it may seem somewhat surprising to treat inerrancy as a subcategory of inspiration, the proper logical home for inerrancy in Henry's economy is within inspiration."[41] To begin at inerrancy is a faulty move, as it elevates the quality of the text over the preceding reality of the truthfulness of God. This was Henry's key concern with the first meeting of the International Council on Biblical Inerrancy, including the Chicago Statement on Biblical Inerrancy in 1978. While Henry agreed with the overall aims of the council, he could not wholeheartedly endorse the final product. Weeks after the statement went public, Henry wrote to Clark Pinnock and expressed that the framers overlooked the importance of inspiration preceding inerrancy: "Then I think the leaping over inspiration to get from authority to a preoccupation with inerrancy (or infallibility which they sometimes equate with and sometimes differentiate from inerrancy) is a weakness, although the document concentrates supposedly on inerrancy."[42] Henry felt that even in a document focused on inerrancy, inspiration should be recognized as the foundation of the doctrine.

Second, alongside inerrancy, Henry affirmed infallibility as a corollary of inspiration. He devoted two chapters to infallibility in Volume 4 of *GRA*, where he defined the term in relation to the transmitted copies of the original autographs.[43] He disagreed with Roger Nicole that no distinction should be made between inerrancy and infallibility; instead, Henry applied infallibility to the copies so as to retain the authority of the inerrant autographs.[44] Inerrancy would be of no benefit if it applied to only the unpossessed originals; however, if the copies are infallible, in that

---

41. White, "Word and Spirit," 133.

42. Carl F. H. Henry, letter to Clark Pinnock, November 14, 1978, CFHHP (box 1978 [box 2]). Henry outlined other disagreements in *GRA*, 4:141.

43. White refers to Henry's views on infallibility as "an innovation in his thought" primarily because, in applying it specifically to the transmission process, Henry deviated from the typical usage of the term. While White does not disagree with Henry's general sentiment, he wonders if using infallibility in this sense causes more problems than it solves. He also critiques Henry for failing to outline the mechanisms by which the Spirit ensures infallible copies. See White, "Word and Spirit," 135–36.

44. Henry, *GRA*, 4:243.

they accurately preserve the original text, then they exist within conti-nuity of the inerrant originals and are capable of communicating God's unchanging truth. The Spirit not only guides the original writer, but he also providentially governs the text's faithful transmission over the millen-nia. Again, one sees that Henry believed the Spirit hovered over both his original creation (Gen 1:2), and the creation and preservation of his word. As Michael White states in evaluating Henry's understanding of infalli-bility (a sentiment Henry would have agreed with): "In the production of Holy Scripture the Spirit's activity is generative, while in the transmission the activity is preservative."[45] For Henry, there existed a pneumatological underpinning that gave the autographs their total trustworthiness (iner-rancy) and a pneumatological hovering that ensures that this quality con-tinues (infallibility). In both cases, Henry's doctrine of special revelation is inconceivable apart from pneumatology.

THE HOLY SPIRIT AS THE "ILLUMINATING EXEGETE": HENRY'S VIEW OF ILLUMINATION

Beyond the Spirit's work in revelation *then* through inspiration, Henry held a thorough view of the Spirit's work *now* in illumination. He summarized the concept in *GRA*:

> God intends that Scripture should function in our lives as his Spirit-illumined Word. It is the Spirit who opens man's being to a keen personal awareness of God's revelation. The Spirit empowers us to receive and appropriate the Scriptures, and promotes in us a normative theological comprehension for a transformed life. The Spirit gives vital current focus to historical revelation and makes it powerfully real.[46]

Henry believed an accurate understanding of illumination to be a pressing issue in his day. He recognized that formidable voices in twentieth-century theology (including Rudolf Bultmann and James Barr) had slowly begun to replace the role of the Spirit in illumination with an

---

45. White, "Word and Spirit," 136.
46. Henry, *GRA*, 4:273.

almost singular focus on the religious, social, and cultural milieus in which the biblical texts were originally penned.[47] This resulted in the elevation of modern man's role in the interpretive task, so much so that, according to Henry:

> The modern critic readily displaces the Holy Spirit as the illuminating exegete by dismissing the apostolic witness to the exceptional divine inspiration of the biblical writers, and by endowing his own verdicts and writings instead with superlative modern wisdom. By thus eliminating the Holy Spirit as the Illuminator who definitively and exactly communicates the Word of God, the critic becomes free to preempt that role.[48]

However, as Paul argues in 1 Corinthians 2:10–16, it is the Spirit who imparts knowledge of spiritual realities to spiritual people. The Spirit does not create new revelation when he illumines the mind and heart of an individual; rather, he causes light to beam from the already inspired text and empowers the mind to absorb and appropriate this truth. As a solar panel transforms light into usable energy, the Spirit causes the individual to absorb Scripture as true and authoritative, and to incorporate it into one's inner life rather than reflecting it away from the heart and mind.

Though Henry was sure of the need for illumination, he was less confident in the particularities of its mechanics:

> If we ask how the Holy Spirit illumines us, we must readily acknowledge that Scripture does not supply much data about the *how* of inspiration or illumination, any more than about the *how* of divine incarnation in Jesus Christ. Yet the ministry of the Spirit of God, distinct in each operation, is as essential and unique in enlivening God's revelation in the lives of his people as it is in the phenomena of divine incarnation and divine inspiration.[49]

---

47. Henry, *GRA*, 4:273.
48. Henry, *GRA*, 4:274.
49. Henry, *GRA*, 4:277.

What Henry was sure of was that illumination did not render the biblical text meaningless apart from the internal work of the Spirit. Unconverted readers may find Scripture unpersuasive, but not unintelligible. According to Henry, "we are not bequeathed a revelation as enigmatic as Mona Lisa's smile," but one that can be rationally formulated.[50] His position here was intimately tied to his understanding of propositional revelation. Though fallen, man is still able to recognize and rationally interpret the propositional nature of biblical truths, including "God is spirit" (John 4:24) and "Christ died for our sins ... [and] was buried ... [and] he was raised on the third day" (1 Cor 15:3–4).[51] This rational activity is necessary but insufficient:

> One need not take a master's degree in biblical theology, nor even read Greek and Hebrew, to know the sense of most scriptural propositions. The revelational truth conveyed by objective scriptural disclosure itself stipulates the need for subjective illumination and appropriation. But to make the fact of illumination and need of appropriation a reason for compromising the perspicacity of scriptural teaching is unjustifiable.[52]

While the intellect is important, apart from the searching Spirit, it remains veiled, unable to sense and appropriate spiritual realities. A pillar of Henry's theological legacy—propositional revelation—was reliant upon illumination by the Spirit. This is one reason he gave illumination such a devoted and detailed treatment. Perhaps Henry's clearest reflection on the Spirit and illumination is found in his 1993 article for *Decision* magazine:

> The controlling reason that I believe the Bible to be the inspired and written truth of God is the compelling witness and testimony of the Holy Spirit. The Spirit of God gives to all believers a vital faith in the self-revealing God and in his revealed Word. Faith is God's gift, not a human achievement. Without the Spirit's enabling power, someone might subscribe to Scripture as a revered and respected

50. Henry, *GRA*, 2:55.
51. Henry, *GRA*, 4:279.
52. Henry, *GRA*, 4:279.

tradition, and even at times defer to some of its content. But that person would halt short of appropriating Scripture as the divine rule of faith and practice.[53]

INSPIRING HENRY'S CHALLENGERS
TOWARD A DIFFERENT READING

It is at the nexus of inspiration and illumination where many of Henry's challengers cry foul. Donald Bloesch, while grateful for Henry's contributions, still counted him as one who reduced "truth to facticity and revelation to conceptuality or logic."[54] According to Bloesch, Henry's tradition possessed a "flat" and "reductionistic" understanding of inspiration and illumination.[55] As referenced in chapter 1, others share Bloesch's critique. Kevin Vanhoozer believes Henry tended to "depersonalize" Scripture.[56] Anthony Thiselton likely would include Henry in the many who "treat the Bible as consisting of 'closed' texts always in propositional form."[57] Alister McGrath found it quite difficult to "make use of some of the foundational theological assumptions that have undergirded the work of some earlier evangelical writers such as Carl Henry."[58] Michael D. White's critique in his dissertation at Wheaton College, written under the supervision of Kevin Vanhoozer, is representative of the above: "The root deficiency of Henry's method is an unintentional, functional separation of Word and Spirit evidenced by various features of Henry's approach."[59] Taken together, these criticisms insinuate that Henry possessed an unhealthy understanding of

---

53. Carl F. H. Henry, "God's Word is God's Word," *Decision* (February 1993): 11.

54. Donald Bloesch, *Holy Scripture: Revelation, Inspiration, and Interpretation*, Christian Foundations (Downers Grove, IL: InterVarsity Press, 1994), 97.

55. Bloesch, *Holy Scripture*, 97.

56. Vanhoozer, *The Drama of Doctrine*, 45. For more on Vanhoozer's appreciations and critiques of Henry's view of Scripture, see Kevin J. Vanhoozer, "Lost in Interpretation? Truth, Scripture, and Hermeneutics," *Journal of the Evangelical Theological Society* 48.1 (2005): 89–114.

57. Thiselton, *Hermeneutics*, 312.

58. Alister E. McGrath, "Engaging the Great Tradition: Evangelical Theology and the Role of Tradition," in *Evangelical Futures: A Conversation on Theological Method*, ed. John G. Stackhouse, Jr. (Grand Rapids: Baker, 2000), 150.

59. White, "Word and Spirit," vii. The core of White's critique is *not* that Henry failed to address the role of the Spirit in inspiration and illumination. White recognizes that Henry did and defends him against those who argue otherwise. White's primary critique is that Henry had a "fundamental misconception" about the Spirit's role in divine revelation and how it is (or is not) perceived and appropriated by fallen humanity. See White, "Word and Spirit," 185–86.

word and Spirit because he had an overdeveloped concept of the former and an underdeveloped concept of the latter.

This view seems to risk overplaying its hand. A surface-level sampling of these critiques might lead one to believe that somewhere along the way somebody took Thomas Jefferson's scalpel and excised all the supernatural elements of Henry's presentation of propositional revelation. Henry's understanding of Scripture and the relationship between word and Spirit have been, at best, underappreciated, and at worst, mischaracterized. He understood both word and Spirit to play a central role in any concept of divine revelation: "Every Christian statement of the knowledge of God makes a central place for two important realities: The Spirit and the Word. No theory of knowledge can be Christian which does not keep the Spirit and the Word at its very center."[60] He was not unaware of the historical debate concerning the relationship between the two, and recognized his own tradition's penchant to downplay the Spirit's role in revelation:

It must be acknowledged that the role of the Spirit is neglected rather than overstated in some Christian circles. Sometimes groups holding a high view of the authority of the Bible allow the Spirit an inadequate role. Evangelical believers have always protested against a mere catechism-Christianity, which treats the memorization of the great doctrines, important as they may be, as if it were the equivalent of a vital Christian experience. The fact is that many an unbeliever has a memory well-stocked with Bible verses and doctrines; the Bible yields a knowledge of God, but the Spirit alone, who uses Scripture as His instrument, is the giver of regenerate life.[61]

Henry devoted an entire chapter in *GRA* to understanding how the Spirit illumines Scripture for the believer and argued that "the Holy Spirit of inspiration and illumination" is "the only key to the Bible."[62] As quoted above, Henry saw the Spirit's role in inspiration and illumination to be "essential and unique in enlivening God's revelation in the lives of people."[63]

---

60. Carl F. H. Henry, "The Spirit and the Written Word," *Bibliotheca Sacra* 111.444 (1954): 302.
61. Henry, "The Spirit and the Written Word," 302.
62. Henry, *GRA*, 4:275.
63. Henry, *GRA*, 4:277.

In discussing Henry's presentation of illumination, Paul House recognizes that "Henry's emphasis on reason and propositional truth in no way intended to put God in a straightjacket."[64] Gregory Thornbury's rebuttal to Henry's challengers merits consideration:

> In light of this, one wonders what would attract evangelicals to look to Barth as opposed, to, say, Henry. If, as John Webster says, the thing one must admire about Barth is his view on the active relationship between God and his creatures, the same is true, if not in great measure, about the Henry corpus, particularly Henry's view on the Spirit's work in the life of the believer to illuminate the meaning of Scripture. After all, as he rightly concludes [in GRA], the lack of "full delineation of the Holy Spirit's work—inspiration, illumination, regeneration, indwelling, sanctification, guidance—nurtures a confused and disabled church. The proliferating modern sects may, in fact, be one of the penalties for the lack of a comprehensive systematic doctrine of the Spirit." *Persistently in his explanation of inerrancy, Henry draws attention to the Spirit as an active and personal stimulant toward understanding, discernment, and regeneration.*[65]

Thornbury concludes: "Powerful observations [concerning the Spirit and the Word] characterize the prose of GRA and, once read, render ridiculous the notion that Carl F. H. Henry embraced some sort of cold, rationalistic view of God, the Spirit, and revelation."[66] Henry thought that we have yet to "'see the worst' in an age that sunders the Spirit from the Scriptures," but he also hoped that we "have yet to 'see the best' of a movement that holds Spirit and Scriptures together as the risen Lord would have us do as he rules his Church through the Spirit by the Scriptures."[67]

To be sure, none of Henry's challengers argue that he said *nothing* about the Spirit's work in special revelation. Many, in fact, express appreciation. For example, White's dissertation is no sledgehammer against Henry but

---

64. Paul R. House, "Remaking the Modern Mind: Revisiting Carl Henry's Theological Vision," *Southern Baptist Journal of Theology* 8.4 (2004): 19.

65. Thornbury, *Recovering Classic Evangelicalism*, 143. Italics added for emphasis.

66. Thornbury, 143–44.

67. Carl F. H. Henry, "The Bible and the Conscience of Our Age," *Journal of the Evangelical Theological Society* 25.4 (1982): 405.

instead a nuanced evaluation of the Spirit's role in Henry's theological method, specifically how humankind receives and appropriates divine revelation. Vanhoozer provides thoughtful and helpful interaction with Henry's understanding of language. Still, it might be that some of Henry's challengers take the volume of his work on propositional revelation—certainly greater than that devoted to illumination—and conclude that he elevated the word over the Spirit.[68] But Henry himself confessed ignorance regarding the precise mechanics of the Spirit's activity. Unsurprisingly, this contributed to a more measured and, as a result, shorter body of work on the topic. This, however, does not mean he found it less important. His own words negate that conclusion.

It is not that Henry merely reserved *a* place for pneumatology in his presentation of special revelation, but that pneumatology has gone unappreciated as *central* to his conception. As stated in the introduction to this chapter, pneumatology served as an aquifer that gave Henry's doctrine of revelation its vibrancy and vitality to such an extent that his concept of special revelation was inconceivable apart from pneumatology. White disagrees with this sentiment and believes that "a fair assessment acknowledges [Henry's] treatment of the Spirit, while also noting that the Spirit often functions peripherally, in contrast to the sure, objective Word of God."[69] He believes Malcolm Yarnell's claim that the Spirit is central to Henry's epistemology to be "exuberant," "misguided," and "unhelpful."[70] But White's conception of Henry's "Christological epistemology" over and against Yarnell's "pneumatological epistemology" is unsatisfactory.[71] Henry would agree, and White quotes *GRA* to the effect that "in the person of Jesus Christ God has given himself to be fully known. This fundamental reality stands behind all forms of revelation, including that of Holy Scripture."[72] But how would one know Jesus Christ, whom God has given to be known, apart from the Holy Spirit, specifically in special revelation? Far from being

---

68. If this theory is correct, White would not be counted among them. He states, "From a certain perspective, and in some segments of his thought, both Word and Spirit receive appropriate development. But the question is not so much on degrees of attention, but of the way the relation between the two terms is construed." See White, "Word and Spirit," 185.

69. White, "Word and Spirit," 185.

70. White, "Word and Spirit," 185.

71. White, "Word and Spirit," 187.

72. White, "Word and Spirit," 115.

"exuberant" and "unhelpful," Yarnell's conception of Henry's "pneumato-logical epistemology" is a thoughtful exposition of how Henry understood Jesus to be made known to believers. It is the Spirit who "makes Christ epistemologically available to us."[73] As Henry stated elsewhere, "The Holy Spirit uses truth as a means of conviction and persuasion."[74] This returns us to Henry's axiomatic theology, outlined at the beginning of this chapter. Henry believed the basic Christian axioms to be two: God *is* (ontological) and God *speaks* (epistemological). The ontological would be inconceivable apart from the epistemological. The ontological triune God is made available epistemically through the past and present ministry of the Spirit. So, Yarnell's "pneumatological epistemology" is a beneficial representation of how Henry understood Christ to be made known, for the Holy Spirit is essential to every step of that process, from inspiration to inerrancy to infallibility to illumination to regeneration.

In sum, this chapter wishes to inspire Henry's challengers to a different reading. While some of their conclusions are due to straightforward disagreement, others regarding Henry's view of special revelation seem to stem from either misunderstanding or unfamiliarity with the intricacies of his work.[75] Of course, this should not insinuate that they have not read Henry at all (though Thornbury approaches this critique in *Recovering Classic Evangelicalism*, as does Doyle in *Carl Henry: Theologian for All Seasons* and Trueman in his article overviewing *GRA*).[76] It is to say that Henry's views concerning language, hermeneutics, genre, and the work of the Spirit in special revelation seem to be downplayed or underappreciated by those who do not share his insistence on propositional revelation and his cognitive-rational bent.

Robert Johnston sees Henry as a prime example of an evangelical who emphasized a theology of the word over (though not against) a theology

---

73. Yarnell, "Whose Jesus? Which Revelation?," 46.

74. Carl F. H. Henry, "Fortunes of the Christian World View," *Trinity Journal* 19.2 (1998): 175. Henry often used language describing the Spirit as the Persuader who used truth as a means of persuasion. He did so five times throughout the pages of *Toward a Recovery of Christian Belief*. See Henry, *Toward a Recovery of Christian Belief*, x, 54, 59, 92, 113.

75. Doyle, *Carl Henry: Theologian for All Seasons*, 92–129.

76. Doyle, 92; Thornbury, *Recovering Classic Evangelicalism*, 132–33; Trueman, "Admiring the Sistine Chapel," 56.

of the Spirit. While both "classic approaches to theology exist in American evangelicalism," Henry preferred the former:

> It is not accidental that Henry chose to begin with knowledge of God through Scripture and then turned to the experiential dimension of the faith. Although the importance of both Word and Spirit are recognized, and although the two are in fact conjoined, a clear priority is evident here, as in other of Henry's writings.[77]

This is accurate as far as it goes, but the categories are too rigid. Henry's theology of the word was a theology of the *Spirit-inspired* word, which required *Spirit-enabled* illumination to take root in the hearer's heart. Henry did not divorce word and Spirit but rather emphasized the Spirit's working in and through the Spirit-inspired Bible. It is *"by* the Spirit, *through* the Scriptures, that the risen Lord rules his Church."[78]

A TWO-C(K)ARL COLLISION: CARL HENRY AND KARL BARTH AS A CASE STUDY

This chapter will conclude by setting Carl F. H. Henry in conversation with Karl Barth regarding inspiration and illumination. This conversation is not new, and no novel interpretation is attempted here. Instead, the goal is to show that pneumatology was not only essential to Henry's doctrine of revelation but also to the feud between these titans.[79] Just as pneumatology played a central role in Henry's disagreements with the charismatic and Jesus People movements, pneumatology was a key point of disagreement between Henry and Barth. Further, by comparing and contrasting their views, Henry's understanding of inspiration and illumination (and the implications thereof) will become clearer and more pronounced.

---

77. Robert K. Johnston, "Varieties of American Evangelicalism," in *Southern Baptists and American Evangelicals: The Conversation Continues*, ed. David S. Dockery (Nashville: B&H, 1993), 50–51.

78. Henry, "God's Word is God's Word," 12. Italics added for emphasis.

79. Of course, Henry had other disagreements with Barth beyond pneumatology and inspiration. He disagreed with Barth's conception of redemption, his articulation of the Trinity, and his use of Reformation sources. See John D. Morrison, "Barth, Barthians, and Evangelicals: Reassessing the Question of the Relation of Holy Scripture and the Word of God," *Trinity Journal* 25 (2004): 205.

Henry and Barth were not outright foes, but nor were they friends. Their disagreements ran deep, and neither was willing to budge. Both were repelled by theological modernism, but each formulated distinct and (almost) diametrically opposed solutions. Their famed verbal bout is worth recounting from Henry's autobiography. After Henry asked Barth a pointed question about the resurrection,

> Barth became angry. Pointing at me, and recalling my identification, he asked: "Did you say *Christianity Today* or *Christianity Yesterday*?" The audience—largely nonevangelical professors and clergy—roared with delight. When countered unexpectedly in this way, one often reaches for a Scripture verse. So I replied, assuredly out of biblical context, "*Yesterday, today and forever.*"[80]

Henry was tickled by his resourceful application of Hebrews 13:8, but Barth was unamused. Shortly after the exchange, Daniel Fuller, a friend and former student of Henry and, at this point, a student of Barth's in Switzerland, wrote to Henry with a comment Barth made that Fuller thought Henry might find interesting:

> I talked with Barth a week ago and tried to get him to say something about his recent trip [to America]. Like other students who have tried this here, I failed, for apparently Barth is disciplining himself to keep any further comments about America from emanating prematurely from Basel. All he said was, "Yes, I was on a panel with a Jew, a Catholic, a liberal, and (with a sneer in his voice) a Fundamentalist."[81]

Was Henry the "Fundamentalist" to whom Barth was referring with a sneer? Possibly. Either way, there was a theological friction that both recognized and from which neither retreated.

Though they shared fundamental disagreements, Henry respected Barth. Henry obviously spent substantial time studying Barth's *Church Dogmatics*, and he was "not afraid to welcome Barth as a theological ally

---

80. Henry, *Confessions of a Theologian*, 211 (italics original). Following the session, Barth apologized for the comment, which Henry gladly accepted.

81. Daniel Fuller, letter to Carl F. H. Henry, June 27, 1962, CFHHP (box 1959 [box 1], file "Correspondence—Fuller, Daniel P.").

and to draw upon his genius."[82] Upon meeting Barth, Henry believed that despite Barth's theological flaws, he was "in the presence of a believer in the gospel."[83] Later, Henry shared his estimation of Barth with William Mueller:

> Now a word about Karl Barth. He was a man of rare courage and beyond doubt the most influential theologian of the 20th century. Three times I had the privilege of an hour with him in his home in Basel, and always in his presence I felt profoundly humble. From his *Dogmatics* I learned many things that I should have learned from evangelical theologians in America, as well as strenuously differing from him.[84]

Still, despite this admiration, Henry critiqued Barth in every conceivable venue. Like two molecules circling the Large Hadron Collider headed for imminent collision, Henry and Barth experienced unavoidable intellectual conflict: "Henry's life-long focus on the issues of revelation and the Bible brought him into direct confrontation with Barth's unique and elusive treatment of these issues."[85] Before evaluating Henry's critiques, it is necessary to briefly outline Barth's conceptions of inspiration and illumination, so as to draw a clear delineation between the two men.[86]

Barth began his chapter on Scripture in *Church Dogmatics* by arguing that "Scripture is holy and the Word of God, because by the Holy Spirit it became and will become to the Church a witness to divine revelation."[87] Here, two key elements of Barth's thought emerge. First, he believed Scripture "will become" the word of God through an encounter with the

---

82. Doyle, *Carl Henry: Theologian for All Seasons*, 103.

83. Henry, *Confessions of a Theologian*, 243.

84. Carl F. H. Henry, to William Mueller, June 25, 1985, CFHHP (box *"God, Revelation and Authority* 1976–1983" [box 1], file "Comments").

85. Mohler, "Evangelical Theology and Karl Barth: Representative Models of Response," 133.

86. A "brief" outline in no way could capture all that is Barth. For a formidable intellectual biography of Barth, see Bruce L. McCormack, *Karl Barth's Critically Realistic Dialectical Theology: Its Genesis and Development 1909–1936* (New York: Oxford University Press, 1995). For Barth's relationship with American evangelicals (including material on Henry's evaluation of Barth), see Bruce L. McCormack and Clifford B. Anderson, eds., *Karl Barth and American Evangelicalism* (Grand Rapids: Eerdmans, 2011).

87. Karl Barth, *Church Dogmatics*, vol. 1, part 2 of The Doctrine of the Word of God, ed. G. W. Bromiley and T. F. Torrance, trans. G. T. Thomson and Harold Knight (London: T&T Clark, 1956), 457.

reader. Second, he believed the Bible to be a witness to divine revelation, rather than the verbal deposit of revelation itself. David Mueller, himself a former student of Barth's, summarized his professor's view by stating, "Barth is always careful to distinguish God in his revelation from the testimony to that revelation which confronts us in the Scriptures."[88]

Barth envisioned a three-fold schema of "the Word of God." He believed the phrase to refer to Christian proclamation, the Bible, or the incarnation. There was a definite order to these three forms. For Barth, the most important form of the revelatory word was the man Christ Jesus. This Barth prioritized in every way. Then, he recognized that the written word of God bore witness to the historical Jesus, for Jesus is the Jesus of the Bible. Finally, when the church bears witness to this Jesus, the church too is a form of the word of God.[89]

It was the second aspect of Barth's three-fold schema with which Henry was most interested—the word of God written. Barth argued that God's inspiring of the Bible does not first speak of a quality of the text, but rather to an event whereby God uses the Bible, as a foreman would use a tool or an artist a brush, to create in a person the knowledge of Christ. He connected the "revelation attested to in Holy Scripture" to "a statement about the occurrence of an event."[90] It is the event, not the textual composition itself, through which the Bible can claim inspiration. The Bible is brought into the circle of God's knowledge, and God superintends this human record of His actions to be a divine portal into the knowledge of God. This led Barth to believe that revelation happened "from time to time" because, by definition, an event is confined to a particular spatial-temporal moment.[91] A 1927 comment Barth made in what would later be adapted into *Church Dogmatics* is representative of his thought: "The Word of God still happens today in the Bible; and apart from this happening [event] the Bible is not

88. David L. Mueller, *Karl Barth*, Makers of the Modern Theological Mind (Waco, TX: Word Books, 1972), 56.

89. Clifford Green, "Karl Barth's Life and Theology," in *Karl Barth: Theologian of Freedom*, ed. Clifford Green, The Making of Modern Theology: Nineteenth- and Twentieth-Century Texts (Minneapolis: Fortress, 1991), 25.

90. Barth, *Church Dogmatics*, vol. 1, part 2, 45.

91. Green, *Karl Barth: Theologian of Freedom*, 25.

the Word of God, but a book like other books."[92] As long as God uses this book for His divine encounter, the Bible can be called inspired. For Barth, "the Bible is the Word of God only in that God chooses to speak through it."[93] He remarked:

> The work of God is done through this text. The miracle of God takes place in this text formed of human words. This text in all its humanity, including all the fallibility which belongs to it, is the object of this work and miracle. By the decision of God this text is now taken and used.[94]

For Barth, the point at which God takes and uses this text for this purpose (the event) is the doctrine of illumination. Therefore, Barth found inspiration and illumination to be inseparable. He thought that apart from illumination, the Bible remained a book with no divine claim or characteristic (other than being the vehicle that gave witness to God's redemptive actions in history). In other words, Barth found the Bible to be inspired only insofar as it illumined. Ultimately, for Barth, these two pneumatological acts—inspiration and illumination—were concurrent and codependent. They could not exist apart from one another. Though Barth refined this view throughout his career, he remained convinced of the fundamental "inseparability" of inspiration and illumination.[95]

While Barth thought inspiration and illumination to be dependent on one another, Henry's fundamental critique of Barth was that he improperly collapsed inspiration and illumination together. Henry believed that Barth "confuses inspiration and illumination, and this misunderstanding adversely affects his exposition of both doctrines."[96] Henry, on the other hand, distinguished inspiration and illumination as separate functions of the same Spirit. While Henry was appreciative that "Barthian theology

---

92. Karl Barth, *Die Lehre vom Worte Gottes. Prolegomena zur christlichen Dogmatik* (Munich: Christian Kaiser, 1927), 63. Quoted in Green, *Karl Barth: Theologian of Freedom*, 25.

93. Mann, "Revelation of the Triune God Through Word and Spirit: A Theological Critique of Karl Barth and Carl Henry," 76–77.

94. Barth, *Church Dogmatics*, vol. 1, part 2, 532.

95. Richard E. Burnett, "Inspiration," in *The Westminster Handbook to Karl Barth*, ed. Richard E. Burnett, The Westminster Handbooks to Christian Theology (Louisville: Westminster John Knox, 2013), 115.

96. Henry, *GRA*, 4:266.

elevated the long-neglected role of the Holy Spirit to new significance in its exposition of divine revelation," he thought Barth's association of inspiration with illumination led him to misconstrue the Spirit's activity in both.[97] Henry found Barth's articulation of inspiration to be too little interested in the actual verbal text *then*, and his articulation of illumination *now* to be focused on the wrong object—the Spirit illumines the text, not merely the believer.[98]

Similarities exist between Henry's disagreements with the charismatic movement and the Jesus People and with Barth. Just as he thought they held too low a view of the Spirit's work, Henry's criticism of Barth took a similar shape. Though Barth thought he was loosening inspiration from a "rigid" connection with Scripture, in doing so he limited the Spirit's role to illumination—a move Henry found unsatisfactory.[99] Barth denied a "fixed, past tense rendering of the text's nature in light of the Spirit's activity [inspiration]."[100] As Barth told a colloquium in 1955, the primary difference between his view of revelation and that of a "fundamentalist" (with Henry likely at the forefront of his mind) was fixated on the work of the Spirit: "For me the Word of God is a *happening*, not a thing. Therefore the Bible must *become* the Word of God, and it does this through the work of the Spirit."[101] Therefore, because Barth denied any historical inspiration of the verbal text by the Spirit, he had to lump inspiration into present-day illumination. But to link inspiration to the occasional event of illumination by the Spirit led Barth beyond the classic Protestant understanding of inspiration:

> It is obvious then that, over against classic evangelical orthodoxy, Barth did not consider the biblical writers to be divinely entrusted transmitters of a verbally-inspired Word of God objectively given

97. Henry, *GRA*, 4:256.

98. Henry, *GRA*, 4:266.

99. Henry, *GRA*, 4:257.

100. David Gibson, "The Answering Speech of Men: Karl Barth on Holy Scripture," in *The Enduring Authority of the Christian Scriptures*, ed. D. A. Carson (Grand Rapids: Eerdmans, 2016), 281.

101. J. D. Godsey, ed., *Karl Barth's Table Talk* (Edinburgh: Oliver & Boyd, 1963), 26. Quoted in Mark D. Thompson, "Witness to the Word: On Barth's Doctrine of Scripture," in *Engaging with Barth: Contemporary Evangelical Critiques*, ed. David Gibson and Daniel Strange (New York: Continuum, 2008), 191.

in Scripture. For him an ongoing sporadic divine encounter is the locus of revelation, and the reality of revelation depends upon one's personal responsive trust. Barth sacrificed the objective inspired-ness of the Bible and linked the reality and truth of revelation not with grammatical-historical exegesis of a divinely vouchsafed body of authoritative teaching but rather with one's inner per-sonal response to a revelational confrontation assertedly attested in Scripture.[102]

In a 1959 radio interview, Henry contrasted his view with Barth's: while Barth could speak of the "inspiring-ness" of the word, Henry found this insufficient. There was a settled "inspired-ness" of the word that had to be appreciated in order to fully comprehend the Spirit's work in rev-elation.[103] Henry was convinced that inspiration relates to Scripture's God-breathed origin, not its present-day function.[104] Attaching "-ing" (Barth) or "-ed" (Henry) to the word "inspire" makes all the difference.

Ultimately, Henry thought Barth found it difficult to escape the verdict that the Spirit is shackled to the reader's faithful response, for only then can the believer be said to be illumined and the Bible inspired. Barth often appealed to the freedom of God, but, in Henry's estimation, Barth's con-cept of revelation enslaved God to the reader's response. Henry, however, had a different vision:

That the Word of God cannot be shackled by human controls, that the Spirit ongoingly manifests the reality of the risen Christ attested to in Scripture, and that the Christian community lives by the free-dom of God's grace and the empowering of the Spirit demands in fact—if we are to possess any valid information about any spiritual

---

102. Carl F. H. Henry, "The Interpretation of the Scriptures: Are We Doomed to Hermeneutical Nihilism?" *Review & Expositor* 71 (1974): 199.

103. Carl F. H. Henry, transcript of interview by Erling Olsen, New York, May 3, 1959, CFHHP (box 1959 [box 2], file "Interview Transcript—Dr. Erling Olsen + Carl Henry WOR, New York"). Henry drew the language of "inspiring-ness" and "inspired-ness" from Geoffrey Bromiley. See Henry, *GRA*, 4:148. For a similar critique of Barth's construction of inspira-tion, see Gibson, "The Answering Speech of Men," 280–82. Gibson concurs with Henry that "Barth's inspiration thesis is exegetically unproven and historically novel." See Gibson, "The Answering Speech of Men," 282.

104. Mann, "Revelation of the Triune God Through Word and Spirit: A Theological Critique of Karl Barth and Carl Henry," 145.

realities whatsoever—an express alternative to the Barthian view
of inspiration. To commend Barth's emphasis on the free, active and
decisive nature of the Word of God *as Barth understands this* arbi-
trarily requires submissive faith as the sine qua non for perceiving
the truth of God's Word.[105]

Henry's view gave the Spirit more room to work, not less, because he did
not limit the Spirit to only the immediate, but instead recognized and
differentiated the past (inspiration) and present (illumination) aspects
of the Spirit's work in revelation. Barth's concept of inspiration was relegated to occasional days on the calendar; Henry's reached back to "In
the beginning."

Despite their disagreements, Henry appreciated Barth's stance that
theology would remain fruitless apart from the Spirit. Therefore, when
Henry devoted the January 4, 1963, issue of *Christianity Today* to the Holy
Spirit, he knew who he was going to recruit to pen the opening article:
Karl Barth. Henry could have commissioned anyone for this role, but he
chose his rival because, though pneumatology lay at the foundation of their
disagreements, both were committed to seeing more engagement with
the Spirit. Henry published Barth's pneumatological reflection because
he agreed with Barth at this point:

> The Holy Spirit is the vital power that bestows free mercy on the-
> ology and on theologians just as on the community and on every
> single Christian. Both of these remain utterly in need of him. Only
> the Holy Spirit himself can help a theology that is or has become
> unspiritual ... *Veni creator Spiritus!* "Come, O come, thou Spirit of
> life!" ... Even the best theology cannot be anything more or better
> than this petition made in the form of resolute work. Theology can
> ultimately only take the position of one of those children who have
> neither bread nor fish, but doubtless a father who has both and
> will give them these when they ask him. [Evangelical theology]
> is rich, sustained, and upheld, since it lays hold on God's promise,
> clinging without skepticism, yet also without any presumption, to

---

105. Henry, *GRA*, 4:260 (italics original).

the promise according to which—not theology, but—"the Spirit searches all things, even the deep things of God."[106]

CONCLUSION

This chapter has argued that pneumatology functioned as an underground aquifer that gave Henry's conception of special revelation its vibrancy and vitality to such an extent that his thought was inconceivable apart from it. In the area of special revelation, the Holy Spirit was "critical to Henry's work."[107] Though Henry is remembered as a defender of biblical inerrancy, he himself did not start there; in fact, he thought it dangerous to leap over inspiration in an effort to arrive at inerrancy. Instead, the Spirit's work in inspiration must be established before the conversation of inerrancy can take hold. This chapter has also sought to redeem Henry from certain criticisms by showing that he was aware of the Spirit's activity in and through the biblical text, and that he sought to balance word and Spirit by showcasing how the Spirit works through the word. Finally, this chapter buttresses the claim that pneumatology played an essential role in Henry's theological and historical context. As demonstrated, pneumatological differences were central not only to Henry and his charismatic counterparts, but between Henry and his perpetual sparring partner, Karl Barth. Overall, this chapter has defended the first third of the book's three-fold thesis thread—that Henry believed a Spirit-inspired Bible (revelation) would order a Spirit-enlivened body (ecclesiology) composed of Spirit-filled believers (ethics). It is to the second element of this thesis—pneumatology and ecclesiology in Henry's thought—that the book will now turn.

---

106. Karl Barth, "When the Spirit Forsakes Theology," *Christianity Today* (January 4, 1963): 3. This was a selection from Barth's soon-to-be-published *Evangelical Theology: An Introduction,* which was released the following week.

107. Mann, "Revelation of the Triune God through Word and Spirit: A Theological Critique of Karl Barth and Carl Henry," 155.

4

—

A SPIRIT-ENLIVENED BODY (PNEUMATOLOGY AND ECCLESIOLOGY)

INTRODUCTION

Carl F. H. Henry was convinced that for evangelicalism to prosper into the future, ecclesiology needed to be a "chief item" of concern.[1] He believed "Christ's word about the church is one that evangelicals just now need most to hear."[2] He gave attention to ecclesiology throughout his academic career, and he devoted much of his life to training future ministers to ensure the ongoing theological health of Christian churches. He was convinced by neither the fundamentalist tendency toward a truncated and schismatic ecclesiology nor the modernist tendency toward a thin one that emphasized social issues at the expense of theological rigor. Instead, Henry articulated an ecclesiology that stressed Spirit-engendered unity at the universal level and Spirit-anointed proclamation at the local one.[3]

Henry believed that a Spirit-inspired Bible (revelation) would order a Spirit-enlivened body (ecclesiology).[4] His doctrine of revelation bore

---

1. Carl F. H. Henry, *The Christian Mindset in a Secular Society* (Portland: Multnomah Press, 1984), 34.

2. Henry, *The Christian Mindset in a Secular Society*, 31.

3. As will be shown, the language of "Spirit-engendered unity" and "Spirit-anointed proclamation" originate with Henry himself.

4. Like the above, the language of a "Spirit-enlivened" body comes directly from Henry as well: "The apostolic portrayal of the church as a *Spirit-enlivened* and Spirit-directed community carried an expectation of the Spirit's special presence and power throughout the body of believers." See Henry, *GRA*, 6:389. Italics added for emphasis. Also: "As incarnate, crucified,

directly on his doctrine of ecclesiology, and both were buttressed by pneu-matology. This chapter will examine how Henry wed pneumatology and ecclesiology; it will demonstrate that, like his understanding of special rev-elation, Henry's conception of ecclesiology was dependent on and incon-ceivable apart from pneumatology. To do so, the chapter will first answer a key question: Did Henry even have a doctrine of the church? If so, what made it unique? Then, the two primary ways Henry incorporated pneu-matology into his ecclesiology will be addressed: Spirit-engendered unity and Spirit-anointed proclamation.

"THE ECCLESIOLOGICAL
AIR TRAFFIC CONTROLLER":
HENRY'S DOCTRINE OF THE CHURCH

While this chapter will argue that Henry's developed pneumatology shaped his unique ecclesiology, he has been critiqued for neglecting both. Previous chapters have defended Henry's pneumatological *bona fides*, but this section will defend him against those who see in his work a dismissal of ecclesiological concerns.[5] Then, the chapter will demonstrate that, far from ignoring pneumatology and ecclesiology, Henry had a rich concept of how they intersect at both the universal level (in unity) and the local level (in proclamation).

Several scholars have challenged Henry's treatment of ecclesiology. Mohler believes that "the most glaring omission in [Henry's] theological project is the doctrine of the church."[6] Garrett also sees too little attention to ecclesiology in Henry's work.[7] Thornbury thinks that "Henry placed too much confidence in big-event and big-organization evangelicalism and could have benefited from thinking more organically and ecclesially."[8] Russell Moore dubbed Henry "the quintessential parachurch academic"

---

risen and exalted, Jesus Christ is the living head of the regenerate church *enlivened by the Holy Spirit.*" See Henry, *GRA*, 1:34. Italics added for emphasis.

5. Some material in this section, including the title, is adapted from the author's previous work on Henry's ecclesiology. See Jesse M. Payne, "An Uneasy Ecclesiology: Carl F. H. Henry's Doctrine of the Church," *Southeastern Theological Review* 10.1 (2019): 95–111.

6. Mohler, "Carl F. H. Henry," 292.

7. Garrett, *Baptist Theology*, 519.

8. Thornbury, *Recovering Classic Evangelicalism*, 23.

and speculated whether he "even had an ecclesiology, and, if so, whether there was anything distinctively Baptist about it."[9]

These critiques are valid in that Henry made collating his views on ecclesiology difficult. He did not produce a typical treatment of ecclesiology, nor did he offer fresh perspective on ecclesiological specifics. *God, Revelation and Authority* is "a theological epistemology of epic proportions, but one that deals little with the Church."[10] His theological interests were often elsewhere. Strachan is correct in recognizing that, "In some cases, [Henry and the neo-evangelicals] considered polity and ecclesiology to be of only glancing importance relative to the gospel and the doctrine of Scripture."[11]

To return to Russell Moore's question—did Henry even have an ecclesiology? Moore answers "Yes," albeit with a certain caveat:

The theological foundations for the universal—or "invisible" (as it is, unfortunately, often called)—church were established in Henry's thought at the most basic levels. What was missing was theological specificity on some of the things that make a church a church—the ordinances, membership, church government, and so forth. It is not debatable that these issues were often intentionally minimized to maintain unity within an evangelical movement seeking to take on Protestant liberalism, separatist fundamentalism, and cultural nihilism.[12]

Moore is right in recognizing that Henry lacked "theological specificity" on ecclesiological distinctives, but this did not mean Henry lacked an

---

9. Russell D. Moore, "God, Revelation, and Community: Ecclesiology and Baptist Identity in the Thought of Carl F. H. Henry," *Southern Baptist Journal of Theology* 8.4 (2004): 27. For more on the critiques of Henry's ecclesiology (and the wider neo-evangelical approach to the doctrine of the church), see Collin Hansen and Justin Taylor, "From Babylon Baptist to Baptists in Babylon: The SBC and the Broader Evangelical Community," in *The SBC and the 21st Century: Reflection, Renewal, and Recommitment*, ed. Jason K. Allen (Nashville: B&H Academic, 2016), 35-39.

10. George, "Evangelicals and Others," 20. This is why, while the previous chapter on Henry's doctrine of revelation drew significantly from *GRA*, this chapter on Henry's ecclesiology will rely more upon his *Christianity Today* catalog, monographs, and various journal articles.

11. Strachan, *Awakening the Evangelical Mind*, 175.

12. Moore, "God, Revelation, and Community," 33.

ecclesiology entirely. He was familiar with the various positions regarding baptism, the Lord's Supper, leadership structures, and church membership. He believed that "[i]t is true that God focuses on life in community,
and particularly on life in the church as a new society of faith, more than
many evangelicals seem to recognize."[13] However, Henry's ecclesiological
presentation took a unique shape because he was committed to a sweeping, trans-denominational neo-evangelicalism that included an array of
conservative denominations willing to cooperate together in their efforts
to articulate the gospel to a new generation.[14] He rallied his evangelical
comrades of differing stripes to a thoughtful defense of vital doctrines
under attack by theological liberalism and neo-orthodoxy.

Despite his work among various Christian traditions, Henry was a
Baptist. He thought that "Baptist distinctives are valid and that the Baptist
mission in the closing decades of the twentieth century is extraordinarily
urgent."[15] His first (and only) pastorate was at Humboldt Park Baptist
Church in Chicago. He moved in Northern Baptist (later American Baptist)
circles for much of his career. However, in the 1980s and 1990s, Henry
"became more closely linked with the Southern Baptist Convention, lecturing in its seminaries, serving on various committees, and quietly supporting the conservative redirection of the denomination during those years."[16]
In 1987, nearing the end of his public ministry, Henry was recognized by
the Southern Baptist Convention Pastors' Conference for his theological
legacy from a Baptist perspective.[17]

---

13. Carl F. H. Henry, "Spiritual? Say It Isn't So!" in *Alive to God: Studies in Spirituality
Presented to James Houston*, ed. J. I. Packer and Loren Wilkinson (Vancouver: Regent College
Publishing, 1992), 10.

14. While aspects of Henry's approach to ecclesiology are worthy of emulation and
commendation, it also had weaknesses. Nathan Hatch, while grateful for Henry's contributions, warned against what he saw to be too strict a focus on intra-denominational alliances.
He thought that movements like neo-evangelicalism risked losing the "riches" of various
denominational traditions. See Nathan O. Hatch, "Response to Carl F. H. Henry," in *Evangelical
Affirmations*, ed. Kenneth Kantzer and Carl F. H. Henry (Grand Rapids: Academie, 1990), 99.

15. Carl F. H. Henry, "Twenty Years a Baptist," *Foundations* 1 (1958): 54.

16. George, "Evangelicals and Others," 20.

17. Mohler, "Carl F. H. Henry," 293. Others have commented on Henry's commitments both
to the Southern Baptist Convention and the wider evangelical world. Henry was not alone in
this dual allegiance: "For example, some of the leading postwar evangelical theologians were
American Baptists but identified most closely with the evangelical seminaries where they
taught. That group included Carl F. H. Henry, Bernard Ramm, Harold Lindsell, and Roger
Nicole. Each of these men also identified with Southern Baptists at various points in their

Still, Henry's voice rang out beyond his Baptist brethren. He spoke of "the evangelical church" in the singular, "not referring to any particular denomination but to all conservative Protestants committed to the formal and material principles of the Reformation."[18] This language was intentional. His vision of ecclesiology required that he lower walls around denominational distinctives in order to strengthen the broader evangelical coalition. His goal for neo-evangelicalism was incompatible with ecclesiological silos. This is why, for example, in the first issue of *Christianity Today*, Henry recruited Addison Leitch, a Presbyterian, to write an article entitled "The Primary Task of the Church."[19] One may assume Henry would secure a Baptist to write *Christianity Today*'s first ecclesiological piece, but it was not so.[20] Though Leitch's article was from a Presbyterian perspective, Henry published it because Leitch articulated the spiritual nature of the universal church and the need for every local church to be tethered to divine inspiration and the Great Commission—views Henry was glad to advance. Leitch ended his article with a conclusion that his Baptist colleagues, including Henry, could affirm:

> The primary task of the Church, therefore, is to bring men into a saving relationship to God through Christ. This is done by Word and

---

lives." See Anthony L. Chute, Nathan A. Finn, and Michael A. G. Haykin, *The Baptist Story: From English Sect to Global Movement* (Nashville: B&H Academic, 2015), 282–83.

18. George, "Evangelicals and Others," 19.

19. Addison Leitch, "The Primary Task of the Church," *Christianity Today* (October 15, 1956): 11–13, 18. One could make the argument that the pillars of Henry's thought are represented by the articles he ran in this inaugural issue. To get a feel for what he was passionate about, look at the lineup and subjects he led off with. Though he wrote only one of the four opening articles, he shaped the topics the first issue covered. Consequently, the articles 1) challenged some of the more dangerous trends emerging from European theology (written by G. C. Berkouwer); 2) argued for biblical authority (in the influential "Biblical Authority in Evangelism" written by Billy Graham); 3) defended the Western concept of freedom through the Judeo-Christian worldview (written by Henry); and 4) urged the church to fulfill her God-given task (written by Leitch). These four topics—challenging European theology, biblical authority and evangelism, the need for a return to the Judeo-Christian worldview, and the church's role in a changing world—encapsulate Henry's career.

20. The first instance in *Christianity Today* of an ecclesiological article from a Baptist perspective (focused on the nature of the church, not how the church should react to a particular social issue) was W. Boyd Hunt's contribution in "The Body Christ Heads: A Symposium." This article combined seven of *Christianity Today*'s contributing editors, all from differing denominations, and outlined their views on ecclesiological issues, especially the unity of the church. See W. Boyd Hunt, "The Body Christ Heads: A Symposium," *Christianity Today* (August 19, 1957): 7–8.

Spirit. Men thus saved must be given the nourishment to grow in Christ; this is Christian education. Such men in communion form the communities which make constant redemptive impact on the world around them.[21]

Later, Henry allowed William Williamson, an Episcopalian, to pen an article entitled "The Doctrine of the Church."[22] In a supplemental note, Henry remarked, "Among the many essays submitted to *Christianity Today*, this exposition of the doctrine of the Church is one of the most significant. Those who do not share its Episcopal orientation will be rewarded nonetheless by its firm reach for New Testament realities."[23] Clearly, Henry allowed ecclesiological traditions different than his own to have a voice in the pages of *Christianity Today* because he believed that a common set of New Testament "realities" united various denominations, and the sooner these realities were recognized, the stronger evangelicalism would be.[24]

Ultimately, Henry's primary calling was not as a shepherd but as a theologian. As such, he saw himself as an evangelical air traffic controller.[25] He left the ecclesiological blueprints to pastors—the mechanics who tweaked and serviced the airplane on the ground.[26] They were best equipped to order the organization after their understanding of Scripture. Henry's role, through writing, teaching, and lecturing, was to help them navigate foggy theological skies and to maintain their convictional coordinates.

With Henry's general approach to ecclesiology addressed, this chapter will turn to his understanding of a Spirit-enlivened church, specifically

---

21. Leitch, "The Primary Task of the Church," 18.

22. William B. Williamson, "The Doctrine of the Church: Part I," *Christianity Today* (December 8, 1961): 11–13.

23. Williamson, "The Doctrine of the Church: Part I," 12.

24. For more on Henry's efforts to create a multi-denominational "alliance for scholarship" even beyond the pages of *Christianity Today*, see Mark A. Noll, *Between Faith and Criticism: Evangelicals, Scholarship, and the Bible in America*, 2nd ed. (Vancouver: Regent College Publishing, 2004), 95–100.

25. Payne, "An Uneasy Ecclesiology," 111.

26. The airplane metaphor is drawn from Henry's own words on the relationship between Spirit and church: "When a church membership is made up of truly twice-born Christians, the minister does not have to 'enrich the mixture' to get his airship off the ground. ... It simply radiates the love of the Saviour and lets the Spirit do the work." See "The Blessings of Faith Include Its Power in Life," unsigned editorial in *Christianity Today* (November 21, 1960): 23.

the Spirit's work in two ways, one universal and one local. On the universal level, Henry understood the Spirit to work through Spirit-engendered unity. On the local level, Henry understood the Spirit to work through Spirit-anointed proclamation.

ONE LORD, ONE FAITH, ONE BAPTISM: SPIRIT-ENGENDERED UNITY

The New Testament overflows with the call for and expectation of unity (John 10:16; 17:21; Acts 4:32; Rom 12:3–7; 1 Cor 1:10–17; 12:12–31; Gal 3:27–28). The oneness of the church was recognized by the Nicene-Constantinopolitan Creed of AD 381, which states that Christians belong to "one, holy, catholic, and apostolic church." This attribute is not to be understood as ancillary or unessential. It is deeply theological: "The church is *one* and is to be one because God is one."[27] When God redeems His image-bearers individually, they are brought into His body, which images His unity corporately. Further, this unity does not originate in the hearts of men but is established by the Holy Spirit (Eph 4:3). As Veli-Matti Kärkkäinen states, "[T]he unity of the church is not primarily a human effort but rather is given from God and as such mandatory for all Christians."[28] It is not a unity of ethnicity, tongue, hobby, or life-stage that unites believers. It is a spiritual unity through their common confession of Christ as Lord (Matt 16:13–20).

Walking through C. S. Lewis's great hall in *Mere Christianity*, one sees occupants in various denominational rooms all connected to this common theological breezeway.[29] The rooms are where the furniture awaits and the fire burns warmest, but they are defined as rooms in relation to the hall; otherwise, they would be altogether separate spaces. But what if certain tenants refused to acknowledge others? Or receded further from the door

---

27. Mark E. Dever, "The Church," *A Theology for the Church*, ed. Daniel L. Akin (Nashville: B&H, 2007), 776.

28. Veli-Matti Kärkkäinen, *An Introduction to Ecclesiology: Ecumenical, Historical, and Global Perspectives* (Downers Grove, IL: InterVarsity Press, 2002), 79.

29. C. S. Lewis, *Mere Christianity* (New York: HarperCollins, 2001), xv: "I hope no reader will suppose that 'mere' Christianity is here put forward as an alternative to the creeds of the existing communions—as if a man could adopt it in preference to Congregationalism or Greek Orthodoxy or anything else. It is more like a hall out of which doors open into several rooms. If I can bring anyone into that hall I shall have done what I attempted. But it is in the rooms, not in the hall, that there are fires and chairs and meals. The hall is a place to wait in, a place from which to try the various doors, not a place to live in."

in isolation? To some, this is the collective personality of Protestantism—a people who continually withdraw from the great hall and are content to express unity with only those who share their primary, secondary, and tertiary beliefs. If one entered a hypothetical "Protestant room," the stereotypical presentation is that they would see various denominations huddled in separate corners, cautious to unify even if the fire got out of hand.[30] To the outside world, Protestants "have a reputation for being schismatic."[31]

Henry, however, had higher hopes for evangelical unity. His ecclesiological impulse toward unity compelled him to address the subject consistently in the pages of *Christianity Today* and other outlets. In his inaugural editorial for the magazine, Henry set the tone for *Christianity Today*'s emphasis upon unity in the Spirit:

> True ecumenicity will be fostered by setting forth the New Testament teaching of the unity of believers in Jesus Christ. External organic unity is not likely to succeed unless the unity engendered by the Holy Spirit prevails. A unity that endures must have as its spiritual basis a like faith, an authentic hope, and the renewing power of Christian love.[32]

This desire for unity never waned, and Henry promoted his vision for decades in various outlets. In so doing, he never disassociated the Spirit, unity, and ecclesiology. About thirty-five years after the first issue of *Christianity Today*, Henry stated, "The doctrine of the church has become for us a neglected article of faith that calls for urgent illumination."[33] He preceded this with a plea for unity:

---

30. However, many Protestants *have* written about how to pursue and maintain unity across denominational lines. Henry himself was a model at this. For a more recent example from a Baptist perspective, see Jonathan Leeman, "A Congregational Approach to Unity, Holiness, and Apostolicity: Faith and Order" and "A Congregational Approach to Catholicity: Independence and Interdependence," in *Baptist Foundations: Church Government for an Anti-Institutional Age*, ed. Mark Dever and Jonathan Leeman (Nashville: B&H Academic, 2015), 333–80.

31. Tom Greggs, "The Catholic Spirit of Protestantism: A Very Methodist Take on the Third Article, Visible Unity, and Ecumenism," *Pro Ecclesia* 26.4 (2017): 353.

32. "Why *Christianity Today*?" unsigned editorial in *Christianity Today* (October 15, 1956): 20.

33. Carl F. H. Henry, "Christianity and Resurgent Paganism: A Death Warrant Hangs Over Modernity," *Vital Speeches of the Day* 57 (1990): 89.

In stressing the need for a manifestation of evangelical unity I need only repeat Jesus' high priestly petition for his disciples to "all be one," even as the persons of the triune Godhead are one, so that the world "may believe that Thou didst send Me." This prayer anticipated no mere sentimental ecumenism that simply rearranges denominational furniture and plays musical chairs with creedal commitments. That recent option was less a witness to the world than an accommodation to it. But if we evangelicals are to bear world witness as the body of believers whose living head is the crucified and risen and returning Jesus we shall need on our own part to wrestle as never before [with] the implications of authentic spiritual and moral unity. We must build network bridges and find ways of reinforcing a mutual witness to a bewildered world.[34]

Three of Henry's key talking points about unity emerge from this paragraph. First, he was convinced that Jesus expected unity among his followers, and a commitment to Christ required a concentrated effort toward unity. In a 1961 editorial entitled "A Plea for Evangelical Unity," Henry was adamant that the pursuit of unity was not a suggestion:

What should be the motivation of [Christian unity]? ... The only motive that will really avail is a biblical one. To put it simply, Christ wills and prays for the unity of his people. ... If this is God's will, it must be also the will of the obedient disciple.[35]

In the same article, Henry wrote, "The one in whom faith is set never alters. Here in God, in the Word and work of God, is an unassailable basis of given unity. Here the people of God have to be one, whether they are prepared for it or not."[36] Elsewhere, drawing on Matthew 16:18 and John 17:11, Henry claimed that "every appeal to an inerrant Bible should humiliate us before the inerrant Christ's insistence on the unity of his church."[37] Second, as will be addressed below, Henry was dissatisfied with the ecumenical

---

34. Henry, "Christianity and Resurgent Paganism," 89.

35. "A Plea for Evangelical Unity," unsigned editorial in *Christianity Today* (March 13, 1961): 24.

36. Unsigned editorial, "A Plea for Evangelical Unity," 24.

37. Henry, *The Christian Mindset in a Secular Society*, 32.

establishment of his day. Finally, Henry sought an authentic spiritual unity that began at the local level, which then radiated out across denominational lines. But what did Henry mean by Christian unity? Examining what he was against will clarify what he was for.

HENRY ON UNITY:
REJECTING "UNCRITICAL ECUMENISM"
AND "FRACTURING INDEPENDENCY"

Carl F. H. Henry agreed with many historians that the ecumenical move- ment was one of—if not the—most important developments in twenti- eth-century Christendom.[40] He consistently evaluated this movement, and he challenged both those who embraced it wholeheartedly and those who dismissed it out of hand. He was opposed to the "two perils" that faced his contemporary ecumenical scene: "uncritical ecumenism and fracturing independency."[39]

REJECTING UNCRITICAL ECUMENISM

Henry warned his fellow evangelicals that they "must not be content to display the defects of the ecumenical establishment."[40] He highlighted the waning numbers, budgets, and effectiveness of multiple denomina- tions that embraced ecumenism.[41] Beyond these visible weaknesses, Henry believed that a theological vacuity blanketed the movement which stifled evangelistic and doctrinal concerns. Here he found commonality with two of his otherwise theological opponents, Emil Brunner and Karl Barth:

In behalf of a spiritual view of the Church, Emil Brunner has fre- quently challenged ecumenical preoccupation with organization

40. Carl F. H. Henry, "The Ecumenical Age: Problems and Promise," *Bibliotheca Sacra* 123:491 (1966): 204, 219. According to Veli-Matti Kärkkäinen, "The purpose and agenda of the ecumenical movement in principle is simple and straightforward: it is the community of all who believe in Christ, and so it purports to promote the unity of Christians and churches." See Kärkkäinen, *An Introduction to Ecclesiology*, 79.

39. "Principles of Church Unity," unsigned editorial in *Christianity Today* (May 26, 1958): 20.

40. Henry, *The Christian Mindset in a Secular Society*, 31.

41. Henry, *The Christian Mindset*, 31. He also argued that one of the major efforts that ecu- menical organizations practiced was to recruit influential media outlets to report positively on their movement in order to paint a strong but inaccurate portrait. All the while, they were bleeding in numbers and their percentage of participation among Protestant denominations was still quite low. See Henry, "The Ecumenical Age," 208.

and externals. Karl Barth's criticisms, if anything, drive even deeper. He protests the ecumenical—or world-wide—restriction of a Church whose real nature is catholic or universal, and hence inclusive of Christians in all times and places. Some modern ecumenists are not on speaking terms with Luther and Calvin and Augustine, or even with the New Testament apostles. Hence they are not genuinely catholic at all; despite their zeal for ecumenism, their devotion to essential Christianity remains in doubt. A further criticism of ecumenism is not wholly unrelated. The unity of the Church is best promoted, Barth contends, through the earnest effort of church dogmaticians, whereas the contemporary ecumenical program is advanced largely through the labor of ecclesiastical politicians.[42]

Two critiques arise from this paragraph. First, Henry questioned whether professing ecumenists embodied genuine ecumenism all that much. How could they claim this title when they swept doctrinal precision under the rug and claimed those who disagreed to be obstinate? By dismissing concerns from those unpersuaded by the ecumenical vision and by relegating rigorous dogmatic debate to the sideline, ecumenists created a movement in their own image, consumed with modernist interests and, therefore, divorced from the historic Christian tradition they claimed to embrace. Henry thought that thorough debate from trained dogmaticians deserved a place at the ecumenical table. But that was quickly jettisoned into the wastebasket marked "irrelevant," substituted with a "least common denominator" theology full of empty calories that was disinterested in securing truth.[43]

Second, Henry thought ecumenism substituted an agile, apostolic church with a web of bureaucracy too cumbersome to address the spiritual needs of the day. This ecumenical oligarchy would eventually swallow the concerns of local clergy committed to their denominational distinctives and their immediate missional context.[44] In doing so, Henry believed the ecumenical movement threatened the spiritual fervor of local

---

42. "Theology in Ecumenical Affairs," unsigned editorial in *Christianity Today* (February 16, 1959): 21.

43. Henry, "The Ecumenical Age," 209.

44. Henry, "The Ecumenical Age," 211–12.

congregations. He feared that ecumenically minded ministers would focus on a worldwide communion at the expense of the local communities to which God had called them. This would eventually limit the effectiveness of gospel proclamation.[45] It was a death pill for evangelical advancement.[46]

REJECTING FRACTURING INDEPENDENCY

Despite concerns with ecumenism, Henry also warned those who scoffed at any semblance of ecumenical sympathies: "Does merely rejecting or absolving oneself of an ecumenical institutional badge justify the lack of evangelical interrelationships and of coordinated fellowship?"[47] As argued above, he was always moving toward a unified evangelical front rather than retreating into ecclesiological cliques.[48] Henry advocated an evangelical ecumenism that embraced a common doctrine and mission for gospel advancement around the world.

The 1966 World Congress of Evangelism in Berlin is one example of Henry's vision for this type of evangelical ecumenism. Chairing the congress remained one of the proudest moments of his career. The event was

45. "[Evangelicals] are not impressed by the enthusiasm for organizational unity shown both by the Second Vatican Council and by the World Council of Churches, while the Lord's evangelistic summons remains on the margin of concern." See Carl F. H. Henry, *Evangelicals at the Brink of Crisis: Significance of the World Congress on Evangelism* (Waco, TX: Word Books, 1976), 81.

46. In reflecting upon the ecumenical movement, Gerald Bray vindicates Henry's concern: "On the whole, it has to be said that these [ecumenical] mergers have favored liberal elements within the participating denominations, which have seized control of the enlarged ecclesiastical structures but done little to promote evangelism. It is also true that more conservative elements have resisted the loss of their particular identity, and that in going against the grain they have been forced to develop firmer convictions about what it is they believe, making them generally stronger and more internally united than they were before." Oddly enough, in other words, ecumenism stifled evangelistic fervor among those who embraced the movement, and it aided theological unity in the denominations that rejected it. See Gerald Bray, *The Church: A Theological and Historical Account* (Grand Rapids: Baker Academic, 2016), 224–25.

47. Henry, *The Christian Mindset in a Secular Society*, 32.

48. Henry was especially interested in how congregations from the free church tradition could embrace his vision of ecumenism. Because churches from this tradition answered to no hierarchical authority, they often needed to be convinced of the importance of ecumenicity in a way that churches that belonged to ecumenically minded denominations did not (for they were bound to follow their authority's lead). This attention to the free church tradition in relation to ecumenism is demonstrated, for example, in Henry's publishing of two back-to-back articles addressing the topic in the May 25, 1962, issue of *Christianity Today*: "Gathered Church, Great Church" by Arthur A. Rouner Jr., and "The Free Churches and Ecumenism" by A. Dale Ihrie. Both argued, like Henry, that the free church tradition indeed had something to offer those inclined to a broad ecumenism.

designed to foster the type of ecumenism that Henry had been working toward for two decades. Roy Fish of Southwestern Baptist Theological Seminary told Henry that "from the viewpoint of a professor of evangelism, those days in Berlin were a time of inestimable value."[49] Henry believed that the congress "gave solid evidence that evangelical ecumenism has already garnered world momentum at the evangelistic level" and that it helped the movement to "gain visibility on a trans-denominational world basis."[50]

The success of the congress—and of Henry's wider hope for evangelical ecumenism—was not because belief was minimized but because mission was emphasized. Henry was convinced that evangelicals must rally together for world evangelization, the publication of religious literature, and the shaping of a biblically informed mind among Christians.

In sum, Henry rejected both an uncritical ecumenism and a fracturing independency. Both were errors at opposite ends of the spectrum. Neither truth nor love could be jettisoned in the pursuit of unity:

> The ecumenical dialogue, moreover, all too often has espoused a unity based on love, a love, however whose definition falls short of theological adequacy. Whether or not "doctrine divides, love unites," to use love as an umbrella to cover doctrinal differences and deficiencies, however hopefully, does not solve the basic problem. ... Doctrine *does* divide. It always has and it always will. And indeed it must, even as the Bible does, in order to separate truth from error. On the other hand the kind of doctrinal jealousy that drives men to strain out a gnat while they swallow a camel is most unfortunate. The quarrel is not with the emphasis on love, but with the implication that since doctrine divides it should be avoided like a plague, and with the idea that doctrine and love in themselves are mutually incompatible. Actually both doctrine *and* love should be emphasized.[51]

---

49. Roy Fish, letter to Carl F. H. Henry, December 9, 1966, CFHHP (box 1966, file "Correspondence—Fish, Roy J.").

50. Henry, *Evangelicals at the Brink of Crisis*, 90.

51. "Unity: Quest and Questions," unsigned editorial in *Christianity Today* (November 24, 1961): 29.

"A UNITY AUTHORED BY THE SPIRIT OF GOD":
THE SPIRIT, THE CHURCH, AND THE BIBLE

With Henry's stance toward ecumenism addressed, it is necessary to tie these various threads into a cohesive account of how his ecclesiology was buttressed by and incomprehensible apart from pneumatology. In his October 26, 1962, *Christianity Today* article "Recasting the Ecumenical Posture," Henry asserted: "It is time for evangelicals to find their ecumenical posture, and to set forth a doctrine of biblical unity which will preserve the vitality of the Gospel without compromising the witness of the Church."[52] What would be the first step toward this end? Henry stressed the Spirit's role in uniting the church:

Where would such an effort begin? In the first place, it would begin by a reaffirmation of the New Testament emphasis upon the essentially spiritual nature of the Church's unity. ... The Church is identified by the permanent indwelling of the Holy Spirit. Paul's exposition of spiritual unity, therefore, is primarily concerned, not with organizational cohesion, but with the "unity of the Spirit," that is, a unity authored by the Spirit of God. As Christians are individually united to Christ, so are they to be united in positive communion with God and to each other by the Spirit.[53]

Henry's language of "a unity authored by the Spirit of God" provides a useful rubric for how to process the relationship between pneumatology and ecclesiology in his thought. He believed the Spirit authored unity in two senses: First, the Spirit authors a spiritual unity. This is a unity among God's people, not based on organizational structure or common demographics, but through the Spirit's bringing men and women to faith in the same Lord. Second, the Spirit authors a theological unity by bringing men and women under the authority of the divinely inspired Bible. This is where the thesis comes to the fore: Henry believed that a Spirit-inspired Bible would order a Spirit-enlivened body.

---

52. "Recasting the Ecumenical Posture," unsigned editorial in *Christianity Today* (October 26, 1962): 24.

53. Unsigned editorial, "Recasting the Ecumenical Posture," 24.

THE SPIRIT AUTHORS A *SPIRITUAL* UNITY

Henry believed the Spirit authors a spiritual unity that connects men and women across the globe through their shared belief in the risen Nazarene. The church's unity is not based on a particular organization or hierarchy; the unity of the church cannot be seen in that sense. But it is very real, and it is owing to the work of the Spirit in the hearts of the redeemed: "The Spirit resides in the Church. The unity he establishes is spiritual, yet not merely mystical or ethereal."[54] It is an actual, genuine unity that should manifest itself in how believers interact and partner together for kingdom causes. In the July 22, 1957, issue of *Christianity Today*, Henry ran an article by J. Marcellus Kik that elaborated on the Spirit's role in constituting this spiritual unity:

> The indwelling Holy Spirit secures the unity of the Church. Establishing and strengthening unity among the people of God falls within the province of the third person of the Holy Trinity. ... The outpouring of the Holy Spirit on Pentecost brought forth a universal spiritual language that could be understood by all nationalities and would bind together the children of God from every nation. In every language, people would understand the mighty works of God: calvary, resurrection, regeneration, justification, reconciliation, sanctification, eternal life and joy. The unity introduced at Pentecost was a foreshadowing of the future unity that would characterize the church under the power of the Holy Spirit.[55]

Henry chastised those denominations that used tradition or bureaucracy as a faux unity, a substitute for the true unity that the Spirit creates. Any ecclesiological conception that relied upon external means for their unity substituted genuine spiritual unity for a man-made forgery that lacked power.[56] He thought the Spirit had a "high disregard for our organized

---

54. "The Winds of the Spirit," unsigned editorial in *Christianity Today* (January 4, 1963): 24.

55. J. Marcellus Kik, "Unity of the Spirit," *Christianity Today* (July 22, 1957): 7.

56. Kik's article shared this same critique: "Supernatural power alone can change human dispositions from evil to good. ... Unity cannot exist without the sanctifying influence of the Holy Spirit. ... Organizational visibility occupies the mind of ecumenists, but what can show forth greater visibility than the manifestation throughout the entire church of love, joy and peace?" See Kik, "Unity of the Spirit," 8.

Christianity" and that "on all fronts the Spirit is breaking old wineskins."[57] The Spirit will not be confined to any one era, church, denomination, tradition, or style. He draws men and women from all corners of the globe and unites them as brothers and sisters together with Christ.[58]

THE SPIRIT AUTHORS A *THEOLOGICAL* UNITY

Beyond a spiritual unity, the Spirit also authors a theological unity. Here, the Spirit's authorship of the Bible is directly relevant for the unity he authors among the body of Christ. Henry cautioned against a unity that stressed the spiritual at the expense of the theological.

In his 1961 *Christianity Today* editorial "A Plea for Evangelical Unity," Henry laid out three theological prerequisites necessary for Christian groups to experience genuine unity. First, "The unity must be that of those who do in fact look only to Jesus Christ and to no other."[59] Second, "It must be a unity of those who follow the authoritative testimony to him in Holy Scripture."[60] Third, "It must be a unity of those who are committed to the great task of world-wide evangelization which he has laid on his disciples."[61] Henry then expanded upon these three theological necessities:

> Without a common looking to the Lord, a common confession of him as Savior, Lord, and God, a common knowledge of God in him, there is no building on the common basis and therefore no hope of unity. Faith in him, however, is not a leap in the dark. It is no blind or chance encounter. It is faith responding to a Word. And this Word is the authentic and authoritative record given concerning him.

---

57. Unsigned editorial, "The Winds of the Spirit," 24. Henry was not critiquing *any* organized Christianity. He himself was the consummate institutional builder, organizing not only media outlets like *Christianity Today*, but also schools, academic societies, and conferences. Here, Henry was critiquing the conceited sense of *merely* organized Christianity, a Christianity that thinks it can build itself up—by its own smarts and resourcefulness—to the heavens, without depending upon the power of God.

58. On the relationship between pneumatology and unity, John Hammett writes, "We call the church the temple of the Spirit because the Spirit is the mortar that holds the stones together. The church is not to be held together by social bonds such as being the same race or class or income, but by the spiritual bond of a common possession of the Holy Spirit." See Hammett, *Biblical Foundations for Baptist Churches*, 47–48.

59. Unsigned editorial, "A Plea for Evangelical Unity," 24.

60. Unsigned editorial, "A Plea for Evangelical Unity," 24–25.

61. Unsigned editorial, "A Plea for Evangelical Unity," 25.

True faith in him is faith in the Jesus of Scripture who embraces both the so-called Jesus of history and the Christ of faith. It is faith enlightened and instructed and impelled by the written Word and its preaching and exposition. ... To build apart from Scripture is to build apart from Jesus Christ himself and therefore to destroy unity. Yet this faith is neither abstract nor ideal. It is busy and active. ... It is given a Great Commission. Outside this Commission, we again pursue isolated and therefore divergent ends. ... The true faith which is loyal to the written Word, however, implies readiness for the Great Commission. The main prerequisites of unity in the Spirit are thus met.[62]

For Henry, the written word (prerequisite two) was a fulcrum upon which the first and third prerequisites depended. Unity demands a common confession of Christ as Lord (prerequisite one) and a shared commitment to the Great Commission (prerequisite three). But where else does one learn of Christ's person and work than from the Bible? And where else is the Great Commission articulated than in Scripture? The Spirit-inspired Bible was essential to unity in the Spirit-enlivened body, for apart from the revealed word there would be nothing to unify around—whether the biblical portrait of Jesus Christ or the biblical call to mission. This is why Henry could claim above that "[t]o build [unity] apart from Scripture is to build apart from Jesus Christ himself and therefore to destroy unity."[63]

One example of how Henry's views are relevant for contemporary Baptists can be found in Christopher A. Graham's article entitled "The Theological Shape of Unity as the Foundation for Southern Baptist Cooperation." He argues that the concept of "spiritual harmony" located in the *Baptist Faith and Message* "would be strengthened if somewhere in the statement there was a *more explicit connection made between pneumatology and ecclesiology* such as is found in [earlier] Baptist confessional statements [such as the 1644 London Baptist Confession or the 1742 Philadelphia Confession]."[64] Graham adds:

---

62. Unsigned editorial, "A Plea for Evangelical Unity," 25.

63. Unsigned editorial, "A Plea for Evangelical Unity," 25.

64. Christopher A. Graham, "The Theological Shape of Unity as the Foundation for Southern Baptist Cooperation," *Criswell Theological Review* 14.2 (2017): 69. Italics added for

Contemporary Baptists may, in fact, find in the thoughts of earlier Baptists, even earlier Southern Baptists, a more robust articulation [of spiritual harmony and cooperation]. ... For example, "spiritual harmony" as a defining aspect of Christian unity found in the *Baptist Faith and Message* would probably have greater import and therefore strengthen the statement on cooperation if it was more clear that this "spiritual harmony" is a result of the Holy Spirit's association with the Church.[65]

Though Graham does not refer to Henry by name, Henry is an excellent model of an earlier Baptist who explored the relationship between the Spirit and the church, and how this relationship between pneumatology and ecclesiology should inform the Baptist conception of "spiritual unity."

So, to tie multiple threads together: Henry's impulse toward a sweeping, trans-denominational ecclesiology was powered by his deep conviction that the Spirit of God authors a spiritual unity among believers of various traditions that is also a theological unity based on the Spirit-inspired Bible. While his ecclesiology is somewhat unique in comparison to some Baptist presentations, it is coherent and logical in light of his understanding of the relationship between pneumatology and ecclesiology.

"THE SPIRIT AND CHURCH PROCLAMATION": SPIRIT-ANOINTED PROCLAMATION

Beyond the unity the Spirit engenders at the universal level, Henry also had a developed understanding of how the Spirit works at the local level through the proclamation of the Spirit-inspired Bible. In Volume 4 of *GRA*, Henry entitled a chapter "The Spirit and Church Proclamation" in which he wrote: "By heralding to the world the message of the Spirit-inspired prophets and apostles, or more expressly, the Spirit-illuminated Word of Scripture, Spirit-anointed couriers carry forward the ongoing task of proclamation."[66] Yarnell sees this concept of Spirit-anointed proclamation

---

emphasis. This helpful article chronicles the development of the *Baptist Faith and Message*, the statement of faith adopted by the Southern Baptist Convention, through its iterations in 1925, 1963, and 2000, especially as it pertains to the cooperative nature of the denomination.

65. Graham, "The Theological Shape of Unity," 68.

66. Henry, *GRA*, 4:476.

as "a major component in Henry's Spirit-based epistemological system."[67] Henry thought the Spirit anoints "couriers" in two senses. First, the Spirit anoints all believers to be carriers of the gospel message to the ends of the Earth. Second, the Spirit anoints preachers to proclaim the Spirit-inspired Bible in the context of the local church.

THE GENERAL CALLING OF ALL COURIERS: EVANGELISM

Without the dynamic power that only the Spirit provides, evangelism would be an impossible endeavor. Henry believed that neglecting the Spirit in the evangelistic task runs the risk of misrepresenting God: "The Spirit's transcendent work in and through us will spare our neighbors from the misimpression that the deity we worship is a vague phantom too much like ourselves."[68] But with the Spirit, men and women can pursue a lost world with unrivaled power. Henry's calls for personal evangelism were always connected to this power available only through the Spirit.

Henry believed that only the Spirit, and therefore a Spirit-enlivened body, possessed the dynamic resources necessary to reach a dark and arid pagan world. This was true in the first century and remains so today: "Alongside the church's confident proclamation of the truth about God and his purposes and its remarkable enthusiasm for holiness, the enduement with power [from the Spirit] was foremost in its spiritual weapons for reaching out into the lost pagan environment that knew God only at a distance."[69] The early church was Henry's favorite example of a people empowered by the Spirit, and he used it often in his writings to spur the modern church toward greater pneumatological dependence and vitality.[70] This emphasis upon the power of Pentecost in relationship to evangelism is evident in *Christian Personal Ethics*,[71] *The Uneasy Conscience of Modern Fundamentalism*,[72] and in the pages of *Christianity Today*:

---

67. Yarnell, "Whose Jesus? Which Revelation?," 45.

68. Henry, "Spiritual? Say It Isn't So!," 13.

69. Henry, *Christian Personal Ethics*, 456.

70. Henry used the same strategy in other areas as well. For example, he thought the New Testament church was the premier model of faithful Christian living in relation to the surrounding culture. See Carl F. H. Henry, "Christian Theology and Social Revolution (II)," *Perkins School of Theology Journal* 21.2–3 (1967–1968): 19–21.

71. Henry, *Christian Personal Ethics*, 454–56.

72. Henry, *The Uneasy Conscience of Modern Fundamentalism*, 88–89: "The evangelical task primarily is the preaching of the Gospel, in the interest of individual regeneration by the

The Protestant Church in our day does not lack numbers. It does not lack programs. It does not lack money. It lacks power for a great spiritual offensive. ... In many ways the Church today resembles the Christian community in the fifty days that followed Easter. This was a different community than the one that had existed before the resurrection. These men knew Christ was risen. They understood the Scriptures. They had received the Great Commission. But there was no power, and there was no outreach. Instead of expanding vigorously, they were gathered together in an upper room. Then came Pentecost and the outpouring of the Holy Spirit. What had before been only a doctrine now became a living reality. Fear gave way to boldness, weakness to strength, and inertia to the dynamic of evangelism. ... Without the power of the Holy Spirit, nothing of value was accomplished in the primitive Church. And it is certain that without the illumination, renewal, and liberation made possible by the Holy Spirit, nothing of spiritual value will be accomplished in the Church of Jesus Christ in our time.[73]

Clearly, this spiritual dependence was the norm in the New Testament era, as demonstrated by texts such as 1 Thessalonians 1:5; Ephesians 6:10; Luke 4:14; 24:49; Acts 1:8; 6:5–10; and 8:18–20.[74] To sacrifice this power today, either through self-dependence or Spirit-indifference, is to lose any hope in fulfilling the God-ordained calling upon individuals and churches:

The church sacrifices more than she knows when she loses her [Spirit-empowered] dynamic. When there is no effective manifestation of the Spirit in her ministry, her message of redemptive theology and morality is perilously near being merely a philosophical

---

supernatural grace of God, in such a way that divine redemption can be recognized as the best solution to our problems, individual and social. This produces within history, through the regenerative work of the Holy Spirit, a divine society that transcends national and international lines. ... *When the twentieth century church begins to 'out-live' its environment as the first century church out-reached its pagan neighbors, the modern mind, too, will stop casting about for other solutions. ... But from the non-evangelical viewpoint, a baptism of Pentecostal fire resulting in a world missionary program and a divinely-empowered Christian community would turn the uneasy conscience of modern evangelicalism into a new reformation*—this time with ecumenical significance." This is the concluding section of the book. Italics added for emphasis.

73. Unsigned editorial, "The Spirit of Pentecost," 28.

74. Henry, *Christian Personal Ethics*, 456.

explanation of life. The church that has only theology and ethics, but is powerless, is the church with a stifled Spirit.[75]

For Henry, the question was not whether all Christians are called to be Spirit-anointed couriers of the gospel of grace. That was settled: they are. The question was whether they would be faithful to do so or not. They would be only as successful as they were dependent upon the Spirit because "the work of the Holy Spirit remains the one indispensable factor in our effective presentation of the Gospel."[76] For this aspect of ecclesiology (the church's mission) to function, the Spirit was of paramount importance. Henry remained convinced that "there is One without which no effective Christian work can be done. There is One who alone supplies that power which is absolutely necessary—the Holy Spirit."[77] In Henry's estimation, "It is high time that we return to the Scriptural teaching that it is 'not by might, nor by power, but by my Spirit saith the LORD of Hosts [Zech 4:6].'"[78]

Henry's bold call for ecclesiological mission, an aspect many have recognized in his work, was inseparable from his call to pneumatological empowerment. Not only did he articulate the need for a Spirit-empowered witness, but he was a model example of just such a life. According to Marsden, "Carl Henry provided the most striking example of [Fuller Seminary's] simultaneous deep commitment to evangelism and to scholarship. Though a leader in reforming fundamentalism, he always remained a true revivalist at heart."[79] Nearing the end of his life, in 1997, Henry began his chapel sermon to students at Southwestern Baptist Theological Seminary with this plea: "If you have never led a soul to Christ, and you are here in seminary preparing for ministry, whether in the pulpit or on the mission field, elevate that among your priorities before another day passes, lest you look upon going into the ministry or to the field as simply the next step after attending a Baptist college, or some other preliminary enterprise."[80] Henry

---

75. Henry, *Christian Personal Ethics*, 456.

76. "Churches and Hidden Persuaders," unsigned editorial in *Christianity Today* (May 25, 1959): 20.

77. "The Spirit the Index to Powerless or Powerful Effort," unsigned editorial in *Christianity Today* (February 4, 1957): 23.

78. Unsigned editorial, "The Spirit the Index to Powerless or Powerful Effort," 23.

79. Marsden, *Reforming Fundamentalism*, 91.

80. Carl F. H. Henry, "The Instability of Twentieth Century Theology" (seminary chapel sermon given at Southwestern Baptist Theological Seminary, Fort Worth, TX, March 4, 1997).

took this call to evangelism upon himself as well. He was eager to turn any conversation toward the cross. As Strachan relates:

> [Henry] did not shy away from personal interaction, but he regularly interrupted his speaking trips to witness to people he befriended. Years later, fellow church member Matt Schmucker remembered Henry's final trip to DC, a trip taken when Henry was frail but still insistent on making it to the Prison Fellowship board meeting. Hours after Henry was supposed to arrive at the home of friends, the elderly theologian was found sharing the gospel with the pilot of the airplane that brought him to Washington. Henry was then in his late eighties. His elderly wife—back in Wisconsin—hadn't heard from him in hours and was frantic. But when Schmucker found Henry at a DC hotel, he saw immediately that Henry was glowing. Though a world-famous theologian, he was thrilled to have been able to share Christ with a fellow sinner.[81]

When Henry and his wife, Helga, selected the gravestone for their Watertown, Wisconsin burial plot, they had a simple phrase inscribed that captured what they thought to be most important about their lives: "Friends of the King."[82] When the stone mason began working on the project, he asked, "What King?"[83] Even in death, Henry was sure to testify to the King of kings and Lord of lords.

THE SPECIAL CALLING OF CERTAIN COURIERS: PREACHING

Beyond this general call to evangelism, Henry also recognized the unique role preachers play in proclaiming the Spirit-inspired word. The preaching ministry of the local church provides the second way Henry understood ecclesiology and pneumatology to intersect and interact.[84]

---

81. Owen Strachan, *The Colson Way: Loving Your Neighbor and Living with Faith in a Hostile World* (Nashville: Nelson Books, 2015), 80.

82. Helga Bender Henry, *Cameroon on a Clear Day: A Pioneer Missionary in Colonial Africa* (Pasadena, CA: William Carey Library, 1999), 169.

83. Henry, *Cameroon on a Clear Day*, 169.

84. For more on the relationship between ecclesiology and pneumatology in worship (beyond preaching) from a Baptist perspective, see James M. Hamilton, Jr., "The Holy Spirit and Christian Worship: The Life-Giving Legacy of the Apostolic Band," *Midwestern Journal of Theology* 18.1 (2019): 69–83.

THE (UNDERAPPRECIATED)
PREACHING OF CARL F. H. HENRY

Before exploring Henry's understanding of the Spirit's role in preaching specifically, it is worthwhile to explore Henry's relationship to preaching more generally.[85] While he was primarily a writer and lecturer, he also carried an active preaching ministry, both in local church contexts and at various conferences, seminars, and chapel services. He was not a dynamic speaker in the typical sense—he spoke methodically, with a static pace that emphasized every syllable. His voice, while readily identifiable, was not strong or booming, and could easily sound shaky or sluggish compared to colleagues like Harold Ockenga or Billy Graham.[86] Thornbury's critique that Henry "was not a good public speaker, as either a preacher or extemporaneous lecturer" is valid insofar as Henry was no soaring orator.[87]

However, Thornbury's claim that Henry "lacked a powerful preaching ministry" is unpersuasive in light of the evidence.[88] While Henry was never at risk of matching Graham's pulpit prominence, neither did he sputter along with a paltry pulpit presence. He was invited to preach at numerous theological institutions throughout his career. He was an instructor at the Stephen Olford Center for Biblical Preaching where he spoke at the Center's Advanced Expository Preaching Institute. Already in the early 1940s, Henry's preaching schedule was at a "punishing level," and it did not

---

85. This represents an area of Henry's corpus that is under-examined and worthy of further treatment. Moore briefly addresses Henry's view of preaching in "God, Revelation, and Community," while Kevin King relates Henry's view of revelation to expositional preaching (though this article is less an examination of Henry's preaching and more a defense of exposition using Henry). See Russell Moore, "God, Revelation, and Community," 29; Kevin King, "The Uneasy Pulpit: Carl Henry, the Authority of the Bible and Expositional Preaching," *Eruditio Ardescens* 2.1 (2015). This is likely because Henry was not primarily a preacher, in either his own eyes or anyone else's. However, he committed many *Christianity Today* editorials to the topic of preaching, and chapter 20 in Volume 4 of *GRA* represents a rich theology of preaching with Henry's typical philosophical slant. Henry's archives are replete with sermon manuscripts spanning decades that represent an awareness of the importance of exegesis, hermeneutics, sermon structure, and illustrations.

86. For more on the preaching ministry of Billy Graham, see Grant Wacker, *America's Pastor: Billy Graham and the Shaping of a Nation* (Cambridge: Harvard University Press, 2014). For more on Ockenga's preaching, see Garth M. Rosell, *The Surprising Work of God: Harold John Ockenga, Billy Graham, and the Rebirth of Evangelicalism* (Grand Rapids: Baker Academic, 2008).

87. Thornbury, *Recovering Classic Evangelicalism*, 23.

88. Thornbury, *Recovering Classic Evangelicalism*, 23.

slow for four decades.[89] Henry took preaching seriously, as demonstrated by an ordination presentation he gave at installation services. The first and primary calling of a new (or any) pastor is to preach the word:

> A pastor without the Word of God to preach is like a surgeon without his scalpel, an author without a pen, a singer without a voice. You can know all philosophy and all literature and all sciences—the physical sciences and the social sciences, but if you do not know the Word of God, you have no right to stand here, Sunday after Sunday, tampering with the souls of men. That God has spoken, has revealed Himself in a special way, that the Bible is His Word to us, and that you proclaim it is the *sine qua non* for any pastor.[90]

Further, Henry's preaching ministry garnered praise from others. He kept three letters from 1978 alone that expressed appreciation for his pulpit supply. Graham Bardsley of The Little Falls Presbyterian Church in Arlington, Virginia, thanked Henry for the "inspiring and stimulating sermon series" he delivered to the church.[91] John Murray Smoot, pastor of Central Presbyterian Church in Baltimore, was grateful for Henry "so admirably edifying the body at Central" through his preaching.[92] He told Henry, "The feedback I have received would have warmed your heart. ... Dottie was especially enthusiastic about what important truths you brought to the surface from a hitherto obscure passage." William Cooper of The First United Methodist Church in Port Huron, Michigan, told Henry:

> It has been several weeks since you were here. The impact of your ministry is still being felt in our church and the community. ... You also made a significant impact upon the uncommitted people in

---

89. Ben Peays, "The Modern Mind and the Uneasy Conscience," in Hall and Strachan, *Essential Evangelicalism*, 152. According to Peays, in 1943 Henry spoke eighty-four times in forty-six different locations. The following year, he spoke ninety-eight times in forty-three different locations. Later in this decade, Henry would commit an entire chapter to kingdom preaching in his 1947 *The Uneasy Conscience of Modern Fundamentalism*.

90. Carl F. H. Henry, "Charge to the Pastor," handwritten note cards (no date), CFHHP (box 1946-1947, file "Charge to the Pastor—Note Cards").

91. Graham F. Bardsley, letter to Carl F. H. Henry, February 22, 1978, CFHHP (box 1978 [box 1], file "Correspondence—Churches and Pastors and Chaplains").

92. John Murray Smoot, letter to Carl F. H. Henry, September 5, 1978, CFHHP (box 1978 [box 1], file "Correspondence—Churches and Pastors and Chaplains").

our congregation. From time to time your statements are quoted in discussion and committee deliberations. The evangelism thrust of our congregation has taken on a new dynamic. ... It was a personal inspiration to me to have you here. I know something of your schedule. I have a feeling for how difficult it is to give so much of yourself to so very few. It could not have been better if the auditorium had been jammed. For all that your coming has meant to us, we give God thanks.[93]

Henry was reserved in evaluating his own preaching, but he recognized that God used him in this role. After preaching a sermon at Hinson Baptist Church in Portland, Henry wrote to his wife Helga: "The sermon went well, though I have done better; the response was good, and everyone seemed pleased. One man came to accept Christ, two girls to reconsecrate, a third for full-time service if led, and two folks to join Hinson."[94]

The above is not meant to elevate Henry to a place of preaching prominence that he neither deserved nor desired. His natural environment was behind the lectern, not the pulpit. However, it does demonstrate that Henry was qualified to address preaching. Even in 1946, Henry told Merrill Tenney of his "passion to be heard beyond the classroom," a passion which would carry Henry around the world preaching the gospel.[95] He was both a theoretician and practitioner. Though Henry was at home in the academy, he also amassed ample experience in preaching, lending credibility to his insight on the topic.

BIBLE-BASED, CHRIST-CENTERED, SPIRIT-BLESSED PREACHING

Henry believed that the Spirit used preaching to transform hearts, but only a particular type of preaching—preaching that was centered on Christ crucified:

---

93. O. William Cooper, letter to Carl F. H. Henry, November 30, 1978, CFHHP (box 1978 [box 1], file "Correspondence—Churches and Pastors and Chaplains").

94. Carl F. H. Henry, letter to Helga Henry, February 18, 1945, CFHHP (box 1945, file "Correspondence—Helga Henry").

95. Carl F. H. Henry, letter to Merrill Tenney, March 18, 1946 (collection 628, box 3, folder 18, The Billy Graham Center Archives, Wheaton College, Wheaton, Illinois).

The Christian fellowship was born in the context of apostolic preaching. The power of that preaching stemmed from the truth of the biblical message, the centrality of the person and work of Jesus Christ, and the dynamic presence of the Holy Spirit. The modern pulpiteer who postpones any reference to "Jesus Christ and him crucified" until the closing moments of his sermon is not following apostolic precedent. Nor will rhetorical cleverness, mastery of crowd psychology, or a parading of knowledge compensate for paucity of gospel content.[96]

The Spirit moved through the sermon only insofar as the sermon was tethered to the Spirit-inspired word and bore witness to the Son. He made the same argument in *Christianity Today*:

> In our day, as in all periods of the Christian Church, a fresh outpouring of the Holy Spirit would result in a renewed and effective proclamation of Jesus Christ—his life and teaching, his sacrificial death, and his bodily resurrection. It is to be added, however, that because the Holy Spirit is actually the Spirit of *Christ*, a fresh outpouring of the Spirit would also mean the exaltation of Christ by the realization of his life in the lives of Christians.[97]

The defenses of Christ-centered preaching are many, but Henry's primary argument was that only such a sermon would invite the blessing of the Spirit of God, for this is a key role of the Spirit—honoring the Son.

Further, this Christ-centered sermon must be derived from the Spirit-inspired Bible. Henry believed that, "The sermon is nothing less than a re-presentation of the Word of God. Sound preaching echoes and reechoes the gospel. ... The preacher no less than the congregation is addressed by the Word of God in the ministry of preaching, for in authentic preaching it is not the preacher alone but God also who speaks, reinforcing his Word given to inspired prophets and apostles."[98] Henry disagreed with the sentiment that the church (only) lives by preaching; while it sounds true

---

96. Henry, *GRA*, 4:476.
97. Unsigned editorial, "The Spirit of Pentecost," 29 (italics original).
98. Henry, *GRA*, 4:479.

enough at face value, Henry knew that it was a specific type of preaching, derived from a specific book, accompanied by the Holy Spirit, that nourishes the church.[99] The church "lives by the Spirit and is nurtured by the Scriptures" through preaching, so that "the sermon is not a segment of the service that permits the pastor to 'perform' ... but a divinely provided opportunity for Spirit and Word to reshape mind and life in the image of Christ."[100] This is one reason that Henry had no tolerance for preaching based on anything but the Scriptures. It lacked transformative power and replaced it with trivial chatter:

> Modernism tended to reduce preaching to pious religious speculation, enlightened opinion, or mere academic lecture. The apostles considered preaching a vehicle for bearing the very Word of God. Preaching is hardly preaching unless enunciated by those personally rescued from spiritual death to new life and whose appropriation of divine revelation knows the crucified and risen Christ as a present living reality.[101]

But Henry not only critiqued modernist preachers who downplayed sturdy biblical preaching; he also challenged those in his own evangelical sphere whose preaching lacked color or warmth. Sermons devoid of life had little chance of being heard or applied:

> The greatest threat today to the Christian pulpit ... comes [not from modernism but] rather from the conservative, evangelical, orthodox preacher whose sermon is dull, irrelevant, and boring. Sermonmaking is an art, and orthodoxy is no guarantee of the practice of that art. Many orthodox preachers simply bore the congregation of the saints.[102]

---

99. Henry, *GRA*, 4:479.

100. Henry, *GRA*, 4:479. Henry believed that the Spirit used another ecclesiological element to reshape hearts and minds: the ordinances. This is one of the only sections in *GRA* that Henry gave attention to the ordinances and their role in ecclesiology. His emphasis was not on specifics, but on their roles in the worship service. Similar to preaching, he gave the Spirit a significant role: "By the ceremonies of worship [in this case the visual nature of the ordinances], and not by preaching alone, the Spirit lifts the hearts of the faithful to the eternal realm where dwells Christ, in whose presence are the saints of earlier generations." See Henry, *GRA*, 4:479.

101. Henry, *GRA*, 4:484.

102. "Crisis in the Pulpit," unsigned editorial in *Christianity Today* (June 4, 1965): 25.

This is another reason Henry believed training preachers to be a vital calling. Affirming the orthodox creeds does not ensure one's preaching will resonate with hearers and build their faith. Henry would have found a minister who consistently delivered dry sermons but who justified himself with the cry, "I am preaching the Bible!" to be at best confused about his call and at worst to have mistaken it entirely. The mechanics of preaching, while never eclipsing the Spirit's work through the word, still mattered because if the sermon was not delivered on a wavelength that could be received, the preacher failed his task. This is why Henry claimed, "While it is probably too much to say that responsive listening attests good preaching, it is nonetheless true that good preaching is 'listenable.'"[103] The preacher's task is to craft a sermon biblical and listenable. The Spirit alone makes it usable.

Again, while the technicalities of sermon formulation and delivery are important, as well as efforts at gospel contextualization in a given time and place, Henry never mistook these elements to be the final source of spiritual power. True power comes through the gospel message itself:

> Many things have been said and could be said about the relevance of the sermon to the needs of the congregation, the necessity for a twentieth century context, proper distinction between committed and uncommitted, and so on. Many more things could be said about presentation and delivery. Yet important as such matters are, there is something even more vital for the preacher to remember: he is a herald, a proclaimer. His message is so much spray in the universe unless it summons men and women worshipfully into the throne room of the King who created them and who now, through the grace that is in Christ Jesus, speaks to them of eternal verities.[104]

Ultimately, Henry believed the preacher must formulate the sermon from the locus of divine speech, the Bible, and anchor it in the death, burial, and

---

103. Henry, *GRA*, 4:480.

104. "Preaching as an Act of Worship," unsigned editorial in *Christianity Today* (September 12, 1960): 21. See also Henry, *GRA*, 4:491: "Preaching must have transactional power to move the modern listener; its goal is decision and response. Yet preaching is not so creatively patterned that all responses to it are welcome or desirable. And neither a prompting to laughter or to tears of itself is a test of authentic proclamation. Faithful Christian preaching judges and/or liberates; speaking in the present tense, the proclaimed law and gospel unmasks the sinner's bondage and press the invitation to liberating conversion and a changed life in the world."

resurrection of Christ so that the Spirit would take and apply his word in the way he sees fit. Anything less fails the litmus test of what it is to "preach the word" (2 Tim 4:2). In this way, preaching was a key way in which a Spirit-inspired Bible formed a Spirit-enlivened body. Flippancy in preaching, through laziness or self-dependency, dishonored the call and left congregations malnourished because the preaching moment was nothing which the Spirit would bless:

> Pulpits also have their ghosts. A clergyman need not sweat over his Sunday sermon; ghostwritten messages are not hard to come by. … Such human ghost writing evidently was not the kind Jesus had in mind when he ordered his disciples to go into all the world and preach. Those disciples were influenced by a Ghost; but he was not a scribe turning out stuff to suit a materialistic world. This Ghost is called Holy, and he is not a professional speech writer. … Not only are ministers commanded to speak; they are also told what to speak and through what dynamic to speak. They are to preach the Word through the power of the Holy Spirit.[105]

CONCLUSION

For Henry, the relationship between pneumatology and ecclesiology was not a flippant matter. It carried eternal consequences: "The contemporary church, it is sometimes remarked, is a Spiritless church. The reference is not so much to its human *esprit de corps*, but rather to its relationship to the Holy Spirit. … The revival that will spare America from devastating divine judgment will come only through a proper rediscovery of the Holy Spirit."[106] This chapter has examined Henry's doctrine of the church, with

---

105. "Ghosts in the Pulpit," unsigned editorial in *Christianity Today* (April 15, 1966): 24. This article provides another example of Henry's use of the early church as the model for pneumatological power and ministry. As can be seen in this article and elsewhere, Henry was particularly concerned with preachers who depended on prepackaged sermons at the expense of the Spirit. In an unpublished presentation (seemingly to clergy), Henry stated, "Tonight, if you suddenly find yourself without time to prepare your Sunday sermon, I can show you where to have one written, on any text, within twenty-four hours, at a price of $3 for each ten minutes' worth. It will be turned out in stirring rhetoric, the canned variety with which many preachers today are supplanting the Holy Spirit." See Carl F. H. Henry, "A Window on World Corruption," CFHHP (box 1935–1939, file "Literary").

106. Henry, "The Acts of the Apostles," 2.

specific attention given to how pneumatology inhabited his ecclesiology at levels both universal (through Spirit-engendered unity) and local (through Spirit-anointed proclamation). Like his conception of special revelation, his conception of ecclesiology was dependent upon and inconceivable apart from pneumatology. Henry believed the Spirit grants a spiritual and theological unity to all believers, while also calling them to Spirit-empowered evangelism and building them up in a particular location through Christ-centered preaching based on Scripture. Henry understood the Bible to be integral to both Spirit-engendered unity and Spirit-anointed proclamation. This supports the first two-thirds of the book's thesis—that Henry believed a Spirit-inspired Bible (revelation) would order a Spirit-enlivened body (ecclesiology) composed of Spirit-filled believers (ethics). It is to the final element of this thesis—pneumatology and ethics in Henry's thought—that the book will turn.

5

—

A SPIRIT-FILLED BELIEVER (PNEUMATOLOGY AND ETHICS)

INTRODUCTION

The converted newspaperman wasted no time leveraging his writing gifts for the spiritual benefit of others. In his very first printed pamphlet as a Christian, Carl F. H. Henry wrote about the relationship between the Holy Spirit and Christian living in a four-page brochure entitled "The Mystery of Living Victoriously." A Post-it note in Henry's hand remains attached to it, housed in his archives, which reads, "My first printed pamphlet (about 1934–35), the year after I was converted in June 1933." In it, he stressed the necessity of a "Spirit-directed life every hour and minute," a life he referred to as "the alps of Christian experience."[1] Though neo-evangelicalism's premier theologian would go on to address numerous other theological issues over the next sixty-five years, the importance of Christian living and ethics would always remain at the forefront of his mind.

This chapter explores how Henry related pneumatology and ethics.[2] Specifically, it will argue that Henry understood the Holy Spirit to be the

---

1. Carl F. H. Henry, "The Mystery of Living Victoriously," CFHHP (box 1935, file "My First Printed Pamphlets 1934–1935").

2. In *Christian Personal Ethics*, Henry referred to Christian ethics as "the divinely-approved pattern for living." See Henry, *Christian Personal Ethics*, 219. Therefore, this chapter will use the term "ethics" and "Christian living" or "the Christian life" synonymously. Of course, ethics proper is a broad field encompassing a variety of disciplines, each with its own subdisciplines. However, Henry's ethical thought was always focused on articulating the good news in a hostile environment through both word and deed, and therefore his conception of ethics was intimately related to Christian living. As seen in Henry and others, using the terms Christian ethics and the Christian life (or Christian ethics and Christian morality) synonymously is not uncommon in Christian ethical literature. For example, David Jones utilizes this approach in his *An Introduction to Biblical Ethics*. Still, Jones recognizes that there is a technical difference between the terms in specialized literature. See David W. Jones, *An Introduction to Biblical*

dynamic power behind ethical living that corresponds to God's revealed word. Similar to previous chapters, this chapter demonstrates that Henry's conception of the Christian life was inconceivable apart from pneumatology. In doing so, the chapter concludes the thesis thread stated in chapter 1: a Spirit-inspired Bible (revelation) would order a Spirit-enlivened body (ecclesiology) composed of Spirit-filled believers (ethics). Henry's ideal vision of the Spirit-filled life is the focus of this chapter.

To showcase how Henry connected the Spirit with Christian ethics, the chapter will first examine the key sources from Henry's corpus on the topic. Then, the chapter will analyze Henry's understanding of the Spirit's work in fostering personal holiness and in cultivating the fruit of the Spirit in an individual.[3] Finally, the chapter will examine Henry himself as a model of Christian ethical living and the Spirit-filled life.

CARL F. H. HENRY'S CONTRIBUTIONS
TO EVANGELICAL ETHICAL THOUGHT

Henry's place among evangelical ethicists has received mixed reviews. Some see Henry holding a prominent place in the field while others think he has gone unappreciated on the issue. For example, Bob Patterson remarked that

---

Ethics, B&H Studies in Christian Ethics, ed. Daniel R. Heimbach (Nashville: B&H, 2013), 5. Scott Rae also notes this difference: "Most people use the terms *morality* and *ethics* interchangeably. Technically, morality refers to the actual content of right and wrong, and ethics refers to the process of determining right and wrong. ... Morality is the end result of ethical deliberation, the substance of right and wrong." See Scott B. Rae, *Moral Choices: An Introduction to Ethics*, 3rd ed. (Grand Rapids: Zondervan, 2009), 15. Because the two are so tightly bound, and because the telos of Christian ethical deliberation is Christian moral living, it is appropriate to use the terms synonymously, especially given Henry's connection between biblical ethics and Christian living. David Clyde Jones affirms this approach when he writes, "Christian ethics ... could be called the doctrine of the Christian life." See David Clyde Jones, *Biblical Christian Ethics* (Grand Rapids: Baker, 1994), 7.

3. Terry L. Cross offers a helpful reminder when he writes that "any evangelical talk of the Spirit in a believer's life needs to consider the specter of individualism (especially in the West)." See Terry L. Cross, "The Holy Spirit," in *The Cambridge Companion to Evangelical Theology*, eds. Timothy Larsen and Daniel J. Treier (New York: Cambridge University Press, 2007), 102. While this chapter focuses on Henry's understanding of the Spirit's work in an individual's life, this was not the only lens through which he saw the relationship between pneumatology and ethics. Henry wrote: "That Christian ethics is the ethics of a body, a community enlivened by the Risen Christ, has implications for the whole moral life. It requires a protest against isolationism in ethical thought and effort. The lone believer does not have adequate reserves for all the ethical demands of life independently of horizontal Christian relations. In ethics, as well as in worship and prayer, Christians need each other for moral discernment, encouragement, and progress." See Henry, *Christian Personal Ethics*, 452.

Henry's influence in "personal and social ethics … is unparalleled among evangelicals."[4] Gabriel Fackre believed that "Henry's work in ethics has given a lasting bequest to the evangelical heritage."[5] However, D. A. Carson believes Henry's understanding of personal and social ethics has gone "almost completely overlooked" because of a hyper focus on the singular topic of epistemology in Henry's thought.[6] How can one figure be both "unparalleled" in a field, while also going "overlooked"?

Both evaluations share a bit of truth. Henry has made significant contributions to evangelical ethical thought. Richard Mouw termed Henry's work in the ethical arena as "pioneering."[7] Henry dedicated three volumes to the topic, each of which will be addressed below: *The Uneasy Conscience of Modern Fundamentalism* (1947), *Christian Personal Ethics* (1957), and *Aspects of Christian Social Ethics* (1964). Henry was also selected to edit the *Baker's Dictionary of Christian Ethics*, showcasing his expertise in the field.[8] D. A. Carson, who counted Henry as a close friend and knew his personal and academic passions, understood that:

> All [Henry's] life he was interested in ethical questions—not only in an academic sense (his *Christian Personal Ethics* was one of the more challenging books I read as an M.Div. student) but in a prophetic sense. This was not only a function of his comprehensive vision of the outworking of the gospel, but a function of his knowledge of Christian views in earlier generations, and his own compassion for the poor and oppressed.[9]

Further, Henry's importance to evangelical ethics can be surmised from his inclusion as a key spokesperson for the viewpoint in multiple volumes.

---

4. Patterson, *Carl F. H. Henry*, 169.

5. Fackre, "Carl F. H. Henry," 603.

6. Carson, "The Compleat Christian," 12.

7. Richard Mouw, "Toward a Full-Orbed Evangelical Ethic," in Hall and Strachan, *Essential Evangelicalism*, 46.

8. Carl F. H. Henry, ed., *Baker's Dictionary of Christian Ethics* (Grand Rapids: Baker Book House Company, 1973). Not only did Henry edit the volume and write the preface, but he also contributed articles on numerous topics, including "Ecumenism and Ethics," "Metaphysics and Ethics," "New Testament Ethics," "Prejudice," "Prison Reform," "Revenge," "Slander," "Terrorism," and "Watergate," among others.

9. Carson, "The Compleat Christian," 16.

For example, Henry is included in *Evangelical Ethics: A Reader*.[10] The editors, who do not share sweeping theological affinity with Henry, nonetheless include selections from *The Uneasy Conscience of Modern Fundamentalism*, demonstrating the weight of Henry's voice. Further, Henry is upheld in the *Dictionary of Scripture and Ethics* as a representative voice for evangelicals on the issue of ethics (again with the focus on *The Uneasy Conscience of Modern Fundamentalism*).[11] Others, including Russell Moore,[12] Augustus Cerillo Jr. and Murray W. Demptster,[13] Miles S. Mullin II,[14] and Mavis Leung[15] have explored Henry's understanding of ethics and its place in his overall theological vision. Mouw argues that engaging Henry's ethical thought is a valuable enterprise for contemporary evangelicals.[16] He believes that through his ethical contributions, "Carl Henry was giving us crucial theological-ethical counsel for present-day evangelicalism."[17] Mouw maintains that Henry's ethical literature (and his theological work more broadly) provides "an exciting expression of a full-orbed Christian ethic" that evangelicals should continue to pursue.[18]

---

10. David P. Gushee and Isaac B. Sharp, eds., *Evangelical Ethics: A Reader*, Library of Theological Ethics (Louisville: Westminster John Knox, 2015), 1–7.

11. Wyndy Corbin Reuschling, "Evangelical Ethics," in *Dictionary of Scripture and Ethics*, ed. Joel B. Green, Jacqueline E. Lapsley, Rebekah Miles, and Allen Verhey (Grand Rapids: Baker Academic, 2011), 284–87.

12. Russell D. Moore, "The Kingdom of God in the Social Ethics of Carl F. H. Henry: A Twenty-First Century Evangelical Reappraisal," *Journal of the Evangelical Theological Society* 55.2 (2012): 377–97.

13. Augustus Cerillo, Jr. and Murray W. Dempster, "Carl F. H. Henry's Early Apologetic for an Evangelical Social Ethic, 1942–1956," *Journal of the Evangelical Theological Society* 34.3 (1991): 365–79.

14. Mullin II, "Evangelicalism as a Trojan Horse," 49–68.

15. Mavis M. Leung, "With What is Evangelicalism to Penetrate the World? A Study of Carl Henry's Envisioned Evangelicalism," *Trinity Journal* 27.2 (2006): 227–44.

16. Despite this praise, Henry's ethical framework has also been challenged. Donald Bloesch thought, "Henry can be criticized for leaping from the absolute to the relative without any mediating principles." The criticism essentially posits that Henry was too reductionistic in how he understood the biblical text to apply directly to modern ethical situations. See Donald Bloesch, *Freedom for Obedience: Evangelical Ethics in Contemporary Times* (Eugene, OR: Wipf & Stock, 2002), 54. David Clyde Jones levied a similar criticism against Henry, in that he thought Henry did not adequately explore how biblical ethical principles play out in complex moral conflicts. Perhaps Henry inherited this from Gordon Clark, as Clark recognized moral conflict was a "lacuna" in his thought, though not one detrimental to his overall theory. See Jones, *Biblical Christian Ethics*, 126.

17. Mouw, "Toward a Full-Orbed Evangelical Ethic," 58.

18. Mouw, "Toward a Full-Orbed Evangelical Ethic," 58.

Despite this attention to Henry's ethical literature, Carson is right to argue that certain elements of his thought have gone overlooked. As the above demonstrates, much of the evaluation of Henry's ethic is derived from a singular work: *The Uneasy Conscience of Modern Fundamentalism*. Even when other resources are consulted, whether they be Henry's *Aspects of Christian Social Ethics* or various articles (*Christianity Today* or otherwise), these are still generally focused on Henry's views of social issues and structures. Little work has been done on his understanding of the personal nature of piety and ethics. This is ironic, considering *Christian Personal Ethics*, a work almost singularly focused on personal virtue as described in the New Testament (as well as the ethical commands upon the believing church), swallows any other ethical volume Henry penned in terms of page count and scholarly interaction. Here, we will seek to fill this gap with an examination of how Henry related the Spirit's work to the individual Christian's life.[19]

AN OVERVIEW OF HENRY'S THREE PRIMARY
CONTRIBUTIONS TO ETHICS

While Henry utilized various forums to discuss ethics, the core of his thought was captured in three key works (in chronological order): *The Uneasy Conscience of Modern Fundamentalism* (1947), *Christian Personal Ethics* (1957), and *Aspects of Christian Social Ethics* (1964). This section will give a brief synopsis of each, with particular attention to the role it played in Henry's ethical vision.

The Uneasy Conscience of Modern Fundamentalism (1947)

If the second edition of Karl Barth's *Romans* commentary "fell like a bomb on the playground of the theologians,"[20] then Henry's *The Uneasy Conscience of Modern Fundamentalism* "acted as a carbon monoxide detector" in the

---

19. To be sure, Henry never divorced individual ethics from social ethics. Though two unique issues, Henry recognized that they are intimately related. This is seen in the final paragraph of *The Uneasy Conscience of Modern Fundamentalism*: "The evangelical task primarily is the preaching of the Gospel, in the interest of individual regeneration by the supernatural grace of God, in such a way that divine redemption can be recognized as the best solution of our problems, individual and social." See Henry, *The Uneasy Conscience of Modern Fundamentalism*, 88–89.

20. This iconic phrase about Barth's *Romans* commentary originated with German Catholic theologian Karl Adam. See Karl Adam, "Die Theologie der Krisis," *Hochland* 23 (1926): 271–86. For a fascinating account of how *The Uneasy Conscience of Modern Fundamentalism* was both conceived and received, see Ben Peays, "The Modern Mind and the Uneasy Conscience," 149–73.

house of American evangelicalism.[21] While twentieth-century fundamentalism did not lack material on ethics, *The Uneasy Conscience of Modern Fundamentalism* was the "first lonely voice" that adopted an intellectual approach, rather than a popular one, to the topic.[22] In what proved to be "in some ways, the most important evangelical book of the twentieth century,"[23] Henry chastised fundamentalists for obsessing over lax personal ethics at the expense of addressing societal ethical challenges.[24] He was concerned that "the sin which Fundamentalism has inveighed, almost exclusively, was individual sin rather than social evil."[25] Henry thought the typical fundamentalist congregation had a stunted spectrum of ethical concern, focused almost single-handedly on avoiding "intoxicating beverages, movies, dancing, card-playing, and smoking."[26] So, from the angle of ethics, *The Uneasy Conscience of Modern Fundamentalism* was meant to illuminate the social dimension of the kingdom of God, so as to spur fundamentalists to a greater awareness of the full range of biblical ethical commands, especially those of a communal nature. He wanted to retrieve the best of the evangelical tradition—a tradition known for its activism—while maintaining the priority of redemptive proclamation.

The *Uneasy Conscience of Modern Fundamentalism* was undoubtedly a work of social ethics.[27] It was a "manifesto" for a movement, not aimed at individual morality, but meant to be appropriated by the entirety of fundamentalism.[28] Henry offered few solutions to the social evils he addressed; instead, his goal was to rally fundamentalism to an interest in pursuing solutions in the first place.

21. Russell D. Moore, afterword to *Has Democracy Had Its Day?* by Carl F. H. Henry, 2nd ed. (Nashville: Leland House Press, 2019), 64. Though Moore was expressing the influence of Henry's *Uneasy Conscience* on himself personally, it is an apt description of the book's wider effect.

22. Kenneth S. Kantzer, "Christian Personal Ethics," in *Evangelical Affirmations*, ed. Kenneth Kantzer and Carl F. H. Henry (Grand Rapids: Academie, 1990), 223.

23. Russell D. Moore, review of 2003 reprint of *The Uneasy Conscience of Modern Fundamentalism*, by Carl F. H. Henry, *Journal of the Evangelical Theological Society* (2005): 182–83.

24. Henry, *The Uneasy Conscience of Modern Fundamentalism*, 1–11.

25. Henry, *Uneasy Conscience*, 7.

26. Henry, *Uneasy Conscience*, 7.

27. Mouw, "Toward a Full-Orbed Evangelical Ethic," 45.

28. George, "Inventing Evangelicalism," 48. Others, including Joel Carpenter, George Marsden, and Russell Moore have applied the terminology of "manifesto" to Henry's brief but explosive volume. See Carpenter, *Revive Us Again*, 202; Marsden, *Reforming Fundamentalism*, 26; Moore, "The Kingdom of God in the Social Ethics of Carl F. H. Henry," 380.

Christian Personal Ethics (1957)

As mentioned, *Christian Personal Ethics* is the heftiest of Henry's ethical literature. *The Uneasy Conscience of Modern Fundamentalism* and *God, Revelation and Authority* receive the press, but *Christian Personal Ethics* remains one of Henry's more substantial theological treatises and was a point of pride for Henry as both a theologian and educator. While *The Uneasy Conscience of Modern Fundamentalism* represented important concepts in Henry's ethical thought, it was "much less rigorous" than *Christian Personal Ethics*, published ten years later.[29] Because scholarly attention to the field of ethics was a "scarce commodity" among twentieth-century North American evangelicals, Richard Mouw sees the publication of *Christian Personal Ethics* as "an important intellectual breakthrough for the North American evangelical movement."[30]

In 1968, over ten years after the publication of *Christian Personal Ethics*, David B. Johnston, pastor of The First Congregational Church in Woodstock, Vermont, wrote to Henry and asked if Henry would recommend a few of his own books to Johnston:

Dear Dr. Henry:

A kind parishioner just gave me a generous check with which to buy a book or two for my library. You have written several but I would be much helped in making my choice if your office would forward a list (with prices listed) of those you have authored and published. Perhaps you might be willing to check the ones you most wished a man in the parish might have in his study.[31]

Henry's reply was surprising—not for what he said but for what he did not say. Henry did not recommend *The Uneasy Conscience of Modern Fundamentalism*, already a celebrated contribution by 1968. Instead, Henry's first recommendation was *Christian Personal Ethics*, the book he thought to be his "most enduring work."[32]

---

29. Mouw, "Toward a Full-Orbed Evangelical Ethic," 45.

30. Richard Mouw, "Evangelical Ethics," in Noll and Thiemann, *Where Shall My Wond'ring Soul Begin?*, 71.

31. David B. Johnston, letter to Carl F. H. Henry, February 19, 1968, CFHHP (box 1968 [box 2], file "Correspondence—Resignation—Churches—Misc.").

32. Carl F. H. Henry, letter to David B. Johnston, February 21, 1968, CFHHP (box 1968 [box 2], file "Correspondence—Resignation—Churches—Misc."). In fact, *The Uneasy Conscience of*

Pastors were not the only ones for whom *Christian Personal Ethics* was a valuable resource. Bernard Ramm, then teaching at Baylor University, wrote to Henry in 1959 with an appreciation for *Christian Personal Ethics*:

Dear Carl:

This is just a word about your book on ethics. I am teaching ethics this semester. I rob daily from your book. I don't have a great collection of works on ethics as this is only the second time I have taught the subject; but yours is my mainstay. You have made some mighty shrewd points from time to time. I look forward to the time when you get out your social ethics.[33]

Other scholars concurred with Ramm. On the back cover of the 1957 publication of *Christian Personal Ethics*, Andrew K. Rule, then professor of apologetics at Louisville Presbyterian Seminary, endorsed the book by stating, "So far superior to other recent works in its field that I have no hesitation in saying it is easily the best treatment of Christian Personal Ethics from the evangelical point of view."

In the first half of *Christian Personal Ethics*, Henry provided a detailed survey of philosophical and ethical schools from antiquity to the modern era. He critiqued secular ethical systems that were "severed" from any fixed or divine standards.[34] He critiqued thinkers such as Marx, Nietzsche, Hobbes, Sartre, Heidegger, and schools including Cynicism, utilitarianism, Epicureanism, and more. In the second half, he addressed issues such as the relationship between divine revelation and ethical living, the image of God in man, the Sermon on the Mount, the atonement in relation to ethics, the fruit of the Spirit, and spiritual disciplines—especially prayer. For a college or seminary-level resource, he left few rocks unturned.[35]

Relevant to this book, Henry devoted an entire chapter to "The Holy Spirit, the Christian Ethical Dynamic" in which he argued that "[t]he

---

Modern Fundamentalism was not among the books Henry recommended at all, as he instead pointed Johnston to his other ethical volume, *Aspects of Christian Social Ethics*, as well as *The God Who Shows Himself* and *Evangelicals at the Brink of Crisis*.

33. Bernard Ramm, letter to Carl F. H. Henry, March 20, 1959, CFHHP (box "*God, Revelation and Authority 1976–1983*" [box 1], file "The Barren Landscape—March 20, 1959").

34. Henry, *Christian Personal Ethics*, 13.

35. For how *Christian Personal Ethics* influenced ethicist Richard Mouw, see Mouw, "Toward a Full-Orbed Evangelical Ethic," 44.

decisive criterion of Christian living is the place of the Spirit in the believer's life."[36] Henry's ethical outlook was intimately connected to pneumatology, and the Spirit occupied the highest place of importance in the pursuit of the virtuous life. While this important aspect of the Spirit's work may be assumed in a textbook of Christian ethics, Henry's elevation of pneumatology in relation to Christian ethics is actually an uncommon approach, further supporting the argument that pneumatology played a vital role in his thought. In *Choosing the Good: Christian Ethics in a Complex World*, ethicist Dennis P. Hollinger argues that "[t]he Holy Spirit receives scant attention in most ethics texts."[37] However, Hollinger recognizes the unique pneumatological shape of Henry's ethical thought: "One exception is Carl F. H. Henry's *Christian Personal Ethics*, in which he devotes an entire chapter to the Holy Spirit and concludes the work with a chapter on prayer."[38] Henry's dependence upon pneumatology in articulating his view of ethics is unmistakable, especially in *Christian Personal Ethics*. (1964)

Aspects of Christian Social Ethics (1964)

The final installment of Henry's ethical trilogy in the seventeen years between 1947–1964 was his *Aspects of Christian Social Ethics*.[39] The book represented an expanded version of his 1963 Payton Lectures at Fuller Theological Seminary.

---

36. Henry, *Christian Personal Ethics*, 441.

37. Dennis P. Hollinger, *Choosing the Good: Christian Ethics in a Complex World* (Grand Rapids: Baker Academic, 2002), 69.

38. Hollinger, *Choosing the Good*, 69. Another exception that Hollinger does not mention is Henlee H. Barnette's 1961 *Introducing Christian Ethics*. In his introduction, Barnette explained the angle he took: "The purpose of this volume—and its justification—is to provide an introduction to Christian ethics which gives more attention to the biblical basis and the role of the Holy Spirit than is usually given in current texts on the subject." See Henlee H. Barnette, *Introducing Christian Ethics* (Nashville: Broadman, 1961), viii. Barnette believed that "[o]ne of the central, yet neglected, doctrines in Christian ethics is that of the Holy Spirit. ... Disregard for this relation of the Spirit to morality has led not only to the loss of the distinctiveness of the Christian ethic but also to the impoverishment of our understanding of its meaning" (87). Writing just four years after Henry's *Christian Personal Ethics*, Barnette used similar language to Henry when describing the role of the Spirit: "The Holy Spirit alone can provide an adequate dynamic for the Christian's ethical life. Without the energizing work of the Spirit, ethics remains abstract and ineffective" (94).

39. Grouping these three volumes into an "ethical trilogy" is simply a way to relate them together as books addressing common themes during a specific part of Henry's career. Henry did not argue that they were a formal trilogy, though he did occasionally connect the latter two together—*Christian Personal Ethics* and *Aspects of Christian Social Ethics*. Henry originally intended to write an equally thorough work on social ethics that complemented *Christian*

In it, Henry returned to similar themes he addressed in *The Uneasy Conscience of Modern Fundamentalism*, but elaborated upon them (and included topics like leisure and work), focused more on concrete solutions, and provided "certain evangelical guidelines in strategic areas of Christian concern."[40]

Four years before the lectures were delivered, in 1959, Henry wrote to Edward John Carnell, then president of Fuller, that he would be leaving the school to serve at *Christianity Today* on a full-time basis (he had been attempting to serve in dual capacities for three years, at both Fuller and *Christianity Today*).[41] In his reply, Carnell expressed his deep appreciation for Henry's tenure at the school and asked him to deliver the Payton Lectures in 1963. Henry replied, expressing both his excitement to deliver the lectures and his disappointment that the evangelical world, including Fuller Seminary, had neglected to take the field of ethics as seriously as was necessary. He told Carnell:

> Dear Ed ... Now it is a most considerate development that the faculty has given me a bid to deliver the Payton Lectures in 1963. I know something of the vision and hopes for that series, and it is with a sense of anticipatory burden that I accept. My present impression is that they will fall into the field of Christian social ethics at that time.[42]

Henry, never one to suppress an opinion about institutions he was formerly associated with, also critiqued Fuller's depreciation of ethics in the seminary's curriculum:

> Let me suggest that the Seminary think seriously about its responsibilities in this field of social ethics. It was one of the great areas of concern that Dr. Ockenga identified with the school in his initial address. You may recall that such a course was at first required, and then was made elective; in my absence, these last years, it has not been offered at all.[43]

Personal Ethics, but his new editorship at *Christianity Today* precluded the project. See Henry, *Confessions of a Theologian*, 151; Mouw, "Toward a Full-Orbed Evangelical Ethic," 45.

40. Carl F. H. Henry, *Aspects of Christian Social Ethics* (Grand Rapids: Eerdmans, 1964; Grand Rapids: Baker, 1980), 9.

41. For Henry's recollection of this time, see *Confessions of a Theologian*, 185–87.

42. Carl F. H. Henry, letter to Edward John Carnell, January 15, 1959, CFHHP (box 1959 [box 1], file "Correspondence—Carnell, Edward John").

43. Carl F. H. Henry, letter to Edward John Carnell, January 15, 1959.

The ethics courses Henry taught at Fuller were a highlight for many students. In this same year, 1959, Daniel Fuller also thanked Henry for his teaching ministry and expressed appreciation for an ethics course Henry taught almost a decade earlier:

> I can never thank you enough for your emphasis on the necessity for propositional as well as personal revelation. Also, the ethics course in 1951, during which you allowed me to read S. K.'s *Works of Love* was a turning point in my life. It seems to me that something essential to the spirit of Fuller Seminary left when you announced your resignation last winter.[44]

Henry, now fully immersed in his work at *Christianity Today* and living on the opposite coast, returned to Fuller in 1963 to present the lectures, and *Aspects of Christian Social Ethics* was published a year later. It functioned as a type of *inclusio* to his ethical body of work while at Fuller, a theological and practical expansion upon the core concepts introduced in *The Uneasy Conscience of Modern Fundamentalism*.[45]

THE OUTPOURING OF THE SPIRIT
AND THE FRUIT OF THE SPIRIT

Turning to the specifics of Henry's thought, this section will defend the chapter's thesis that Henry understood the Holy Spirit to be the dynamic power behind ethical living that corresponds to God's revealed word. While others have considered the social dimensions of Henry's ethical thought, this section will focus on personal ethics, specifically the Spirit's work in establishing a new ethical age in distinction to ancient and modern

---

44. Daniel P. Fuller, letter to Carl F. H. Henry, October 9, 1959, CFHHP (box 1959 [box 1], file "Correspondence—Fuller, Daniel P."). "S. K.'s *Works of Love*" refers to Søren Kierkegaard's work from 1847.

45. In writing about Henry's body of ethical literature, Erickson sees *Christian Personal Ethics* as his "chief contribution." Further, he argues that "most of [Henry's] treatment of substantive issues of ethics has appeared in editorials and other writings in *Christianity Today*." Erickson is correct in recognizing that Henry utilized *Christianity Today* as an avenue for addressing specific ethical situations, but these articles were penned ad hoc and tended to be relatively concise. The intellectual infrastructure of his ethical system was found not in *Christianity Today*, but in the three volumes outlined above. See Millard J. Erickson, "Carl F. H. Henry," in *A New Handbook of Christian Theologians*, ed. Donald W. Musser and Joseph L. Price (Nashville: Abingdon, 1996), 215.

ethical systems, and his ongoing work of fostering the fruit of the Spirit in a Christian's life.

CHRISTIAN ETHICS AND THE OUTPOURING OF THE SPIRIT

Throughout his career, Henry was concerned with the diminishing ethical climate that was enveloping the American landscape, including that of evangelicalism. Beginning in the 1970s, he began to articulate this concern in published works, an era marked by numerous jeremiads sounding the alarm at increasing cultural corrosion.[46] In one such volume, Henry wrote, "Appalling social vices thrust us ever nearer a national doomsday. Only a pseudotheologian would ignore the emptiness that sweeps much of American life today and the deep social problems and injustices that scar our land."[47] He critiqued the degradation of the nuclear family, sexual licentiousness, obsession with material wealth, and multiple elements of American popular culture, primarily raunchy television that no longer raised an eyebrow among self-professing evangelicals.[48] Even in one of *Christianity Today's* earliest editorials, Henry began drawing attention to increasing immorality and the eternal consequences at stake:

> Americans are now faced with immorality paraded in attractive guise by almost every media of entertainment. That the Church seldom speaks out against this evil is a strange phenomenon. Why this silence? The Bible says that because of these very things the holy anger of God falls on those who refuse to obey. By this token God's judgement hangs over America at this very minute[.] ...

---

46. For more on the pessimistic trajectory of Henry's cultural commentary (including in the thought of his colleagues Francis Schaeffer and Charles Colson), see James A. Patterson, "Cultural Pessimism in Modern Evangelical Thought: Francis Schaeffer, Carl Henry, and Charles Colson," *Journal of the Evangelical Theological Society* 49.4 (2006): 807–20. Patterson argues that Henry's pessimistic posture actually made his program of invigorating the evangelical mind more difficult and less effective. Moore, however, balances this evaluation with a personal conversation he had with Henry while Henry was in his eighties. Henry stated, "the future is always bright, because the future always belongs to Jesus Christ." In reflecting on the conversation, Moore concluded, "He was in his eighties, and I in my twenties, but I was the curmudgeon in that situation and he was the idealist." See Moore, afterword to *Has Democracy Had Its Day?*, 68.

47. Henry, *The Christian Mindset in a Secular Society*, 12.

48. Carl F. H. Henry, "The Uneasy Conscience 45 Years Later: The Spiritual Predicament," *Vital Speeches of the Day* 58 (May 1992): 475–80.

[U]nless there is a Spirit-led return to those moral standards so plainly stated in the Bible, and from which we have departed so far, how can God's holy wrath be deferred?[49]

Henry believed that a worldview disconnected from biblical truth led to "the moral failure of paganism."[50] The light of the early church shone brightly not only because of their redemptive message but because of the striking juxtaposition of their way of life with that of the surrounding culture. Though separated by a chronological distance, Henry believed his century and that of the apostles to be similar in spiritual darkness and opportunity.

Much like he saw the early church as a model for evangelism, so too did he see the early church as a prime example of pneumatologically empowered ethics.[51] The decisive ethical difference between followers of the Way and their pagan counterparts was the outpouring of the Spirit at Pentecost. This event marked a new era that, "compared and contrasted with the past ... towers in spiritual privileges far above those of pre-Pentecostal times."[52] Now, "life in the Spirit has become the Christian community's daily prerogative (Rom. 8:2, 10–11; 2 Cor. 3:6; Gal. 5:16–18)."[53] As Henry wrote in the *Baker's Dictionary of Christian Ethics*, "Christian virtue finds its center in the Spirit outpoured at Pentecost by the Risen Head of the church."[54] Ancient and modern philosophical systems failed to match the ethical dynamic offered by the Holy Spirit in Christianity.[55] Henry argued that the Holy Spirit provided the power that neither secular philosophy nor Hebrew religion possessed to live a virtuous life:

---

49. "Is the Church Too Silent on Personal Morality?" unsigned editorial in *Christianity Today* (November 12, 1956): 23.

50. Henry, *Christian Personal Ethics*, 437.

51. Whereas the early church represented a strong example of ethical living empowered by the Spirit, Henry recognized that the ultimate embodiment of Christian ethics is found in the life of Jesus Christ alone. Henry wrote, "[Jesus] was more than the great Teacher of ethics. He was its great Liver. ... [In Jesus] the moral life is unveiled with no discordant note, with nothing that is less than ethically superlative. ... [He] is the faultless example of virtue ... the lone exhibition of ethical excellence to be found in the history of the fallen race." See Carl F. H. Henry, "Jesus as the Ideal of Christian Ethics," *Christianity Today* (February 4, 1957): 12.

52. Henry, *GRA*, 3:22.

53. Henry, *GRA*, 3:22.

54. Carl F. H. Henry, "New Testament Ethics," in *Baker's Dictionary of Christian Ethics*, ed. Carl F. H. Henry (Grand Rapids: Baker Book House Company, 1973), 456.

55. Henry, *Christian Personal Ethics*, 438.

It was the Holy Spirit alone who had transformed the inescapable and distressing "I ought" which philosophical ethics was compelled to acknowledge and the tormenting "thou shalt" which Hebrew religion adduced as its complement into the "I will" of New Testament ethical dedication and zeal. ... Christianity holds before man the absolute perfection of a revealed ethics, and through the power of redemption and the Spirit-sustained life it supplies man with hitherto-unknown reservoirs of moral energy.[56]

Henry's view of ethics cannot be separated from the new ethical capacity empowered by the indwelling Spirit. He was convinced that ethical systems dependent upon secular philosophy simply did not have the capacity to account for the givenness of ethical demands and living. Therefore, he believed that "Pentecost marked the beginning of a distinct era in the moral history of man."[57] The sending of the Spirit should radically alter the ethical outlook of individual believers and the corporate church. As Henry noted in a set of handwritten reflections: "Only of John the Baptist and of Jesus do the gospels use the phrase 'filled with the Holy Spirit'; after Pentecost, the [Christian] church is characteristically depicted as a 'Spirit-filled body.' "[58]

From the above, it becomes clear that Henry's view of ethics was radically pneumatological, in that the Holy Spirit occupies the central place of importance for ethical living. But how did that manifest itself in one's individual life? The next section explores how Henry understood the Spirit to foster spiritual fruit in a Christian's life.

CHRISTIAN ETHICS AND THE FRUIT OF THE SPIRIT

For Henry, the Holy Spirit was not an impersonal force that introduced only a minor distinction between Christian ethics and other systems. Instead, the Spirit is the personal, indwelling God who takes up residence in the heart of redeemed humankind, the dynamic enabler of ethical living

---

56. Henry, *Christian Personal Ethics*, 438.

57. Henry, *Christian Personal Ethics*, 438.

58. Carl F. H. Henry, "Pneumatology = The Holy Spirit," CFHHP (unprocessed box). From the manuscript, it seems that Henry may have been quoting from Leon Morris's "The Holy Spirit" in the *New International Dictionary of the Christian Church*, ed. J. D. Douglas (Grand Rapids: Zondervan, 1974).

apart from which true biblical virtue is impossible. The New Testament teaching that the Spirit abides in the believer as in a temple should reorient the Christian's life around honoring God in thought, word, and deed (1 Cor 6:19-20). In one unpublished sermon on 1 Corinthians 6:19-20 (possibly from his early pastorate at Humboldt Park Baptist Church), Henry remarked, "This truth, that the believer's body is the temple of the Holy Spirit, should quicken our abhorrence of sensual vice. Nowhere are disorder and neglect more unseemly than in a temple."[59]

In his chapter entitled "The Distinctive New Testament Virtues" in *Christian Personal Ethics*, Henry focused on two sections of Scripture that relate to holiness and ethics: the Beatitudes of Christ in Matthew 5:1-12 and Galatians 5:22-25. In both cases (and in other passages Henry appealed to), he argued that "[t]he Christian virtues all cohere in a harmonious whole. One is not lifted up at the expense of another; they do not work against each other. It is the Holy Spirit who fits each in place in the good life."[60] Again, the Spirit lay at the center of one's ethical development: "Ethical achievement is correlated by the pervasive influence of the Spirit in the life of the believer."[61]

In *Christian Personal Ethics*, Henry addressed numerous virtues and multiple aspects of the fruit of the Spirit, including love, purity, faith, humility, hope, joy, peace, kindness, meekness, and contentment.[62] However, both in the pages of *Christian Personal Ethics* and in other works, two elements of the fruit of the Spirit listed above receive increased attention: love and joy.

THE SPIRIT AND LOVE IN THE
LIFE OF THE BELIEVER

Theologians have long recognized that one defining mark of the Spirit's indwelling presence is a clear love for God and neighbor.[63] Henry shared this understanding of love and the manifestation of the Holy Spirit in

---

59. Carl F. H. Henry, "The Temple of the Spirit," CFHHP (box "Early Sermons," file "Sermon Series—First Corinthians").

60. Henry, *Christian Personal Ethics*, 474.

61. Henry, *Christian Personal Ethics*, 475.

62. Henry, *Christian Personal Ethics*, 472-508.

63. For more on the intersection of pneumatology, love, and the church throughout history, especially in the thought of Augustine and Aquinas, see Matthew Levering, *Engaging the*

one's life. He believed that "love for another is the whole sum of Christian ethics."[64] In *Christian Personal Ethics*, Henry devoted an entire chapter to "Love, The Divine Imperative in Personal Relations," in which he wrote, "The distinctive feature of Christian ethics is its operation on a principle of universal love—love that is extended alike to believers and unbelievers."[65] Contrary to common cultural conceptions of love, Henry argued that love as a fruit of the Spirit is based not on an internal human experience but rather originates from an alien source: God himself through the Holy Spirit's work.[66] Appealing to Galatians 5:22, Henry argued that true agape love "exits only as the Holy Spirit's gift. ... Pure love is not man-made but a divinely accomplished virtue."[67]

One helpful source for evaluating Henry's thought on the relationship between the Holy Spirit and Christian love is the manuscript of his 1990 presentation at an evening dinner for Prison Fellowship.[68] While not a published theological piece, Henry nonetheless gave sustained attention to love not only in a general sense but to the Spirit's activity in birthing and forming the virtue in one's heart. His presentation entitled "Love at Its Best" contained three points. First, Henry argued that God is the source and example of true love. Second, Jesus declared true love to be a hallmark of his disciples. Third, the Holy Spirit imparts true love as the primary Christian virtue.

Doctrine of the Holy Spirit: Love and Gift in the Trinity and the Church (Grand Rapids: Baker, 2016). One example of this connection between love and the Spirit is found in Jonathan Edwards's *Charity and Its Fruits*: "That Christian love is one in its principle, to whatever objects it flows out, appears by the following things. ... It is all from the same Spirit influencing the heart. It is from the breathing of the same Spirit that the Christian's love arises, both towards God and men. The Spirit of God is a spirit of love. And therefore when the Spirit of God enters into the soul, love enters. God is love, and he who has God dwelling in him by his Spirit will have love dwelling in him. The nature of the Holy Spirit is love; and it is by communicating himself, or his own nature, that the hearts of the saints are filled with love or charity." See Jonathan Edwards, *Charity and Its Fruits: Living in Light of God's Love*, ed. Kyle Strobel (Wheaton, IL: Crossway, 2012), 40.

64. Henry, *Christian Personal Ethics*, 486.

65. Henry, *Christian Personal Ethics*, 220.

66. Henry also stressed that genuine love would be congruent with God's revealed word in the Bible. He believed that "love gains its direction from the commandments of God." See Carl F. H. Henry, "The Bible and the New Morality," *Christianity Today* (July 21, 1967): 9.

67. "The Paganizing of Love," unsigned editorial in *Christianity Today* (February 3, 1958): 21.

68. Carl F. H. Henry, "Love at Its Best," CFHHP (box 1990 [box 1], file "Love At Its Best").

This third point, focused on the Holy Spirit, occupied the majority of Henry's attention. He reiterated that "[t]he Spirit is the single unifying source of the whole panoply of virtues. It is in and through the Holy Spirit that we bear any and all moral fruit characteristic of the Christian life."[69] Moving from the general animating power of the Spirit to the specific virtue of love, Henry stated:

> I speak now only of one of the Christian virtues, namely, love or agape. Paul puts it first in Galatians for the same reason that he puts it last in the great Love Chapter, 1 Corinthians 13—that is, because it is most important. Without love all the other virtues break down; to the Colossians Paul depicts love as "the bond of perfectness" ... the string on which all the pearls are strung and without which they scatter.[70]

Henry recognized the Holy Spirit to be crucial to the development and flourishing of Christian love.

THE SPIRIT AND JOY IN THE
LIFE OF THE BELIEVER

The second virtue that Henry concentrated on in relation to the Holy Spirit was that of joy. When *The Christian Herald* interviewed Henry in 1986 and asked him what distinctly Christian contribution believers offered to their contemporary scene, he responded with an appeal for joy:

> There's an absence of joy in contemporary life. The gospel is among other things an infectious source of joy in a world pervaded by a sense of melancholy and gloom. ... Contemporary Christians need to understand again that joylessness is a sin. It betrays a great deal about the shallowness of spiritual experience when joy is absent. We in Western society tend to be preoccupied with material things which give us only a transient happiness, as it were, if indeed happiness is the term for it, but joy is something that has its roots in

---

69. Henry, "Love at Its Best."

70. Henry, "Love at Its Best." Henry incorrectly cited Colossians 2:14 in the paragraph, but he clearly meant to refer to Colossians 3:14.

the transcendent world, surpassing anything material things can provide or take away.[71]

Appealing to Romans 14:17 and 15:13, Henry believed that because joy arises "in the power of the Spirit," it is one of the Spirit's "characteristic fruits."[72] In contradistinction to other ethical systems that devalued joy or saw it as a liability (here Henry specifically targeted Stoicism), Christianity offers not only a firm foundation for joy but also an expectation that joy characterizes the life of a believer.[73] The Spirit's cultivation of joy in an individual serves as an apology for the hope within them (1 Pet 3:15). Henry reminded his fellow evangelicals that they should be a joyful band in a gloomy world. Christian joy was integral for both an outward witness and for inward spiritual health:

> With all the needed emphasis upon obedience and responsibility in the Christian life, we are apt to forget that God's best witnesses are light-hearted Christians, and that the oil of joy is the only lubricant God has provided to keep the church's machinery from clanking. Pentecost Sunday is a great time to rediscover it.[74]

He was convinced that the Spirit's presence in one's soul would result in an unshakable joy. In fact, Henry was willing to go so far as to argue that joy represented a necessary disposition that would help carry the church down through the ages: "The power of the Christian faith does not always lie in its theological validity, tremendously important though that be; nor in its vast constituencies and institutional thrust. It lies also in the Spirit's power to create an inner ecstasy to override human agony."[75]

Again, as he was prone to do, Henry appealed to the apostolic church as the exemplar of a body of joyful, Spirit-filled believers. To the outside world, an "inexplicable joy irradiated the lives of these ordinary mortals," to such an extent that others could no longer ignore their message

---

71. Carl F. H. Henry, *Conversations with Carl F. H. Henry*, vol. 18 of The Symposium Series (Lewiston, NY: Mellen, 1986), 191.

72. Henry, *Christian Personal Ethics*, 495.

73. Henry, *Christian Personal Ethics*, 493–94.

74. "It is Time for Rejoicing," unsigned editorial in *Christianity Today* (May 23, 1960): 20.

75. "The Power of Joy," unsigned editorial in *Christianity Today* (July 19, 1968): 35.

or assume it to be impotent or irrelevant.[76] It was clear that they were a "holy people, graced by the Holy Spirit."[77]

To this point, the chapter has argued that Henry understood the Holy Spirit to be the animating and dynamic source of all Christian ethical living, with special attention paid to how he understood the Spirit to foster the fruit of the Spirit in the life of the individual. He had great confidence in the Spirit's ethical influence upon one's life. In a set of handwritten notes, Henry wrote, "The Spirit transforms babes into giants in a year."[78] And while Henry's timetable may be extended to recognize some level of progressive sanctification, he remained convinced of the ethical metamorphosis possible through the Spirit. Believers are "a new creation" (2 Cor 5:17) who spend their remaining days, by the power of the Spirit, growing in the good works for which God has created them (Eph 2:10). There is an established newness and a progressive continuation, both of which are dependent upon the Holy Spirit.

With Henry's view of the relationship between pneumatology and ethics addressed, the book will turn to a concrete case study of a Spirit-filled believer: Henry himself. The intention is not to provide a hagiographical account of the man. His weaknesses will be noted. Rather, it is meant to demonstrate that Henry was not detached from the practicalities of Christian ethics; instead, he applied all he taught about ethics to himself first.

THE PNEUMATOLOGICAL LIFE: HENRY AS A CASE STUDY OF THE SPIRIT-FILLED BELIEVER

As mentioned, B. B. Warfield coined John Calvin "The Theologian of the Spirit." However, Timothy George expresses surprise that "few studies have been written on the 'spirituality of John Calvin,' " given the attention Calvin devoted to this theme throughout his life and the lengths he went to in outlining the Spirit's work.[79] A similar curiosity arises when one considers the scant studies of Henry's spirituality, given his own published work

---

76. Carl F. H. Henry, "The Christian-Pagan West," *Christianity Today* (December 24, 1956): 4.
77. Henry, "The Christian-Pagan West," 4.
78. Carl F. H. Henry, untitled lecture notes, CFHHP (undated, unprocessed box).
79. Timothy George, *Theology of the Reformers*, rev. ed. (Nashville: B&H, 2013), 231–32.

on the ethical life and the remarks that many evangelical colleagues have made about his devotion to the Lord and yielded-ness to the Spirit. About fifty-five years after his pamphlet on "The Mystery of Living Victoriously," Henry penned another piece advocating an authentic spirituality among Christians. He was alarmed that "theologians today do not write much about spirituality, preachers do not preach much about it, and churchgoers do not much practice it."[80] In his writing as a theologian, speaking as a preacher, and life as a churchgoer, Henry aimed to reverse this trend by explaining and embodying a genuine, biblical spirituality. Because spirituality "flows spontaneously and mellifluously as an overflow of the Spirit's fullness," Henry believed that "spirituality is a quality, indeed an excellence, that every believer ought to treasure and manifest."[81] This section will put Henry forward as a model example of the pneumatological life, a life lived by the dynamic power of the Holy Spirit and bearing the fruit of the Spirit as a Spirit-filled believer. It will show that he was not only an educator of the Spirit's role in ethics but also a partaker of this same power. Though no substantial study yet exists on Henry's spirituality, friends and colleagues have written about the effect his life and person had on them. His ethical life and spiritual devotion were well known in his circles, as demonstrated by numerous personal accounts and letters.

One testimony of Henry's spirituality comes from Henry's friend Kenneth Kantzer. Kantzer's chapter in *God and Culture: Essays in Honor of Carl F. H. Henry* is entitled "Carl Ferdinand Howard Henry: An Appreciation." Kantzer chronicled how he and Henry intersected at various points throughout their careers, from their early days in Boston as graduate students to a genuine friendship based on mutual interests and admiration. Kantzer stressed that beyond Henry's academic accomplishments and theological impressiveness, "Christian piety ... represented a crucial part of the warp and woof of Carl's inner soul."[82] Kantzer also commented on Henry's personal integrity and commitment to his wife and children. Kantzer, one

---

80. Henry, "Spiritual? Say It Isn't So!," 13.

81. Henry, "Spiritual? Say It Isn't So!," 13.

82. Kenneth S. Kantzer, "Carl Ferdinand Howard Henry: An Appreciation," in *God and Culture: Essays in Honor of Carl F. H. Henry*, ed. D. A. Carson and John Woodbridge (Grand Rapids: Eerdmans, 1993), 374.

who saw and heard and walked alongside Henry, was convinced that "Carl Henry is truly a man of God."[83]

Another dear friend of Henry, Chuck Colson, also commented on Henry's piety and spirituality. In his foreword to *Carl Henry at His Best: A Lifetime of Quotable Thoughts*, Colson remarked that "Carl Henry as a man embodies the things he has taught and believed."[84] He was impressed by Henry's authenticity and genuineness, and believed that this aspect of his personal life "made him the giant that he is."[85] He also commented on Henry's willingness to serve the Lord in any capacity—nothing was below him. He would speak to thousands or to ten with the same passion, resolve, and carefulness. Colson thought that "this desire to help others is ingrained in the man's character."[86]

Others too have taken note of Henry's personal piety. Paul House remembers Henry as a "serious Christian" who "was a hospitable man, a caring husband, an encourager of younger people, a constant witness of the resurrected Christ, and a very hard worker."[87] He thinks Henry's character "serves as an excellent example to other believers in general and to other theologians in particular."[88] House concludes his essay by describing Henry as "an exemplary theologian and a fine human being."[89] John Woodbridge was struck by Henry's "urbanity, broad sense of fair play, humanity, personal kindness, and grace."[90] Woodbridge saw Henry as "one of the most godly, humble, gracious men I ever knew" and recognized him as "a man of deep prayer and great faith."[91] D. A. Carson summarizes the consensus regarding the integration of Henry's ethical teaching and his personal piety: "All his life, he strove to practice what he preached. The stories that are told in this arena are legion."[92]

---

83. Kantzer, "Carl Ferdinand Howard Henry," 377.

84. Colson, "Foreword," 12.

85. Colson, "Foreword," 13.

86. Colson, "Foreword," 13.

87. House, "Hope, Discipline, and the Incarnational Scholar," 118.

88. House, "Hope, Discipline, and the Incarnational Scholar," 118.

89. House, "Hope, Discipline, and the Incarnational Scholar," 132.

90. John D. Woodbridge, "A Biblically Faithful Theologian Evangelist," in Hall and Strachan, *Essential Evangelicalism*, 87.

91. Woodbridge, "A Biblically Faithful Theologian Evangelist," 87.

92. D. A. Carson, "The *SBJT* Forum: Testimonies to a Theologian," *Southern Baptist Journal of Theology* 8.4 (2004): 84.

Throughout published accounts and unpublished correspondence, two aspects of Henry's Spirit-filled life are consistently mentioned: Henry's strong prayer life and his passion for personal encouragement.

CARL F. H. HENRY AS A MAN OF PRAYER

It is noteworthy that Henry devoted the final chapter of *Christian Personal Ethics* to "Christian Morality and the Life of Prayer." He wanted prayer to be the final note that sounded from a volume that explored various features of ethical living. He argued that "[t]he very breath of prayer sustains the Christian life."[93] The believer who routinely neglects prayer not only walks in sin but also "leases body and soul to idols."[94] He ended the book with a soaring description of prayer in relation to ethical living:

> Eternity alone will disclose the effect of prayer in the turning-points of human history and in the great decisions that have shaped the affairs of the successive centuries. Say what one will about Christian action, its main roots are to be found in the soil of efficacious prayer. For prayer remains the hinterland of Christian moral advance. It is the one language of heaven translated into the multi-lingual speech of earth, the redeemed race's spiritual counterpart to the secular world's Babel, and the multiplied tongues of Pentecost turned upward again toward the glory.[95]

Henry articulated the need for prayer not only in the academic *Christian Personal Ethics* but also in the popular pages of *Christianity Today*. For example, leading up to Billy Graham's 1957 New York crusade, Henry reminded his *Christianity Today* readers of the intimate connection between prayer and the Holy Spirit: "The difference between a spurious revival and a genuine one is the Holy Spirit. ... Pray that God may send the Spirit with regenerating power. Pray that God may turn New York City upside down. Pray without ceasing."[96]

---

93. Henry, *Christian Personal Ethics*, 573.
94. Henry, *Christian Personal Ethics*, 573.
95. Henry, *Christian Personal Ethics*, 582–83.
96. "Prayer and the Spirit the Door to New York," unsigned editorial in *Christianity Today* (May 13, 1957): 24.

Henry also utilized the pulpit to communicate the importance of prayer. On April 8, 1990, at the evening service of Capitol Hill Baptist Church, Henry preached a message entitled "Does Prayer Really Make a Difference?" His handwritten manuscript indicates that he shared with the congregation about powerful movements of God initiated by prayer, especially contemporary situations including the toppling of Communism in Eastern Europe (a relevant issue at the time of the message). After elaborating upon God's power in prayer, Henry remarked, "Prayer can move mountains, but we often behave as if God can't move an anthill."[97] At the end of the message, Henry called the congregation to pray alongside one another for various topics including personal needs, their local church, spiritual sensitivities, and sick loved ones. In another sermon (undated), focused on Romans 8:26, Henry stated:

> Beloved, we shall never reach the fullness of God's plan for us until we permit the Holy Spirit so fully to possess us that He can pray within us as He will. The Christian who shuns the place of prayer in time of adversity and trouble adds to his burden; he who hurries to the secret place enters into the haven of God. The one quenches the Spirit, the other is brought by the Spirit to the place of victory. There are times when the burden is so great that we know not how to pray. These are the hours in which the Spirit leads the submissive soul to the place of trust, of power, of victory.[98]

He utilized the pulpit and his brief pastorate to reiterate the place of prayer in parishioners' lives. As pastor of Humboldt Park Baptist Church, Henry wrote to his congregation with the reminder that "your prayers cause a glow in the hearts of your Lord, your pastor, your fellow-Christians, and yourself."[99]

But prayer was not something Henry reserved only for academic investigation, as preparation for a Graham crusade, or as merely homiletical fodder. Instead, it saturated his entire life. Kantzer captured Henry's prayer

---

97. Carl F. H. Henry, "Does Prayer Really Make a Difference?" handwritten manuscript, CFHHP (box 1990 [box 1], file "Does Prayer Really Make a Difference?").

98. Carl F. H. Henry, "The Groans of Romans 8," sermon manuscript, CFHHP (undated, unprocessed box).

99. Carl F. H. Henry, letter to Humboldt Park Baptist Church, November 18, 1940, CFHHP (box 1940–1941, file "Humboldt Park Baptist Church").

life when he wrote: "Carl was also a man of prayer. ... [I]n all my relationships with him, I knew him as a man of prayer. Across the years, he lived
each day, and he still continues to live today, in constant dependence upon
and in unbroken communion with his Lord. Prayer was neither a public
pose nor simply a private duty. It was a way of life, the normal Christian
life."[100] Henry was known to walk into Charles Woodbridge's office at Fuller
Seminary, and the two would pray for students by name.[101] The topic of
prayer even occupied a place in the young Henry's poetry collection, written soon after his conversion. One poem, from the mid-1930s, highlighted
his dependence upon prayer in seasons of trial:

> Out in the milling throng I tried
>> To shake the burden from my soul,
>> But like my flesh it clung
>> And as a mood it hung
>> Upon me still.
>
> I called up to the star-lit skies
>> For nature's balm to heal the wound,
>> But thorny sorrow stayed
>> And bitter midnight weighed
>> Upon me still.
>
> With friends who had shed tears I spoke
>> To find a torch across the way,
>> But handclasp, sympathy
>> And words left agony
>> Upon me still.
>
> The secret place of prayer remained;
>> The Man of Sorrows tarried there.
>> Though how I cannot say,
>> He took the hurt away
>> And there, from all the world apart,
>> The waves were stilled within my heart.[102]

100. Kantzer, "Carl Ferdinand Howard Henry," 374.
101. Woodbridge, "A Biblically Faithful Theologian Evangelist," 87.
102. Carl F. H. Henry, untitled poem (no date), CFHHP (box 1935–1939, file "Literary").

About sixty years later, in an essay written for a new generation of Christian leaders (and in what would be one of the final pieces he published in his career), Henry again reflected upon the role of prayer throughout his life (and how, despite his commitment to the practice, he wished he could have prayed more):

> Don't forget to pray. I've always believed in prayer; more than that, I have prayed. But not enough. Nobody told me that in those supposedly 'golden years' (when one turns over what little gold he has to doctors, dentists, and hospitals) that the loss of memory and recollection would unexpectedly puncture holes in my prayer list. I start out praying for Russia and find myself wandering through Hong Kong. My petitions get shorter while my prayer list gets longer. I wish I could be steeped in prayer even if I can no longer easily shift my knees from first to overdrive. But God sees me, and he is not hard of hearing.[103]

Henry wrote, preached, and modeled dependence upon the Spirit through prayer. Prayer represented an integral aspect of Henry's pneumatological life—a life lived as a Spirit-filled believer.

CARL F. H. HENRY AS A MAN OF ENCOURAGEMENT

Commenting on Romans 12:7–8 and the spiritual gift of encouragement (rendered as "exhortation" in some translations), Robert H. Mounce writes, "If teaching provides guidance for what people ought to do, encouragement helps them achieve it."[104] Henry was gifted in both—he was a master teacher and a master encourager. He actively sought to encourage others and build them up through personal conversation and correspondence.

Henry's collection of letters at Trinity Evangelical Divinity School is bursting with correspondence he sent to evangelical leaders, spurring them on in their gospel efforts. Paul House's recollection of this aspect of Henry's ministry is illuminating:

---

103. Carl F. H. Henry, "Learning to Avoid Subtle Temptations," in *Lessons in Leadership: Fifty Respected Evangelical Leaders Share Their Wisdom on Ministry*, ed. Randal Roberts (Grand Rapids: Kregel Publications, 1999), 136–37.

104. Robert H. Mounce, *Romans: An Exegetical and Theological Exposition of Holy Scripture*, vol. 27 of The New American Commentary (Nashville: B&H, 1995), 235.

Henry's correspondence likewise proves his concern for others. It was conducted on paper, and it was massive. He typed many letters on an old portable typewriter. Many letters he wrote by hand. I do not know why he chose to do one or the other. But I know his letters to me were encouraging, challenging, chastening, and always welcome.[105]

D. A. Carson also recognizes Henry's extensive encouragement via letters:

[Henry] was a great encourager of others, not least younger men and women. His correspondence was voluminous, much of it cast in the guise of encouragement. Both he and Helga penned thousands, probably tens of thousands, of personal notes and letters to encourage other Christians along their way.[106]

While thousands of examples exist, two selections from Henry's letters demonstrate the nature of his encouragement. First, he routinely encouraged Billy Graham in Graham's varied ministry efforts, especially from 1940 to 1960. Henry was convinced that Graham's ministry represented an important movement of God. While he was cautious about Graham's theological and academic endeavors—Henry told Graham biographer William Martin that he "keeps his fingers crossed about the books Billy writes"— he appreciated Graham's unique calling as an evangelist and was an ally to his ministry.[107]

For many years, Henry served as both an encourager and sounding board for Graham's sweeping ministry interests. Henry encouraged Graham by both affirming Graham's positive instincts and cautioning him on avenues to avoid. Henry spoke into Graham's crusade ministry, the vision for *Christianity Today*, Graham's work at educational institutions, and multiple other projects. Graham began many of his letters to Henry with "Beloved Carl" or "My Dear Carl," indicating his trust in and appreciation for Henry's friendship. In 1976, after the two had turned their focus from mutual projects to other ministry pursuits, Graham told Henry,

---

105. House, "Hope, Discipline, and the Incarnational Scholar," 127.
106. Carson, "The *SBJT* Forum: Testimonies to a Theologian," 84–85.
107. William Martin, *A Prophet with Honor: The Billy Graham Story*, rev. ed. (Grand Rapids: Zondervan, 2018), 583.

"There are times that I miss our fellowship so much. You will never know what your friendship, counsel, and advice meant to me during those early years when you were editor of *Christianity Today*. ... There are so many times I have needed your counsel. I hope I don't have to remind you that I love you in the Lord as few men I have ever known."[108] In 1980, Graham again reiterated to Henry that, "Your counsel and advice to me during the 50s and 60s were of immense value to me and my ministry."[109] About thirty years earlier, Graham told Henry, "There is no man in America that I have admired more than I have you."[110] This admiration stemmed from Henry's consistent encouragement and wise counsel to Graham.

Another example of Henry's encouragement is the attention he gave to Edward Carnell during a difficult season in Carnell's life.[111] In 1959, when Carnell resigned the presidency of Fuller Seminary in order to return full time to the classroom, he experienced a deep melancholy due to the circumstances at Fuller and to wider criticism that he received in the academy. It all left him severely unsettled and with a bout of insomnia.[112] While Henry thought Carnell's gifts were better utilized in the classroom than in administration, he stood by his friend and affirmed his calling to teaching, writing, and scholarship. In March of that year, Henry encouraged Carnell by reminding him of the important role he played in evangelicalism, even if that did not include the presidency of Fuller: "Dear Ed ... I am troubled you are not well. I had heard this, during my last visit, and it was confirmed during our chance meeting. ... Take care of yourself, Ed. The Church needs you, especially in these critical days."[113] This series of letters demonstrates

---

108. Billy Graham, letter to Carl F. H. Henry, November 19, 1976, CFHHP (box 1976 [box 1], file "Correspondence—Graham, Billy").

109. Billy Graham, letter to Carl F. H. Henry, September 24, 1980, CFHHP (box 1980 [box 1], file "Correspondence—Graham, Billy").

110. Billy Graham, letter to Carl F. H. Henry, January 14, 1948, CFHHP (box 1948, file "Correspondence—Graham, William [Billy]").

111. For more on the life and story of Edward J. Carnell, see Rudolph Nelson, *The Making and Unmaking of an Evangelical Mind: The Case of Edward Carnell* (Cambridge: Cambridge University Press, 1987). For more on the intramural relationships between budding neo-evangelical leaders in the 1940s, including Carnell, see Strachan, *Awakening the Evangelical Mind*, 82–89.

112. Carl F. H. Henry, letter to Edward J. Carnell, December 10, 1959, CFHHP (box 1959 [box 1], file "Correspondence—Carnell, Edward John").

113. Carl F. H. Henry, letter to Edward J. Carnell, March 30, 1959, CFHHP (box 1959 [box 1], file "Correspondence—Carnell, Edward John").

a caring, concerned friend in Henry.[114] In January of that year, Carnell told Henry, "I count it a privilege to know you as friend."[115] Henry's friendship was manifested in encouragement to Carnell at one of the lowest professional moments of Carnell's life.[116]

Examples span far beyond the above, but these are a representative sample of the encourager that Henry was. Further, Henry's encouragement to others carried on until the end of his life. When Timothy George and Greg Waybright visited the aging Henry at his Wisconsin residence, George remembers, "Though he could no longer walk, his eyes still sparkled with the joy of Christ, and, in his high, wispy voice, he whispered words of encouragement and blessing to both of us."[117]

Like any fallen sinner, Henry had his flaws.[118] He could remember perceived slights in high definition. Despite the positive virtues stated above, his drive and conviction occasionally led to inflexibility and tension among colleagues. He could have burdensome expectations of those who did not share his intellectual fortitude. Though by all accounts he had a sweet and healthy home life, he was a self-professed workaholic who spent large amounts of time away from his family due to vocational demands. His pneumatological life was one of progress, not arrival.

CONCLUSION

The constitution of Henry the man resembled the constitution of neo-evangelicalism the movement: bold and confident, lively and upbeat. His prayer life and encouragement are two indicators that he lived by the dynamic power of the Spirit, the same power he encouraged others to depend on in their daily lives. Though a fallen sinner, Henry modeled a pneumatological life worthy of emulation today. His ethical framework was undergirded by

---

114. Strachan demonstrates that beyond Henry, Harold Ockenga also served as an encourager for Carnell in these difficult days. See Strachan, *Awakening the Evangelical Mind*, 160–62.

115. Edward J. Carnell, letter to Carl F. H. Henry, January 12, 1959, CFHHP (box 1959 [box 1], file "Correspondence—Carnell, Edward John").

116. For more on the specifics of Carnell's depression and the circumstances surrounding his tragic death, see Marsden, *Reforming Fundamentalism*, 256–59.

117. Timothy George, "The *SBJT* Forum: Testimonies to a Theologian," *Southern Baptist Journal of Theology* 8.4 (2004): 86.

118. Thornbury, *Recovering Classic Evangelicalism*, 23–24; House, "Hope, Discipline, and the Incarnational Scholar," 132.

pneumatology, and he believed the Holy Spirit to be the dynamic power behind ethical living that corresponds to God's revealed word. In his teaching, writing, and living, Henry communicated that "the Christian life is that of a man born of the Spirit, walking in the Spirit, led of the Spirit, filled by the Spirit."[119] This chapter has served to defend the final element of the three-fold thesis thread—that Henry believed a Spirit-inspired Bible (revelation) would order a Spirit-enlivened body (ecclesiology) composed of Spirit-filled believers (ethics).

---

119. Henry, *Christian Personal Ethics*, 508.

Conclusion

—

CARL F. H. HENRY AS A THEOLOGIAN OF THE SPIRIT

This book has argued that despite criticism that he possessed an underdeveloped pneumatology, Carl F. H. Henry understood the Holy Spirit to play a vital role in three key areas: revelation, ecclesiology, and ethics. In this, he believed that a Spirit-inspired Bible (revelation) would order a Spirit-enlivened body (ecclesiology) composed of Spirit-filled believers (ethics). Further, the book has demonstrated that pneumatology was central to the context in which Henry was writing, and that his historical milieu is significant for understanding his pneumatological thought. Overall, the goal has been to demonstrate that, while not claiming the mantle of *the* theologian of the Spirit, Henry deserves to be remembered as *a* theologian of the Spirit. This understanding provides a new angle through which to interpret his significant writings on revelation, ecclesiology, and ethics, along with his wider work on various subjects. Further, Henry's pneumatology is a portal through which one can understand and evaluate his own inner life and apply his contributions to a new generation.

A THEOLOGIAN OF THE SPIRIT:
DEFINED AND DEFENDED

While pneumatology is not the only rubric by which to evaluate Henry's overall thought (nor even the primary one), it provides an undergirding effect to his conceptions of revelation, ecclesiology, and ethics, giving each vitality and resonance. Much of what Henry is known for was built upon his prior doctrine of the Spirit. The Life-Giver gave life to these aspects of Henry's thought.

Henry is usually remembered for his refined articulation of inerrancy, his attempt to revive an atrophying theological mind, his call for evangelical social awareness, his construction of an institutional network, and his renunciation of foreign theological trends that were eroding evangelicalism. This book argues that Henry should also be remembered for possessing a rich pneumatology, and that pneumatology was central to his historical context and many of his own important moments—from his sparring with Barth, to his evaluations of the charismatic and Jesus People movements, to one of his proudest contributions, *Christian Personal Ethics*. Unfortunately, while the doctrine of the Spirit occupied much of Henry's thinking, it does not occupy much of the thinking about Henry. However, to discount the role of pneumatology in Henry's overall theological vision is to limit one's understanding of an important aspect of his work. This book utilized unpublished data from Henry's archives and untapped published material to analyze relatively uncharted space in his thought, offering a unique contribution to the growing body of literature on Henry.

With the above stated, the question arises: Is it appropriate, as chapter 1 suggests, to recognize Henry as a theologian of the Spirit? There are, of course, no standardized criteria by which to make this judgement. However, by comparing Calvin (whom many have referred to as "the theologian of the Spirit") with Henry, there is justification for recognizing Henry as a theologian of the Spirit in a similar vein as Calvin.

Certainly, differences exist between the two. Whereas Calvin bestowed to the church a significant pneumatological legacy in his teaching on the internal witness of the Spirit, Henry bequeathed no novel insight to the doctrine. And whereas others have confirmed Warfield's claim of Calvin as "the theologian of the Spirit,"[1] there is no movement to view Henry as such. Care is required anytime we correlate one's thought to Calvin's, who, in the words of Karl Barth, was a "primeval forest," a "phenomenon" who descended "straight down from the Himalayas."[2] Tread lightly, Barth would tell us.

And yet, they share striking similarities. Calvin is remembered as a theologian of the Spirit for a combination of at least five reasons: he was the first to systematize biblical data on the Spirit, he integrated pneumatology

1. Herman J. Selderhuis, ed., *The Calvin Handbook*, trans. Henry J. Baron, Judith J. Guder, Randi H. Lundell, and Gerrit W. Sheeres (Grand Rapids: Eerdmans, 2009), 299.

2. Eberhard Busch, *Karl Barth: His Life from Letters and Autobiographical Texts*, trans. John Bowden (Eugene, OR: Wipf & Stock, 2005), 138.

into other theological loci, he examined at length the relationship between word and Spirit, he wrote during a time of pneumatological controversy (and combatted those who claimed divine revelation apart from Scripture),[3] and he presented the entirety of Christian ethics in light of the Holy Spirit.[4]

As this book has argued, Henry shared commonalities at each of these points. First, while not a systematician in the same way that Calvin was, Henry still devoted ample attention to biblical and theological exposition of the Holy Spirit: over 250 pages in *God, Revelation and Authority* directly related to the Spirit, and another 50 in *Christian Personal Ethics*. Add to these Henry's various academic and *Christianity Today* articles that addressed pneumatology. Though not systematic in the traditional sense, Henry's pneumatological writings are still substantive. Further, as noted in chapter 1, Studebaker places Henry alongside Calvin as two rare theologians who explicitly address the authority of the Holy Spirit in their work.[5] Second, Henry also related pneumatology to various theological loci—specifically, as this book has argued, to revelation, ecclesiology, and ethics. Third, as noted in chapter 3, a proper understanding of the relationship between word and Spirit was vital for Henry, an impulse he gleaned from Calvin. Fourth, Henry also wrote during a time of pneumatological controversy. Calvin and Henry's opponents both risked supplanting the Scriptures with the Spirit (for Calvin, the 'Enthusiasts,' and for Henry, the charismatic and Jesus People movements). In similar pneumatological climates (though separated by 400 years), both men struck a healthy, biblical balance between word and Spirit. And finally, Henry and Calvin both elevated the role of the Holy Spirit as central to their conceptions of Christian ethics.

Overall, this book argues that it is appropriate to recognize Henry as *a* theologian of the Spirit who took pneumatological cues from Calvin, *the* theologian of the Spirit. Henry appreciated Calvin's pneumatology (he devoted a section to Calvin and the Spirit in *GRA*), and he appropriated something of Calvin's approach, perhaps because he encountered similar

---

3. These first four reasons are drawn from Augustus Nicodemus Lopes and José Manoel da Conceicao, "Calvin, Theologian of the Holy Spirit: The Holy Spirit and the Word of God," *Scottish Bulletin of Evangelical Theology* 15.1 (1997): 38–49.

4. This fifth reason is drawn from Paul S. Chung, *Christian Spirituality and Ethical Life: Calvin's View on the Spirit in Ecumenical Context* (Eugene, OR: Pickwick, 2010), 7.

5. Studebaker, *The Lord Is the Spirit*, 19.

pneumatological challenges in the twentieth century as did Calvin in the sixteenth. While a modest connection—and one that should not be pressed to the extreme—it is still valid to recognize Henry as a theologian of the Spirit in the vein of Calvin (though not in the exact same ways nor to the same extent). Henry's Calvinism was both soteriological and pneumatological, and the spirit of Calvin's doctrine of the Spirit lives on in Henry.

A THEOLOGIAN OF THE SPIRIT
FOR EVANGELICALS TODAY

But does Henry's pneumatology bear a timestamp, relegated to an era of pneumatological expression that has since matured two decades into the twenty-first century? Or, as evangelicals continue to wrestle with the role of the Holy Spirit in their theology and practice, might Henry be an untapped well of doctrinal and experiential insight?

A THEOLOGIAN OF THE SPIRIT AMONG
CONTINUATIONISTS AND CESSATIONISTS

Evangelicals are not of one accord regarding the supernatural gifts of the Spirit. And this is understandable, given that there is room to disagree on the specifics of these positions. But it seems that disagreements are the central point of discussion anytime continuationists and cessationists gather, rather than a recognition of their respective strengths and, perhaps, their ability to shed light on the other's blind spots.[6] Worse still, caricatures of each are parroted far too often, if not verbally then imaginatively, making productive dialogue all the more difficult. About thirty years ago, D. A. Carson recognized this dilemma and painted the stereotypes in ways still identifiable today:

> As judged by the charismatics, noncharismatics tend to be stodgy traditionalists who do not really believe the Bible and who are not really hungry for the Lord. They are afraid of profound spiritual

---

6. Granted, some would rather avoid these two classifications entirely, though their beliefs and practices still fall somewhere along the spectrum. A hesitancy at being immediately sorted into corners because of terminology is understandable. However, in an effort to avoid endless caveats and exceptions, these two terms will be used as indicative of the perspectives, with full awareness that the situation is not so straightforward.

experience, too proud to give themselves wholeheartedly to God, more concerned for ritual than for reality, and more in love with propositional truth than with the truth incarnate. ... [T]hey are defeatist in outlook, defensive in stance, dull in worship, and devoid of the Spirit's power in their personal experience. The noncharismatics themselves, of course, tend to see things a little differently. The charismatics, they think, have succumbed to the modern love of "experience," even at the expense of truth. Charismatics are thought to be profoundly unbiblical, especially when they elevate their experience of tongues to the level of theological and spiritual shibboleth. If they are growing, no small part of their strength can be ascribed to their raw triumphalism, their populist elitism, their promise of shortcuts to holiness and power. They are better at splitting churches and stealing sheep than they are at evangelism, more accomplished in spiritual one-upmanship before other believers than in faithful, humble service.[7]

Of course, Carson knew that neither was correct. Caricatures should be rejected from whatever corner they originate. But Carson's words cut because they remind us that disagreements here can easily bleed into questioning another's commitments to God and his word. But I think Henry embodies this conversation at its best rather than rekindling it at its worst, and that, as a Spirit-attuned cessationist, he offers a pneumatological blueprint that deserves appreciation. Henry would concur with M. James Sawyer (who, as noted, challenged Henry's views of revelation) that "we in the cessationist tradition need to reconceptualize the work of the Spirit in far broader terms that we have in the past."[8] Similarly, Henry would wholeheartedly endorse the words of another critic, Alister McGrath:

We need to see the relationship between classical evangelicalism and the charismatic movement, or between perhaps "word-centered" and "spirit-centered" evangelicalism. Moreover, they can learn from

---

7. D. A. Carson, *Showing the Spirit: A Theological Exposition of 1 Corinthians 12–14* (Grand Rapids: Baker, 1987), 12.

8. Sawyer, "The Father, the Son, and the Holy Scriptures?," 275.

and complement each other. There is always a danger that the charismatic movement will become so experiential that it has no contact with the world of thought, not contact with scripture, no contact with Jesus Christ. And there is a danger that a more word-centered theology may simply be "right thoughts" about Jesus, lacking the real experiential dimension that was so important to Wesley before us and that has reemerged as important in our own day.[9]

However, whereas Sawyer and McGrath see Henry as part of the problem, I see him as part of the solution. Certainly, Henry is not the final word on word and Spirit, but his thought was more textured and sympathetic to their concerns than has been appreciated. Where the Western world continues to drift into personal experience as the defining metric of reality (and charismatics are not immune to this), Henry offers a corrective. And where Scripture becomes merely a deposit of linguistic signs and the Christian life lacks a supernatural and experiential basis (and cessationists are not immune to this), Henry offers a corrective.

Specific to Henry's own cessationist views, I think he is a prime embodiment of what Daniel B. Wallace and M. James Sawyer refer to as "*pneumatic* Christianity" in *Who's Afraid of the Holy Spirit? An Investigation into the Ministry of the Spirit of God Today*. They contend that "the way evangelical cessationism has developed was reactionary and reductionistic," with too little regard for the Holy Spirit as "a deep presence within the soul."[10] In their rejection of an overemphasis on experience in certain Pentecostal and charismatic expressions, cessationists tossed the Spirit out with the proverbial bathwater of the second baptism. But Wallace and Sawyer, cessationists themselves, "have become convinced that the ministry of the Spirit is far wider and deeper but more subtle than even the Pentecostal/charismatic tradition envisions it."[11] Interestingly, as mentioned in chapters 2 and 3, this was *precisely* what Henry thought of the charismatic and

---

9. Alister McGrath, "Trinitarian Theology," in Noll and Thiemann, *Where Shall My Wond'ring Soul Begin?*, 55.

10. Daniel B. Wallace and M. James Sawyer, preface to *Who's Afraid of the Holy Spirit? An Investigation into the Ministry of the Spirit of God Today*, ed. Daniel B. Wallace and M. James Sawyer (Dallas: Biblical Studies Press, 2005), v.

11. Wallace and Sawyer, *Who's Afraid of the Holy Spirit?*, vi.

Jesus People movements, as well as the views of Karl Barth—the Spirit was larger and more active than they recognized. Wallace and Sawyer's volume is a helpful resource that "attempt[s] to steer a middle ground between the sterile cessationism that essentially locks the Spirit in the pages of scripture, and an anything-goes-approach that has characterized parts of the Pentecostal/charismatic/Third Wave movements."[12] This is a welcome addition to literature supporting the cessationist position. Perhaps another step might be a renewed appreciation for a figure who embodied this approach: Carl Henry. It remains a formidable task to unearth the gems of his pen, many of which are buried deep within GRA, but mining them could bring fresh insight that will strengthen both cessationism and continuationism in the years to come.

A THEOLOGIAN OF THE SPIRIT FOR SPIRITUAL FORMATION

Not only is Henry's pneumatological body of work valuable for the cessationist and continuationist conversation, but it is also worthy of attention amid increased interest in spiritual formation. Gordon Fee argues that "most expressions of the Protestant tradition have ended up being trinitarian in name only, but not in practice[.] … [I]n belief Protestants maintain their trinitarianism, but in practice many of them are thoroughgoing binitarians."[13] Gordon Smith agrees: "The problem or issue at hand is that it would seem that for so many Christians, they live without an awareness, on any level, of the immediacy of God in their lives. They live, one might say, in a binitarian rather than trinitarian world; they have, at best, a truncated pneumatology. They have little consciousness of the Spirit's agency in their lives."[14] Richard Lovelace explains the situation with colorful phrasing:

> Even where Christians know about the Holy Spirit doctrinally, they have not necessarily made a deliberate point of getting to know him personally. … The typical relationship between believers and

---

12. Wallace and Sawyer, Who's Afraid of the Holy Spirit?, vi.

13. Gordon D. Fee, "On Getting the Spirit Back into Spirituality," in Life in the Spirit: Spiritual Formation in Theological Perspective, ed. Jeffrey P. Greenman and George Kalantzis (Downers Grove, IL: InterVarsity Press, 2010), 43.

14. Gordon T. Smith, Evangelical, Sacramental, and Pentecostal: Why the Church Should Be All Three (Downers Grove, IL: IVP Academic, 2017), 98–99.

the Holy Spirit in today's church is too often like that between the husband and wife in a bad marriage. They live under the same roof, and the husband makes constant use of his wife's services, but he fails to communicate with her, recognize her presence and celebrate their relationship with her. ... What should be done to reverse this situation? We should make a deliberate effort at the outset of every day to recognize the person of the Holy Spirit, to move into the light concerning his presence in our consciousness and to open up our minds and to share all our thoughts and plans as we gaze by faith into the face of God. [15]

In an effort to reclaim the role of the Spirit in the life of individual believers and in the corporate body of Christ, evangelicals would do well to consult Henry. Though he is not often considered a relevant voice in this area, Henry has much to contribute.[16] Language about formation, purity, holiness, evangelism, peace, and inner strength are weaved into his work, and he himself exhibited a strong pneumatological life. In fact, as demonstrated in chapter 5, Henry tied pneumatology to the very same virtues

---

15. Lovelace, *Dynamics of Spiritual Life*, 130–31. Allison and Köstenberger offer similar counsel: "What if our concrete plan would be to establish regular rhythms of 'spiritual breathing': crying out 'Spirit, direct my steps today' as we tumble out of bed, listening to the voice of the Spirit as we meditate on Scripture, checking for sins to confess, creating margins for divine appointments arranged by the Spirit, voicing simple phrases like 'Spirit, I adore you' and 'Spirit, thank you,' praying for the Spirit's guidance, obeying him when he directs us, and the like? While this may appear to be just another list of things to do, these rhythms are actually expressions of a lifestyle that flows from walking with the Holy Spirit moment by moment." See Allison and Köstenberger, *The Holy Spirit*, 482.

16. One fruitful area of further research would be an examination of the role of the Keswick Movement (either consciously or subconsciously) on Henry (and neo-evangelicalism as a whole). There seems to be an appropriation of the Keswick legacy in Henry's work, but he also expressed dissatisfaction with certain components of Keswickian thought. See Henry, *Christian Personal Ethics*, 463–68. Douglas Weaver has done a fine job of relating the Keswick Movement to Baptists in America (see Weaver, *Baptists and the Holy Spirit*), but more work can be done specifically on the relationship between Keswick theology and neo-evangelicalism. Along these lines, other neo-evangelical leaders are primed for an examination of their pneumatological thought, Harold Ockenga first among them. He held to a "modified" version of the Pentecostal second blessing and was something of a chronological enigma in that he was characterized by neo-evangelicalism's intellectual ethos but also advocated for more popular expressions of charismaticism. See Owen Strachan, "Reenchanting the Evangelical Mind: Park Street Church's Harold Ockenga, the Boston Scholars, and the Mid-Century Intellectual Surge" (PhD diss., Trinity Evangelical Divinity School, 2011), 86–87; Strachan, *Awakening the Evangelical Mind*, 30–33.

that Smith identifies with the charismatic and Pentecostal movements—love and joy:

But this [errors in some charismatic and Pentecostal expressions] should not discourage the church from seeking and living in dynamic fellowship with the Spirit, a fellowship that will be evident in two things, love—the experience of God's love that radiates within the faith community and to the world—and second, the experience of a deep and resilient joy.[17]

Those who, like Smith, advocate an increased awareness of the immediacy of the Spirit in the individual and corporate Christian life find an ally and resource in Henry. For the willing reader, Henry offers more contemplation on spiritual formation in the second half of *Christian Personal Ethics* alone than is available on pallets of Christian living books at the local bookstore.

CONCLUSION: THE PROFOUND ROLE OF THE "FULL, FURIOUS WIND OF GOD"

Carl F. H. Henry, neo-evangelicalism's titanic theologian, a man known for his intellect, wit, and sheer force of theological personality, was a man also dependent upon the Holy Spirit in his own life and held space in his theological presentation for a thorough conception of pneumatology. Despite criticism that he possessed an underdeveloped pneumatology, Henry understood the Holy Spirit to play a vital role in three key areas: revelation, ecclesiology, and ethics. In this, he believed that a Spirit-inspired Bible (revelation) would order a Spirit-enlivened body (ecclesiology) composed of Spirit-filled believers (ethics). Though pneumatology has gone underappreciated (or entirely unnoticed) in previous evaluations of his work, this book is an effort to reclaim the doctrine of the Spirit as a subsidiary, yet significant, element of his thought. In doing so, it has pressed for a new understanding of Henry as a theologian of the Spirit. Henry recognized the Spirit as the "full, furious wind of God," both theologically and experientially.[18] Further, he believed that "the New Testament most surely

---

17. Smith, *Evangelical, Sacramental, and Pentecostal*, 105.

18. Henry, *GRA*, 6:336

assigns a profound role to the Holy Spirit in the Christian era."[19] This book has argued that the Holy Spirit should also maintain a profound role in the theological legacy of Carl F. H. Henry.

We return to Henry's 1967 *Christianity Today* editorial, quoted at the beginning of chapter 1:

> If the Church is stricken today, it is not the soul that is dying. The Spirit is alive. There may yet be healing. There may yet be resurrection. It will depend on whether the churches really want this outpouring of the Holy Spirit in our day. Do we? Or do we merely want to get along as we have always done?[20]

Carl Henry asked questions of his readers then, and he does so now. Will we make room for the Holy Spirit of God in our hearts, homes, and churches? Will we plead for his unique and abiding presence in our lives? Are we willing to be shaped into greater conformity to the fruit of the Spirit? Or do we want to simply get along as we always have? Do we really want an outpouring of the Spirit in our day? The Spirit is alive, and he is willing.

Are we?

---

19. Henry, *GRA*, 4:499.
20. Unsigned editorial, "The Spirit of Pentecost," 29.

BIBLIOGRAPHY

—

ARCHIVAL MATERIAL

Carl F. H. Henry Papers. Rolfing Library, Trinity Evangelical Divinity School, Deerfield, Illinois.

The Billy Graham Center Archives. Wheaton College, Wheaton, Illinois.

PRIMARY SOURCES

Carl F. H. Henry. "The Acts of the Apostles: An Introduction to the Quarter's Lessons." Pages 2–4 in *The All Bible Graded Series of Sunday School Lessons: Studies in the Book of Acts.* Edited by James DeForest Murch. Chicago: Scripture Press, 1951.

———. *Aspects of Christian Social Ethics.* Grand Rapids: Eerdmans, 1964; Grand Rapids: Baker, 1980.

———, ed. *Baker's Dictionary of Christian Ethics.* Grand Rapids: Baker, 1973.

———. "The Bible and the Conscience of Our Age." *Journal of the Evangelical Theological Society* 25.4 (1982): 403–7.

———. "The Bible and the New Morality." *Christianity Today* (July 21, 1967): 5–9.

———. *The Christian Mindset in a Secular Society.* Portland: Multnomah Press, 1984.

———. "The Christian-Pagan West." *Christianity Today* (December 24, 1956): 3–5, 34.

———. *Christian Personal Ethics.* Grand Rapids: Eerdmans, 1957.

———. "Christian Theology and Social Revolution (II)." *Perkins School of Theology Journal* 21.2–3 (1967–1968): 13–23.

———. "Christianity and Resurgent Paganism: A Death Warrant Hangs Over Modernity." *Vital Speeches of the Day* 57 (1990): 81–91.

———. *Confessions of a Theologian.* Waco, TX: Word Books, 1986.

———. *Conversations with Carl F. H. Henry.* Vol. 18 of The Symposium Series. Lewiston, NY: Mellen, 1986.

———. "Does Genesis 9 Justify Capital Punishment?" Pages 230–50 in *The Genesis Debate: Persistent Questions about Creation and the Flood.* Edited by Ronald Youngblood. Nashville: Thomas Nelson, 1986.

———. "Dr. Henry Tackles Pros and Cons of the Charismatic Movement." *Evangelical Thrust* (June 1978): 16–19.

———. "The Ecumenical Age: Problems and Promise." *Bibliotheca Sacra* 123:491 (1966): 204–19.

———. "Editor's Note." *Christianity Today* (July 5, 1968): 2.

———. *Evangelicals at the Brink of Crisis: Significance of the World Congress on Evangelism.* Waco, TX: Word Books, 1976.

———. "Fortunes of the Christian World View." *Trinity Journal* 19.2 (1998): 163–76.

———. *God, Revelation and Authority.* 6 vols. Waco, TX: Word Books, 1976–1983; Wheaton, IL: Crossway, 1999.

———. *The God Who Shows Himself.* Waco, TX: Word Books, 1966.

———. "God's Word is God's Word." *Decision* (1993): 11–12.

———. "I Believe ..." *Christianity Today* (January 30, 1961): 23.

———. *The Identity of Jesus of Nazareth.* Nashville: Broadman & Holman, 1992.

———. "The Instability of Twentieth Century Theology." Seminary Chapel sermon. Southwestern Baptist Theological Seminary, Fort Worth, TX, March 4, 1997.

———. "The Interpretation of the Scriptures: Are We Doomed to Hermeneutical Nihilism?" *Review and Expositor* 71 (1974): 197–215.

———. "Jesus as the Ideal of Christian Ethics." *Christianity Today* (February 4, 1957): 12–14, 26.

———. "Jesus Freaks Seen as Test of Christian Belief." *Los Angeles Times* (January 15, 1972).

———. "Justification: A Doctrine in Crisis." *Journal of the Evangelical Theological Society* 38.1 (1995): 57–65.

———. "Learning to Avoid Subtle Temptations." Pages 136–37 in *Lessons in Leadership: Fifty Respected Evangelical Leaders Share Their Wisdom on Ministry*. Edited by Randal Roberts. Grand Rapids: Kregel, 1999.

———. "Let's Sharpen Our Word Power: Real Piety is Never Mossy." *Christianity Today* (November 7, 1960): 26–27.

———. "Natural Law and Nihilistic Culture." *First Things* (1995): 54–60.

———. "The Priority of Divine Revelation: A Review Article." *Journal of the Evangelical Theological Society* 27.1 (1984): 77–92.

———. "The Spirit and the Written Word." *Bibliotheca Sacra* 111.444 (1954): 302–16.

———. "Spiritual? Say It Isn't So!" Pages 8–14 in *Alive to God: Studies in Spirituality Presented to James Houston*. Edited by J. I. Packer and Loren Wilkinson. Vancouver: Regent College Publishing, 1992.

———. *Toward a Recovery of Christian Belief: The Rutherford Lectures*. Wheaton, IL: Crossway, 1990.

———. "Twenty Years a Baptist." *Foundations* 1 (1958): 46–54.

———. *The Uneasy Conscience of Modern Fundamentalism*. Grand Rapids: Eerdmans, 1947; 2003.

———. "The Vagrancy of the American Spirit." *Faculty Dialogue: Journal of the Institute for Christian Leadership* 22 (1994): 5–18.

———. "What Is Man on Earth For?" Pages, 155–61 in *Quest for Reality: Christianity and the Counter Culture*. Edited by Carl F. H. Henry. Downers Grove, IL: InterVarsity Press, 1973.

CHRISTIANITY TODAY EDITORIALS

"A Plea for Evangelical Unity." Unsigned editorial in *Christianity Today* (March 13, 1961): 24–25.

"The Blessings of Faith Include Its Power in Life." Unsigned editorial in *Christianity Today* (November 21, 1960): 23.

"Churches and Hidden Persuaders." Unsigned editorial in *Christianity Today* (May 25, 1959): 20–22.

"Crisis in the Pulpit." Unsigned editorial in *Christianity Today* (June 4, 1965): 24–25.

"Ghosts in the Pulpit." Unsigned editorial in *Christianity Today* (April 15, 1966): 24–25.

"Is the Church Too Silent on Personal Morality?" Unsigned editorial in
    Christianity Today (November 12, 1956): 23.

"It is Time for Rejoicing." Unsigned editorial in *Christianity Today* (May 23, 1960): 20.

"The Paganizing of Love." Unsigned editorial in *Christianity Today* (February 3,
    1958): 20–21.

"The Power of Joy." Unsigned editorial in *Christianity Today* (July 19, 1968): 34–35.

"Prayer and the Spirit the Door to New York." Unsigned editorial in *Christianity
    Today* (May 13, 1957): 24.

"Preaching as an Act of Worship." Unsigned editorial in *Christianity Today*
    (September 12, 1960): 20–21.

"Principles of Church Unity." Unsigned editorial in *Christianity Today* (May 26,
    1958): 20–22.

"Recasting the Ecumenical Posture." Unsigned editorial in *Christianity Today*
    (October 26, 1962): 24–25.

"Revelation in History." Unsigned editorial in *Christianity Today* (October 9, 1964):
    31–33.

"The Spirit and the Church." Unsigned editorial in *Christianity Today* (March 30,
    1959): 20–21.

"The Spirit of Pentecost: Will a Powerless Church Recover Its God-Given Soul?"
    Unsigned editorial in *Christianity Today* (April 14, 1967): 28–29.

"The Spirit the Index to Powerless or Powerful Effort." Unsigned editorial in
    Christianity Today (February 4, 1957): 23.

"Theology in Ecumenical Affairs." Unsigned editorial in *Christianity Today*
    (February 16, 1959): 20–21.

"Unity: Quest and Questions." Unsigned editorial in *Christianity Today* (November
    24, 1961): 28–30.

"Why *Christianity Today*?" Unsigned editorial in *Christianity Today* (October 15,
    1956): 20–23.

"The Winds of the Spirit." Unsigned editorial in *Christianity Today* (January 4,
    1963): 24.

SECONDARY SOURCES

Adam, Karl. "Die Theologie der Krisis." *Hochland* 23 (1926): 271–86.

Allison, Greg R., and Andreas J. Köstenberger. *The Holy Spirit. Theology for the People of God.* Edited by David S. Dockery, Nathan A. Finn, and Christopher W. Morgan. Nashville: B&H, 2020.

Alsdurf, Phyllis. "*Christianity Today* Magazine and Late Twentieth-Century Evangelicalism." PhD diss., The University of Minnesota, 2004.

———. "The Founding of Christianity Today Magazine and the Construction of An American Evangelical Identity." *Journal of Religious and Theological Information* 9 (2010): 20–43.

Anderson, Allan. *An Introduction to Pentecostalism: Global Charismatic Christianity.* Cambridge: Cambridge University Press, 2004.

Barnette, Henlee H. *Introducing Christian Ethics.* Nashville: Broadman, 1961.

Barrett, Matthew. "'We Believe in the Holy Spirit': Revisiting the Deity of the Spirit." *Southern Baptist Journal of Theology* 16.4 (2012): 32–53.

Barth, Karl. *Church Dogmatics.* Vol. 1, part 2, of The Doctrine of the Word of God. Edited by G. W. Bromiley and T. F. Torrance. Translated by G. T. Thomson and Harold Knight. London: T&T Clark, 1956.

———. *Die Lehre vom Worte Gottes. Prolegomena zur christlichen Dogmatik.* Munich: Christian Kaiser, 1927.

———. *Ethics.* Edited by Dietrich Braun. Translated by Geoffrey W. Bromiley. Eugene, OR: Wipf & Stock, 2013.

———. *Homiletics.* Translated by Geoffrey W. Bromiley and Donald E. Daniels. Louisville: Westminster John Knox, 1991.

Bebbington, David. *Evangelicalism in Modern Britain: A History from the 1730s to the 1980s.* London: Unwin Hyman Ltd., 1989.

Bloesch, Donald. *Freedom for Obedience: Evangelical Ethics in Contemporary Times.* Eugene, OR: Wipf & Stock, 2002.

———. *Holy Scripture: Revelation, Inspiration, and Interpretation.* Christian Foundations. Downers Grove, IL: InterVarsity Press, 1994.

Blumhofer, Judith L. and Joel A. Carpenter, eds. *Twentieth-Century Evangelicalism: A Guide to the Sources*. New York: Garland, 1990.

Brand, Chad Owen. "Is Carl Henry a Modernist? Rationalism and Foundationalism in Post-War Evangelical Theology." *Trinity Journal* 20 (1999): 3–21.

Bray, Gerald. *The Church: A Theological and Historical Account*. Grand Rapids: Baker Academic, 2016.

Brockway, Dan. "Transforming Presence: The Holy Spirit in Baptist Theological Ethics." *American Baptist Quarterly* 31.2 (2012): 263–75.

Bruner, Fredrick Dale, and William Hordern. *The Holy Spirit: Shy Member of the Trinity*. Eugene, OR: Wipf & Stock, 2001.

Burgess, Stanley M., Gary B. McGee, and Patrick H. Alexander, eds. *Dictionary of Pentecostal and Charismatic Movements*. Grand Rapids: Zondervan, 1990.

Burnett, Richard E. "Inspiration." Pages 115–17 in *The Westminster Handbook to Karl Barth*. The Westminster Handbooks to Christian Theology. Edited by Richard E. Burnett. Louisville: Westminster John Knox, 2013.

Busch, Eberhard. *Karl Barth: His Life from Letters and Autobiographical Texts*. Translated by John Bowden. Eugene, OR: Wipf & Stock, 2005.

Bustraan, Richard. *The Jesus People Movement: A Story of Spiritual Revolution Among the Hippies*. Eugene, OR: Pickwick, 2014.

Caldwell, Robert W. *Communion in the Spirit: The Holy Spirit as the Bond of Union in the Theology of Jonathan Edwards*. Paternoster Studies in Evangelical History and Thought. Eugene, OR: Wipf & Stock, 2006.

Carpenter, Joel A. *Revive Us Again: The Reawakening of American Fundamentalism*. New York: Oxford University Press, 1997.

Carson, D. A. "The Compleat Christian: The Massive Vision of Carl F. H. Henry." *Trinity Journal* 35 (2014): 9–18.

———. "The *SBJT* Forum: Testimonies to a Theologian." *Southern Baptist Journal of Theology* 8.4 (2004): 82–98.

Carswell, Robert. "A Comparative Study of the Religious Epistemology of Carl F. H. Henry and Alvin Plantinga." PhD diss., The Southern Baptist Theological Seminary, 2007.

Cerillo Jr., Augustus, and Murray W. Dempster. "Carl F. H. Henry's Early Apologetic for an Evangelical Social Ethic, 1942–1956." *Journal of the Evangelical Theological Society* 34.3 (1991): 365–79.

Chinn, Jack J. "May We Pentecostals Speak?" *Christianity Today* (July 17, 1961): 8–9.

Chung, Paul S. *Christian Spirituality and Ethical Life: Calvin's View on the Spirit in Ecumenical Context*. Eugene, OR: Pickwick, 2010.

Chute, Anthony L., Nathan A. Finn, and Michael A. G. Haykin. *The Baptist Story: From English Sect to Global Movement*. Nashville: B&H Academic, 2015.

Cole, Graham A. *He Who Gives Life: The Doctrine of the Holy Spirit*. Foundations of Evangelical Thought. Edited by John S. Feinberg. Wheaton, IL: Crossway, 2007.

Colson, Charles W. Foreword to *Carl Henry at His Best: A Lifetime of Quotable Thoughts*. Edited by Steve Halliday and Al Janssen. Portland: Multnomah Press, 1989.

Cross, Terry L. "The Holy Spirit." Pages 93–108 in *The Cambridge Companion to Evangelical Theology*. Edited by Timothy Larson and Daniel J. Treier. New York: Cambridge University Press, 2007.

Daane, James. "The Christ-Centered Spirit." *Christianity Today* (January 4, 1963): 4–5.

Dayton, Donald W. "Some Doubts about the Usefulness of the Category 'Evangelical.'" Pages 245–51 in *The Variety of American Evangelicalism*. Edited by Donald W. Dayton and Robert K. Johnston. Knoxville: University of Tennessee Press, 1991.

Dempster, Murray. "The Role of Scripture in the Social-Ethical Writings of Carl F. H. Henry." PhD diss., The University of Southern California, 1969.

Dever, Mark E. "The Church." Pages 766–856 in *A Theology for the Church*. Edited by Daniel L. Akin. Nashville: B&H, 2007.

Dockery, David S. *Southern Baptist Consensus and Renewal: A Biblical, Historical, and Theological Proposal*. Nashville: B&H, 2008.

Dockery, David S., and David P. Nelson. "Special Revelation." Pages 118–74 in *A Theology for the Church*. Edited by Daniel L. Akin. Nashville: B&H, 2007.

Dorrien, Gary. *Social Ethics in the Making: Interpreting an American Tradition*. Chichester: Wiley-Blackwell, 2009.

Doyle, G. Wright. "Carl Henry and the Chinese Church." *Evangelical Review of Theology* 38.1 (2014): 33–53.

———. *Carl Henry: Theologian for All Seasons—An Introduction and Guide to Carl Henry's God, Revelation, and Authority*. Eugene, OR: Pickwick, 2010.

Duesing, Jason G. "'Power in the Seminary': 20th Century Pneumatological Distinctives at Southwestern Baptist Theological Seminary." White Paper 11. Fort Worth: The Center for Theological Research at Southwestern Baptist Theological Seminary, 2006.

Edwards, Jonathan. *Charity and Its Fruits: Living in Light of God's Love*. Edited by Kyle Strobel. Wheaton, IL: Crossway, 2012.

Ellington, Scott A. "Pentecostalism and the Authority of Scripture." Pages 149–70 in *Pentecostal Hermeneutics: A Reader*. Edited by Lee Roy Martin. Leiden: Brill, 2013.

Erickson, Millard J. "Carl F. H. Henry." Pages 214–20 in *A New Handbook of Christian Theologians*. Edited by Donald W. Musser and Joseph L. Price. Nashville: Abingdon, 1996.

———. *Christian Theology*. Grand Rapids: Baker Academic, 1995.

Eskridge, Larry. *God's Forever Family: The Jesus People Movement in America*. Oxford: Oxford University Press, 2013.

Fackre, Gabriel. "Carl F. H. Henry." Pages 583–607 in *A Handbook of Christian Theologians*. Edited by Dean G. Peerman and Martin E. Marty. Enl. ed. Nashville: Abington Press, 1984.

———. *The Doctrine of Revelation: A Narrative Interpretation*. Edinburgh Studies in Constructive Theology. Edinburgh: Edinburgh University Press, 1997.

Fee, Gordon D. "On Getting the Spirit Back into Spirituality." Pages 36–44 in *Life in the Spirit: Spiritual Formation in Theological Perspective*. Edited by Jeffrey P. Greenman and George Kalantzis. Downers Grove, IL: InterVarsity Press, 2010.

Feinberg, John S. *No One Like Him: The Doctrine of God*. Foundations of Evangelical Theology. Edited by John S. Feinberg. Wheaton, IL: Crossway, 2001.

Ferguson, Sinclair B. *The Holy Spirit*. Contours of Christian Theology. Edited by Gerald Bray. Downers Grove, IL: InterVarsity Press, 1996.

Finn, Nathan A. "Curb Your Enthusiasm: Martin Luther's Critique of Anabaptism." *Southwestern Journal of Theology* 56.2 (2014): 163-81.

Gaffin, Richard B. "A Cessationist View." Pages 23-64 in *Are Miraculous Gifts for Today? Four Views*. Edited by Stanley N. Gundry and Wayne A. Grudem. Grand Rapids: Zondervan, 1996.

Garrett, James Leo. *Baptist Theology: A Four-Century Study*. Macon, GA: Mercer University Press, 2009.

———. "Representative Modern Baptist Understandings of Biblical Inspiration." *Review and Expositor* (1974): 179-95.

———. *Systematic Theology: Biblical, Historical, and Evangelical*. 2nd ed. North Richland Hills, TX: Bibal Press, 2000.

George, Timothy. "Evangelicals and Others." *First Things* (2006): 15-23.

———. "Inventing Evangelicalism." *Christianity Today* (March 2004): 48-51.

———. "The Reformation Roots of the Baptist Tradition." *Review and Expositor* 86 (1989): 9-22.

———. *Theology of the Reformers*. Rev. ed. Nashville: B&H, 2013.

Gibson, David. "The Answering Speech of Men: Karl Barth on Holy Scripture." Pages 266-91 in *The Enduring Authority of the Christian Scriptures*. Edited by D. A. Carson. Grand Rapids: Eerdmans, 2016.

Goatley, David Emmanuel. "The Charismatic Movement Among Baptists Today." *Review and Expositor* 94 (1997): 31-40.

Godsey, J. D., ed. *Karl Barth's Table Talk*. Edinburgh: Oliver & Boyd, 1963.

Graham, Christopher A. "The Theological Shape of Unity as the Foundation for Southern Baptist Cooperation." *Criswell Theological Review* 14.2 (2017): 47-69.

Green, Clifford, ed. *Karl Barth: Theologian of Freedom*. The Making of Modern Theology: Nineteenth and Twentieth Century Texts. Edited by John W. de Gruchy. Minneapolis: Fortress Press, 1991.

Green, Gene L. "Introduction: The Spirit over the Earth: Pneumatology in the Majority World." Pages 1-12 in *The Spirit over the Earth: Pneumatology in the Majority World*. Edited by Gene L. Green, Stephen T. Pardue, and K. K. Yeo. Grand Rapids: Eerdmans, 2016.

Green, Joel B., Jacqueline E. Lapsley, Rebeckah Miles, and Allen Verhey, eds. *Dictionary of Scripture and Ethics*. Grand Rapids: Baker Academic, 2011.

Greggs, Tom. "The Catholic Spirit of Protestantism: A Very Methodist Take on the Third Article, Visible Unity, and Ecumenism." *Pro Ecclesia* 26.4 (2017): 353–72.

Grenz, Stanley J. *Theology for the Community of God*. Grand Rapids: Eerdmans, 2000.

Grenz, Stanley J., and Roger E. Olson. *20th-Century Theology: God and The World in a Transitional Age*. Downers Grove, IL: InterVarsity Press, 1992.

Grudem, Wayne. Preface to *Are Miraculous Gifts for Today? Four Views*. Counterpoints Bible and Theology. Edited by Stanley N. Gundry and Wayne A. Grudem. Grand Rapids: Zondervan, 1996.

———. *Systematic Theology: An Introduction to Biblical Doctrine*. Grand Rapids: Zondervan, 1994.

Gushee, David P., and Isaac B. Sharp, eds. *Evangelical Ethics: A Reader*. Library of Theological Ethics. Louisville: Westminster John Knox, 2015.

Hall, Matthew J., and Owen Strachan, eds. *Essential Evangelicalism: The Enduring Influence of Carl F. H. Henry*. Wheaton, IL: Crossway, 2015.

Hamilton Jr., James M. *God's Indwelling Presence: The Holy Spirit in the Old and New Testaments*. NAC Studies in Bible and Theology. Edited by Ray Clendenen. Nashville: B&H, 2006.

———. "The Holy Spirit and Christian Worship: The Life-Giving Legacy of the Apostolic Band." *Midwestern Journal of Theology* 18.1 (2019): 69–83.

Hammett, John S. *Biblical Foundations for Baptist Churches: A Contemporary Ecclesiology*. Grand Rapids: Kregel, 2005.

Hancock-Stefan, George. "Fifty Years of Baptist Pneumatological Publications (1960–2010): A Historical Review." *American Baptist Quarterly* (2012): 163–78.

Hankins, Barry. *Uneasy in Babylon: Southern Baptist Conservatives and American Culture*. Tuscaloosa: University of Alabama Press, 2002.

Hansen, Collin, and John Woodbridge. *A God-Sized Vision: Revival Stories that Stretch and Stir*. Grand Rapids: Zondervan, 2010.

Hansen, Collin, and Justin Taylor. "From Babylon Baptist to Baptists in Babylon: The SBC and the Broader Evangelical Community." Pages 33-49 in *The SBC and the 21st Century: Reflection, Renewal, and Recommitment.* Edited by Jason K. Allen. Nashville: B&H Academic, 2016.

Hatch, Nathan O. *The Democratization of American Christianity.* New Haven: Yale University Press, 1989.

———. "Response to Carl F. H. Henry." Pages 95-101 in *Evangelical Affirmations.* Edited by Kenneth S. Kantzer and Carl F. H. Henry. Grand Rapids: Academie, 1990.

Haykin, Michael A. G., and Kenneth Stewart, eds. *The Advent of Evangelicalism: Exploring Historical Continuities.* Nashville: B&H Academic, 2008.

Heltzel, Peter Goodwin. *Jesus and Justice: Evangelicals, Race, and American Politics.* New Haven: Yale University Press, 2009.

Henry, Helga Bender. *Cameroon on a Clear Day: A Pioneer Missionary in Colonial Africa.* Pasadena, CA: William Carey Library, 1999.

Hollinger, Dennis P. *Choosing the Good: Christian Ethics in a Complex World.* Grand Rapids: Baker Academic, 2002.

Holmes, Christopher J. *The Holy Spirit.* New Studies in Dogmatics. Edited by Michael Allen and Scott R. Swain. Grand Rapids: Zondervan, 2015.

Holmes, Stephen R. *Baptist Theology.* London: T&T Clark, 2012.

Horton, Michael. "'Lord and Giver of Life': The Holy Spirit in Redemptive History." *Journal of the Evangelical Theological Society* 62.1 (2019): 47-63.

———. "Prologue: What Are We Celebrating?" Pages 13-35 in *Reformation Theology: A Systematic Summary.* Edited by Matthew Barrett. Wheaton, IL: Crossway, 2017.

———. *Rediscovering the Holy Spirit: God's Perfecting Presence in Creation, Redemption, and Everyday Life.* Grand Rapids: Zondervan, 2017.

House, Paul R. "Hope, Discipline, and the Incarnational Scholar." Pages 115-33 in *Essential Evangelicalism: The Enduring Influence of Carl F. H. Henry.* Edited by Matthew J. Hall and Owen Strachan. Wheaton, IL: Crossway, 2015.

———. "Remaking the Modern Mind: Revisiting Carl Henry's Theological Vision." *Southern Baptist Journal of Theology* 8.4 (Winter 2004): 4-24.

Hunt, W. Boyd. "The Body Christ Heads: A Symposium." *Christianity Today* (August 19, 1957): 7–8.

Ihrie, A. Dale. "The Free Churches and Ecumenism." *Christianity Today* (May 25, 1962): 12–14.

Ireland, Jerry M. "Evangelism and Social Concern in the Theology of Carl F. H. Henry." PhD diss., Liberty University, 2015.

Jenson, Robert W. "You Wonder Where the Spirit Went." *Pro Ecclesia* 2.3 (1993): 296–304.

Johnston, Robert K. "Varieties of American Evangelicalism." Pages 40–51 in *Southern Baptists and American Evangelicals*. Edited by David S. Dockery. Nashville: B&H, 1993.

Jones, David Clyde. *Biblical Christian Ethics*. Grand Rapids: Baker, 1994.

Jones, David W. *An Introduction to Biblical Ethics*. B&H Studies in Christian Ethics. Edited by Daniel R. Heimbach. Nashville: B&H, 2013.

Kantzer, Kenneth S. "Carl Ferdinand Howard Henry: An Appreciation." Pages 369–77 in *God and Culture: Essays in Honor of Carl F. H. Henry*. Edited by D. A. Carson and John D. Woodbridge. Grand Rapids: Eerdmans, 1993.

———. "Christian Personal Ethics." Pages 195–239 in *Evangelical Affirmations*. Edited by Kenneth S. Kantzer and Carl F. H. Henry. Grand Rapids: Academie, 1990.

Kärkkäinen, Veli-Matti. *An Introduction to Ecclesiology: Ecumenical, Historical and Global Perspectives*. Downers Grove, IL: InterVarsity Press, 2002.

———. *Pneumatology: The Holy Spirit in Ecumenical, International, and Contextual Perspective*. 2nd ed. Grand Rapids: Baker Academic, 2018.

Kidd, Thomas S. "The Bebbington Quadrilateral and the Work of the Holy Spirit." *Fides et Historia* 47.1 (2015): 54–57.

———. *Who Is an Evangelical? The History of a Movement in Crisis*. New Haven: Yale University Press, 2019.

Kik, J. Marcellus. "Unity of the Spirit." *Christianity Today* (July 22, 1957): 7–8, 22.

Kim, JinHyok. *The Spirit of God and the Christian Life: Reconstructing Karl Barth's Pneumatology*. Minneapolis: Fortress Press, 2014.

King, Gerald W. *Disfellowshiped: Pentecostal Responses to Fundamentalism in the United States, 1906-1943.* Princeton Theological Monograph Series. Eugene, OR: Pickwick, 2011.

King, Kevin. "The Uneasy Pulpit: Carl Henry, the Authority of the Bible and Expositional Preaching." *Eruditio Ardescens* 2.1 (2015): 1-17.

Küng, Hans. *The Church.* New York: Burns & Oates, 1968.

Kuyper, Abraham. *The Work of the Holy Spirit.* Translated by Henri De Vries. New York: Funk & Wagnalls, 1900.

Leeman, Jonathan. "A Congregational Approach to Catholicity: Independence and Interdependence." Pages 367-80 in *Baptist Foundations: Church Government for an Anti-Institutional Age.* Edited by Mark Dever and Jonathan Leeman. Nashville: B&H Academic, 2015.

———. "A Congregational Approach to Unity, Holiness, and Apostolicity: Faith and Order." Pages 333-66 in *Baptist Foundations: Church Government for an Anti-Institutional Age.* Edited by Mark Dever and Jonathan Leeman. Nashville: B&H Academic, 2015.

Leitch, Addison. "The Primary Task of the Church." *Christianity Today* (October 15, 1956): 11-13, 18.

Leung, Mavis M. "With What is Evangelicalism to Penetrate the World? A Study of Carl Henry's Envisioned Evangelicalism." *Trinity Journal* (2006): 227-244.

Levering, Matthew. *Engaging the Doctrine of the Holy Spirit: Love and Gift in the Trinity and the Church.* Grand Rapids: Baker, 2016.

Lewis, C. S. *Mere Christianity.* New York: HarperCollins, 2001.

Lewis, Gordon R., and Bruce A. Demarest. *Integrative Theology.* Grand Rapids: Zondervan, 1996.

Lopes, Augustus Nicodemus, and José Manoel da Conceicao. "Calvin, Theologian of the Holy Spirit: The Holy Spirit and the Word of God." *Scottish Bulletin of Evangelical Theology* 15.1 (1997): 38-49.

Lovelace, Richard F. *Dynamics of Spiritual Life: An Evangelical Theology of Renewal.* Downers Grove, IL: InterVarsity Press, 1979.

Machen, J. Gresham. "The Eternal Verities: The Holy Spirit." *Christianity Today* (March 12, 1956): 27.

Macklin, George Benjamin. "Pneumatology: A Unifying Theme of B. H. Carroll's Theology." PhD diss., Southwestern Baptist Theological Seminary, 2007.

Mann, John B. "Revelation of the Triune God through Word and Spirit: A Theological Critique of Karl Barth and Carl Henry." PhD diss., Southwestern Baptist Theological Seminary, 2018.

Marsden, George. *Fundamentalism and American Culture: The Shaping of Twentieth Century Evangelicalism: 1870–1925.* New York: Oxford University Press, 1980.

———. *Reforming Fundamentalism: Fuller Seminary and the New Evangelicalism.* Grand Rapids: Eerdmans, 1987.

———. *The Twilight of the American Enlightenment: The 1950s and the Crisis of Liberal Belief.* New York: Basic Books, 2014.

———. *Understanding Fundamentalism and Evangelicalism.* Grand Rapids: Eerdmans, 1991.

Marshall, I. Howard. *Biblical Inspiration.* Vancouver: Regent College Publishing, 2004.

Martin, William. *A Prophet with Honor: The Billy Graham Story.* Rev. ed. Grand Rapids: Zondervan, 2018.

McCormack, Bruce L. *Karl Barth's Critically Realistic Dialectical Theology: Its Genesis and Development 1909–1936.* New York: Oxford University Press, 1995.

McCormack, Bruce L., and Clifford B. Anderson, eds. *Karl Barth and American Evangelicalism.* Grand Rapids: Eerdmans, 2011.

McGrath, Alister E. "Engaging the Great Tradition: Evangelical Theology and the Role of Tradition." Pages 139–58 in *Evangelical Futures: A Conversation on Theological Method.* Edited by John G. Stackhouse, Jr. Grand Rapids: Baker, 2000.

———. "Trinitarian Theology." Pages 51–60 in *Where Shall My Wond'ring Soul Begin? The Landscape of Evangelical Piety and Thought.* Edited by Mark A. Noll and Ronald F. Thiemann. Grand Rapids: Eerdmans, 2000.

Mitchell, C. Ben. "The Vulnerable: Abortion and Disability." Pages 481–96 in *The Oxford Handbook of Evangelical Theology.* Edited by Gerald R. McDermott. Oxford: Oxford University Press, 2010.

Mohler, R. Albert. "Carl F. H. Henry." Pages 279–96 in *Theologians of the Baptist*

Tradition. Edited by Timothy George and David S. Dockery. Nashville: B&H, 2001.

———. "Evangelical Theology and Karl Barth: Representative Models of Response." PhD diss., The Southern Baptist Theological Seminary, 1989.

Moore, Russell D. Afterword to *Has Democracy Had Its Day?* 2nd ed, by Carl F. H. Henry. Nashville: Leland House, 2019.

———. "God, Revelation, and Community: Ecclesiology and Baptist Identity in the Thought of Carl F. H. Henry." *Southern Baptist Journal of Theology* 8.4 (2004): 26–43.

———. "The Kingdom of God in the Social Ethics of Carl F. H. Henry: A Twenty-First Century Evangelical Reappraisal." *Journal of the Evangelical Theological Society* 55.2 (2012): 377–97.

———. "Kingdom Theology and the American Evangelical Consensus: Emerging Implications for Sociopolitical Engagement." PhD diss., The Southern Baptist Theological Seminary, 2002.

———. Review of 2003 reprint of *The Uneasy Conscience of Modern Fundamentalism*, by Carl F. H. Henry. *Journal of the Evangelical Theological Society* (2005): 182–83.

Morrison, John D. "Barth, Barthians, and Evangelicals: Reassessing the Question of the Relation of Holy Scripture and the Word of God." *Trinity Journal* 25 (2004): 187–213.

Mounce, Robert H. *Romans: An Exegetical and Theological Exposition of Holy Scripture*. Vol. 27 of The New American Commentary. Nashville: B&H, 1995.

Mouw, Richard. "Evangelical Ethics." Pages 71–86 in *Where Shall My Wond'ring Soul Begin? The Landscape of Evangelical Piety and Thought*. Edited by Mark A. Noll and Ronald F. Thiemann. Grand Rapids: Eerdmans, 2000.

———. Foreword to *The Uneasy Conscience of Modern Fundamentalism*, by Carl F. H. Henry. Grand Rapids: Eerdmans, 2003.

———. "Toward a Full-Orbed Evangelical Ethic." Pages 43–58 in *Essential Evangelicalism: The Enduring Influence of Carl F. H. Henry*. Edited by Matthew J. Hall and Owen Strachan. Wheaton, IL: Crossway, 2015.

Mueller, David L. *Karl Barth*. Makers of the Modern Theological Mind. Waco, TX: Word Books, 1972.

Mullin II, Miles S. "Evangelicalism as Trojan Horse: The Failure of Neo-
Evangelical Social Theology and the Decline of Denominationalism."
Criswell Theological Review (2014): 49–68.

Mullins, E. Y. *Baptist Beliefs.* 2nd ed. Louisville: Baptist World, 1913.

Murch, James DeForest. *Cooperation without Compromise: A History of the National
Association of Evangelicals.* Grand Rapids: Eerdmans, 1956.

Naselli, Andrew David. "Keswick Theology: A Survey and Analysis of the
Doctrine of Sanctification in the Early Keswick Movement." *Detroit Baptist
Seminary Journal* 13 (2008): 17–67.

———. *No Quick Fix: Where Higher Life Theology Came From, What It Is, and Why It's
Harmful.* Bellingham: Lexham Press, 2017.

Nelson, Rudolph. *The Making and Unmaking of an Evangelical Mind: The Case of
Edward Carnell.* Cambridge: Cambridge University Press, 1987.

Noll, Mark A. "Evangelicalism at Its Best." Pages 1–26 in *Where Shall My Wond'ring
Soul Begin? The Landscape of Evangelical Piety and Thought.* Edited by Mark
A. Noll and Ronald F. Thiemann. Grand Rapids: Eerdmans, 2000.

———. *Faith and Criticism: Evangelicals, Scholarship, and the Bible in America.* 2nd ed.
Vancouver: Regent College Publishing, 2004.

Oden, Thomas C. *A Change of Heart: A Personal and Theological Memoir.* Downers
Grove, IL: InterVarsity Press, 2014.

Olson, Jonathan. "The Quest for Legitimacy: American Pentecostal Scholars
and the Quandaries of Academic Pursuit." *Intermountain West Journal of
Religious Studies* 4.1 (2013): 93–115.

Packer, J. I. *"Fundamentalism" and the Word of God: Some Evangelical Principles.*
Leicester: InterVarsity Press, 1958.

———. *Keep in Step with the Spirit: Finding Fullness in our Walk with God.* Grand
Rapids: Baker, 2005.

Patterson, Bob E. *Carl F. H. Henry.* Makers of the Modern Theological Mind.
Peabody, MA: Hendrickson, 1983.

Patterson, James A. "Cultural Pessimism in Modern Evangelical Thought:
Francis Schaeffer, Carl Henry, and Charles Colson." *Journal of the
Evangelical Theological Society* 49.4 (2006): 807–20.

Payne, Jesse M. "An Uneasy Ecclesiology: Carl F. H. Henry's Doctrine of the Church." *Southeastern Theological Review* 10.1 (2019): 95–111.

Peays, Benjamin Thomas. "Carl F. H. Henry's Understanding of the Formation of Evangelical Self-Identity from 1945 to 1948." PhD diss., Trinity Evangelical Divinity School, 2015.

———. "The Modern Mind and the Uneasy Conscience." Pages 149–73 in *Essential Evangelicalism: The Enduring Influence of Carl F. H. Henry*. Edited by Matthew J. Hall and Owen Strachan. Wheaton, IL: Crossway, 2015.

Pinnock, Clark H. *Flame of Love: A Theology of the Holy Spirit*. Downers Grove, IL: InterVarsity Press, 1996.

Rae, Scott B. *Moral Choices: An Introduction to Ethics*. 3rd ed. Grand Rapids: Zondervan, 2009.

Ramm, Bernard. *Rapping about the Spirit*. Waco, TX: Word Books, 1974.

Reeves, Michael. *Delighting in the Trinity: An Introduction to the Christian Faith*. Downers Grove, IL: IVP Academic, 2012.

Richardson, Alan, and John Bowden, eds. *The Westminster Dictionary of Christian Theology*. Philadelphia: Westminster, 1983.

Roach, William C. *Hermeneutics as Epistemology: A Critical Assessment of Carl F. H. Henry's Epistemological Approach to Hermeneutics*. Eugene, OR: Wipf & Stock, 2015.

Rosell, Garth M. *The Surprising Work of God: Harold John Ockenga, Billy Graham, and the Rebirth of Evangelicalism*. Grand Rapids: Baker Academic, 2008.

Rouner Jr., Arthur A. "Gathered Church, Great Church." *Christianity Today* (May 25, 1962): 9–11.

Sasse, Hermann. "Inspiration and Inerrancy—Some Preliminary Thoughts." *Concordia Journal* (2010): 107–19.

Saucy, Mark R. "*Regnum Spiriti*: The Role of the Spirit in the Social Ethics of the Kingdom." *Journal of the Evangelical Theological Society* 54.1 (2011): 89–108.

Sawyer, M. James. "The Father, the Son, and the Holy Scriptures?" Pages 253–77 in *Who's Afraid of the Holy Spirit? An Investigation into the Ministry of the Spirit of God Today*. Edited by Daniel B. Wallace and M. James Sawyer. Dallas: Biblical Studies Press, 2005.

Schäfer, Axel R. *Countercultural Conservatives: American Evangelicalism from the Postwar Revival to the New Christian Right*. Madison: University of Wisconsin Press, 2011.

Schreiner, Thomas R. *Spiritual Gifts: What They Are & Why They Matter*. Nashville: B&H, 2018.

Selderhuis, Herman J., ed. *The Calvin Handbook*. Translated by Henry J. Baron, Judith J. Guder, Randi H. Lundell, and Gerrit W. Sheeres. Grand Rapids: Eerdmans, 2009.

Siecienski, A. Edward. *The Filioque: History of a Doctrinal Controversy*. Oxford Studies in Historical Theology. Oxford: Oxford University Press, 2010.

Smeaton, George. *The Doctrine of the Holy Spirit*. Edinburgh: T&T Clark, 1882.

Smedes, Lewis B., ed. *Ministry and the Miraculous: A Case Study at Fuller Theological Seminary*. Pasadena, CA: Fuller Seminary Press, 1987.

Smith, Gordon T. *Evangelical, Sacramental, and Pentecostal: Why the Church Should Be All Three*. Downers Grove, IL: IVP Academic, 2017.

Spittler, Russell P. "Are Pentecostals and Charismatics Fundamentalists? A Review of American Uses of These Categories." Pages 103–16 in *Charismatic Christianity as a Global Culture*. Edited by Karla Poewe. Columbia: University of South Carolina Press, 1994.

Stafford, John K. "Richard Hooker's Doctrine of the Holy Spirit." PhD diss., The University of Manitoba, 2005.

Stanghelle, Jason S. "God, History, and Authority? History and Revelation in the Thought of Carl F. H. Henry." *Trinity Journal* 35 (2014): 39–59.

Strachan, Owen. *Awakening the Evangelical Mind: An Intellectual History of the Neo-Evangelical Movement*. Grand Rapids: Zondervan, 2015.

———. "Carl F. H. Henry's Doctrine of the Atonement: A Synthesis and Brief Analysis." *Themelios* 38.2 (2013): 215–31.

———. *The Colson Way: Loving Your Neighbor and Living with Faith in a Hostile World*. Nashville: Thomas Nelson, 2015.

———. "Light from the Third Great Awakening: Harold Ockenga and the Call to Future Pastor-Theologians." *Journal of Biblical and Theological Studies* 3.1 (2018): 93–110.

———. "Reenchanting the Evangelical Mind: Park Street Church's Harold Ockenga, The Boston Scholars, and the Mid-Century Intellectual Surge." PhD diss., Trinity Evangelical Divinity School, 2011.

Studebaker, John A. *The Lord Is the Spirit: The Authority of the Holy Spirit in Contemporary Theology and Church Practice.* The Evangelical Theological Society Monograph Series. Eugene, OR: Pickwick, 2008.

Sutton, Matthew Avery. *American Apocalypse: A History of Modern Evangelicalism.* Cambridge: Harvard University Press, 2014.

Sweeney, Douglas A. *The American Evangelical Story: A History of the Movement.* Grand Rapids: Baker Academic, 2005.

———. "The Essential Evangelicalism Dialectic: The Historiography of the Early Neo-Evangelical Movement and the Observer-Participant Dilemma." *Church History* 60.1 (1991): 70–84.

———. "Fundamentalism and the Neo-Evangelicals." *Fides et Historia* 24 (1992): 81–95.

———. "One in the Spirit? Evangelicals Are Still Searching for the Elusive Ideal of Unity." *Christian History and Biography* 92 (2006): 42–43.

Synan, Vinson. *The Holiness-Pentecostal Tradition: Charismatic Movements in the Twentieth Century.* Grand Rapids: Eerdmans, 1997.

Thiselton, Anthony C. *Hermeneutics: An Introduction.* Grand Rapids: Eerdmans, 2009.

———. *The Holy Spirit—In Biblical Teaching, Through the Centuries, and Today.* Grand Rapids: Eerdmans, 2013.

Thompson, Mark D. "Witness to the Word: On Barth's Doctrine of Scripture." Pages 168–97 in *Engaging with Barth: Contemporary Evangelical Critiques.* Edited by David Gibson and Daniel Strange. New York: Continuum, 2008.

Thompson, Philip Edward. "Toward Baptist Ecclesiology in Pneumatological Perspective." PhD diss., Emory University, 1995.

Thornbury, Gregory Alan. *Recovering Classic Evangelicalism: Applying the Wisdom and Vision of Carl F. H. Henry.* Wheaton, IL: Crossway, 2013.

———. "Vain Philosophy? Carl F. H. Henry's Plea for a Philosophically Informed Ministry." Pages 135–47 in *Essential Evangelicalism: The Enduring Influence of*

Carl F. H. Henry. Edited by Matthew J. Hall and Owen Strachan. Wheaton, IL: Crossway, 2015.

Trueman, Carl R. "Admiring the Sistine Chapel: Reflections on Carl F. H. Henry's *God, Revelation and Authority*." *Themelios* 25.2 (2000): 48–58.

———. "Uneasy Consciences and Critical Minds: What the Followers of Carl Henry Can Learn from Edward Said." *Themelios* 30.2 (2005): 32–45.

Turner, John G. *Bill Bright and Campus Crusade for Christ: The Renewal of Evangelicalism in Postwar America*. Chapel Hill: University of North Carolina Press, 2008.

Umstattd, Rustin. *The Spirit and the Lake of Fire: Pneumatology and Judgement*. Eugene, OR: Wipf & Stock, 2017.

Vanhoozer, Kevin J. *The Drama of Doctrine: A Canonical-Linguistic Approach to Christian Theology*. Louisville: Westminster John Knox, 2005.

———. "Lost in Interpretation? Truth, Scripture, and Hermeneutics." *Journal of the Evangelical Theological Society* 48.1 (2005): 89–114.

Vanhoozer, Kevin J., Craig G. Bartholomew, Daniel J. Trier, and N. T. Wright. eds. *Dictionary for Theological Interpretation of the Bible*. Grand Rapids: Baker Academic, 2005.

Wacker, Grant. *America's Pastor: Billy Graham and the Shaping of a Nation*. Cambridge: Harvard University Press, 2014.

———. *Heaven Below: Early Pentecostals and American Culture*. Cambridge: Harvard University Press, 2001.

———. *One Soul at a Time: The Story of Billy Graham*. Library of Religious Biography. Edited by Mark A. Noll and Heath W. Carter. Grand Rapids: Eerdmans, 2019.

———. "Travail of a Broken Family: Evangelical Responses to Pentecostalism in America, 1906–1916." *Journal of Ecclesiastical History* 47.3 (1996): 505–28.

Wagner, C. Peter. *The Third Wave of the Holy Spirit: Encountering the Power of Signs and Wonders*. Ann Arbor: Vine Books, 1988.

Waita, Jonathan. "Carl F. H. Henry and the Metaphysical Foundations of Epistemology." PhD diss., Dallas Theological Seminary, 2012.

Wallace, Daniel B., and M. James Sawyer. Preface to *Who's Afraid of the Holy Spirit: An Investigation into the Ministry of the Spirit of God Today*. Edited by Daniel B. Wallace and M. James Sawyer. Dallas: Biblical Studies Press, 2005.

Walvoord, John F. "Contemporary Issues in the Doctrine of the Holy Spirit—Part III: New Morality." *Bibliotheca Sacra* (1973): 213-22.

Warfield, B. B. *Counterfeit Miracles*. New York: Charles Scribner's Sons, 1918.

———. "John Calvin the Theologian." Pages 481-507 in *Calvin and Augustine*. Edited by Samuel G. Craig. Philadelphia: Presbyterian and Reformed, 1956.

Watson, Edward. "A History of Influence: The Charismatic Movement and the SBC." *Criswell Theological Review* (2006): 15-30.

Weaver, C. Douglas. *Baptists and the Holy Spirit: The Contested History with Holiness-Pentecostal-Charismatic Movements*. Waco, TX: Baylor University Press, 2019.

———. "Baptists, The Holy Spirit, and Corporate Worship." *American Baptist Quarterly* 31 (2014): 179-98.

Webster, John. "Illumination." *Journal of Reformed Theology* 5 (2011): 325-40.

———. "Introduction: Systematic Theology." Pages 1-15 in *The Oxford Handbook of Systematic Theology*. Edited by John Webster, Kathryn Tanner, and Iain Torrance. Oxford: Oxford University Press, 2007.

Weeks, David Lee. "The Political Thought of Carl F. H. Henry." PhD diss., Loyola University of Chicago, 1991.

Wells, David F. *No Place for Truth: Or Whatever Happened to Evangelical Theology?* Grand Rapids: Eerdmans, 1993.

Wellum, Stephen J. "The Glorious Work of God the Holy Spirit." *Southern Baptist Journal of Theology* 16.4 (2012): 2-3.

White, Michael D. "Word and Spirit in the Theological Method of Carl Henry." PhD diss., Wheaton College, 2012.

Williamson, William B. "The Doctrine of the Church: Part I." *Christianity Today* (December 8, 1961): 11-13.

Wilson, Andrew. *Spirit and Sacrament: An Invitation to Eucharismatic Worship*. Grand Rapids: Zondervan, 2018.

Wood, Jonathan. "Revelation, History, and the Biblical Text in the Writings of
    Carl F. H. Henry." PhD diss., Southwestern Baptist Theological Seminary,
    2015.

Woodbridge, John D. "A Biblically Faithful Theologian Evangelist." Pages 81–101 in
    Essential Evangelicalism: The Enduring Influence of Carl F. H. Henry. Edited by
    Matthew J. Hall and Owen Strachan. Wheaton, IL: Crossway, 2015.

———. "Carl F. H. Henry: Spokesperson for American Evangelicalism." Pages
    378–93 in *God and Culture: Essays in Honor of Carl F. H. Henry*. Edited by D. A.
    Carson and John D. Woodbridge. Grand Rapids: Eerdmans, 1993.

Worthen, Molly. *Apostles of Reason: The Crisis of Authority in American
    Evangelicalism*. Oxford: Oxford University Press, 2014.

Yarnell III, Malcom B., "The Person and Work of the Holy Spirit." Pages 483–540
    in *A Theology for the Church*. Rev. ed. Edited by Daniel L. Akin. Nashville:
    B&H Academic, 2014.

———. *Who Is the Holy Spirit? Biblical Insights into the Divine Person*. Hobbs College
    Library. Edited by Heath A. Thomas. Nashville: B&H Academic, 2019.

———. Whose Jesus? Which Revelation?" *Midwestern Journal of Theology* 1.1–2
    (2003): 33–53.

Yong, Amos. "Pentecostalism and the Theological Academy." *Theology Today* 64
    (2007): 244–50.

SUBJECT / AUTHOR INDEX

—

SCRIPTURE INDEX

—

Old Testament

STUDIES IN HISTORICAL & SYSTEMATIC THEOLOGY

Studies in Historical and Systematic Theology is a peer-reviewed series of contemporary monographs exploring key figures, themes, and issues in historical and systematic theology from an evangelical perspective.

—

Learn more at LexhamPress.com/SHST